Rhetorical Analysis:
A Brief Guide for Writers

Mark Garrett Longaker
University of Texas at Austin

Jeffrey Walker
University of Texas at Austin

Longman

Boston   Columbus   Indianapolis   New York   San Francisco   Upper Saddle River
Amsterdam   Cape Town   Dubai   London   Madrid   Milan   Munich   Paris
Montréal   Toronto   Delhi   Mexico City   São Paulo   Sydney   Hong Kong   Seoul
Singapore   Taipei   Tokyo

Executive Editor: Lynn Huddon
Senior Marketing Manager: Sandra McGuire
Production Manager: Denise Phillip
Project Coordination, Text Design, and Electronic Page Makeup:
S4Carlisle Publishing Services, Inc.
Cover Designer/Manager: Wendy Ann Fredericks
Cover Photo: © Science Faction/SuperStock
Photo Researcher: Jullie Chung
Senior Manufacturing Buyer: Dennis J. Para
Printer and Binder: Edwards Brothers
Cover Printer: The Lehigh Press/Phoenix Color Corporation

Library of Congress Cataloging-in-Publication Data
Longaker, Mark Garrett, 1974-
    Rhetorical analysis : a brief guide for writers / Mark Garrett
Longaker, Jeffrey Walker.
        p. cm.
    ISBN 978-0-205-56570-2
    1. English language—Rhetoric. 2. Persuasion (Rhetoric)
I. Walker, Jeffrey, 1949- II. Title.
    PE1408.L67 2011

    808'.042—dc22   2010041524

Longman   5 6 7 8 9 10—EDW—13 12
is an imprint of

ISBN-13: 978-0-205-56570-2
www.pearsonhighered.com ISBN-10:   0-205-56570-0

Contents

Preface

As its title suggests, this is a book about rhetorical analysis. It introduces particular rhetorical concepts (both classical and modern) relevant to analysis, while also demonstrating how to analyze. It has broader aims as well. One, for example, is improving student judgment. This aim is not novel, of course; it has an ancient, as well as modern, pedigree. Aristotle contended that rhetoric benefits the judge just as much as the advocate (see *Rhetoric* 1354a). Echoing Aristotle, Wayne Booth has cautioned against "rhetrickery": "passionate proofs for this or that false belief" (*A Rhetoric of Rhetoric: The Quest for Effective Communication* [Malden MA: Blackwell, 2004], p. 109). Both Booth and Aristotle worry about persuasion's ability to warp human judgment. Both propose the same method of making us more capable of assessing an act of persuasion: rhetorical analysis. Rhetoric as an analytic art is very much, as Aristotle said, a "faculty of observing the possibly persuasive in each case" (*Rhetoric* 1355b): a faculty of assessing not only what forms of appeal have been applied and how, but also *what else* is possible in the given situation.

The chapters introduce undergraduates to rhetorical analysis through a series of lessons, each building on the last. These chapters also teach and exemplify analytic writing through rhetorical lenses. At the ends of Chapters 2–5, you will find undergraduate essays that reflect our efforts at teaching students to write rhetorical analysis. Within the chapters themselves, you will find theoretic discussion of concepts, analytic applications of those concepts, and explanations of how contemporary rhetorical theory is an extension of classical notions. *Rhetorical Analysis* does not cover all methods or theories, but it does systematically and progressively introduce undergraduates to classical and contemporary ideas about and approaches to rhetorical criticism. Finally, within the chapters, you will find supplementary material: questions to guide students writing their own analyses, in the "Questions for Analysis" boxes; directions about how this material might be applied in a classroom discussion, in the "For Further Discussion" boxes; suggestions for students wanting to write their own rhetorical analyses, in the "Write an Analysis" boxes, and specific modes of analysis not covered by the chapters themselves, in the "Methods of Analysis" boxes.

We were initially inspired to write this book when our department invented an undergraduate major in Rhetoric and Writing. We found ourselves teaching and imagining many lower- and upper-division courses that required substantial writing and that emphasized classical and contemporary rhetorical theory. We both teach Principles of Rhetoric, the gateway course for Rhetoric and Writing majors at the University of Texas at Austin. This class is designed to explore core principles that can benefit students both in other writing classes (such as Advanced Writing and Principles of Technical Writing) and in other rhetoric classes (such as History of Public Argument; Multimedia: Remaking Invention; and Nonargumentative Rhetoric in Zen). In the past academic year, we have used various iterations of this textbook in our classes. In our experience, the book works very well for a sophomore- or junior-level undergraduate class with a strong emphasis on classical and contemporary rhetorical theory and with a series of challenging analytic writing assignments.

But you don't need to be working in a department of writing and rhetoric to use this textbook. We hope to offer something to any instructor interested in teaching rhetorical analysis in any department. In a lower-division writing class with a large analysis component, for instance, *Rhetorical Analysis* could be used to introduce certain concepts and to exemplify analytic writing. We concede that there is more material than can be covered easily in such a lower-division class. (We have had trouble covering everything in our own upper-division classes.) But you need not teach all of the concepts or analytic methods. We've had great success emphasizing the ideas and methods that most suit our purposes.

Furthermore, though *Rhetorical Analysis* is not designed for adoption in a class with a strict emphasis on writing, the book can be and has been used in this pedagogical arena. For instance, we have used *Rhetorical Analysis* to teach writing by asking students to compose and then to analyze their own writing through the lenses provided in the chapters that follow. In one assignment sequence, for instance, we asked students to write an opinion piece for their local student newspaper. For the next seven weeks, students wrote reports about their kairos, their argument, their arrangement, and their style. Each report used vocabulary from this textbook to explain what the writers were trying to accomplish and how they could revise their opinion articles to better achieve those ends. By the end of the assignment sequence, each student had written five reports (each with recommendations about revision) and six versions of the initial opinion article. Each student had also completed numerous exercises, all derived from the first five chapters of *Rhetorical Analysis*. You are welcome to consider, borrow from, and improve upon this assignment sequence. Simply go to: http://instructors.cwrl.utexas.edu/ longaker/node/102 and read the material under the "Persuasion Portfolio" heading.

We also believe that *Rhetorical Analysis* has potential in a course that addresses a range of analytic methods (a survey of literary, cultural, or rhetorical criticism). The book is brief and can be excerpted, making it manageable in tandem with another book or with a series of other texts (primary or secondary). Finally, *Rhetorical Analysis* has potential in the graduate classroom. We have used sections of the textbook to teach rhetorical theory and analysis to graduate instructors who are teaching the required first-year writing course at UT, a class that is premised upon classical rhetorical pedagogy and that includes a rhetorical-analysis unit. Because the textbook presents rhetorical theory and analysis without watering down the material, it serves as a useful primer for advanced students who are nevertheless newcomers to rhetoric.

We hope you see the same potential that we imagine and that we have found in this textbook. Writing the book and using it in our classes has certainly improved our teaching.

A CourseSmart eTextbook

Note that *Rhetorical Analysis* is also available as a CourseSmart eTextbook (www.coursesmart.com). Students can subscribe to and search the eText, make notes online, print out assignments that incorporate lecture notes, and bookmark important passages for later review.

Acknowledgments

At this point, we feel it is appropriate to offer brief acknowledgments to all those who have contributed to this textbook's composition. First, and foremost, we would like to thank our students. Many read and gave feedback on early drafts of the manuscript. Many volunteered their work for reproduction between these covers. Due to restrictions on the book's total length, we were unable to reprint the good work produced and volunteered by so many. Nevertheless, the following students wrote work that especially inspired us and that we wanted, and in some cases were abe, to reprint between these covers: Eric Ormsby, Benjamin Orlansky, Tara Hall, Haley Faulkner, Rebecca Reilly, David Daniel, and Tatum Fritz. They have inspired us to think about rhetorical analysis in new and interesting ways. Our students energize and revitalize the familiar classical and modern concepts by offering their own insights, by finding application in their own lives, by asking difficult questions, and by solving impossible riddles. Students make our classes enjoyable. Students make our textbook readable. Students make our jobs rewarding. Students teach us. And we are grateful for the lesson.

Our spouses and children deserve thanks as well. They sacrificed time with us, as we stared at computer screens and notebooks—writing, revising, and rethinking. And they supported us with their affection and their attention.

Our colleagues deserve our thanks. The stimulating intellectual environment at UT and in the discipline of rhetoric and writing has motivated us and instigated our thoughts for many years. The cornucopia of ideas and analyses in these pages testifies to the boisterous conversations in the hallways that join our offices and in the hotels that host our conferences.

The editorial staff at Pearson deserves our thanks. Lynn Huddon, our editor, has served as more of a collaborator than an editor. Lynn has offered invaluable insights into the textbook market as well as prudent advice about how to write such a book, how to address readers' comments, and how to arrange and present our material. Others deserve specific mention as well: Michael Kopf directed the book's production, and Pat Eichhorst copyedited every page. Their efforts are reflected in the quality of the final project. And countless reviewers read, commented on, and made suggestions about this book: Matthew Abraham, DePaul University; Danika Brown, University of Texas, Pan American; Susan H Delagrange, The Ohio State University, Mansfield; Rebecca Dingo, University of Missouri; Doug Downs, Montana State University; Richard Leo Enos, Texas Christian University; Gracia Grindal, Luther Seminary; Marguerite Helmers, University of Wisconsin, Oshkosh; Patricia Marie Malesh, University of Colorado; Peter Marston, California State University, Northridge; Susan Miller-Cochran, North Carolina State University; Richard Nordquist, Armstrong Atlantic State University; Stephen Schneider, University of Alabama; and Elizabeth Weiser, The Ohio State University. They have shaped the project in many ways. We are grateful for their patience and for their advice.

Finally, we would like to thank Doug Day—once our textbook representative, now our friend. Doug listened to our ideas when they were little more than random suggestions made at a faculty party. He encouraged us to write a proposal and has celebrated every stage of the writing process with us.

Mark Garrett Longaker
Jeffrey Walker

1

Introduction to Rhetoric and Rhetorical Analysis

On March 23, 2010, while signing into law the most significant piece of legislative healthcare reform in more than forty years, President Barack Obama said, "In a few moments, when I sign this bill, all of the over-heated rhetoric over reform will finally confront the reality of reform." Regardless of how you feel about America's Affordable Health Choices Act of 2009, we would guess that, like many other U.S. citizens, you share President Obama's feelings about rhetoric. "Rhetoric" is the opposite of "reality." Rhetoric is spin. Rhetoric is dangerous. Rhetoric inflames. Rhetoric deceives.

When many people hear the word *rhetoric*, they think of a television show that features two (or three or four) people seated at an oblong table, spouting empty catchphrases at one another in an effort to "win the argument" about some issue. They think of a politician standing behind a podium, trying to mask something unpopular (perhaps a scandal, a failed policy, or a recent vote on a contentious piece of legislation) using "spin," obfuscation, or empty appeals. Or they think of the stereotypical used car salesman who encourages the buyer not to worry about a vehicle's six-digit odometer reading because those are all "highway miles." For such people, rhetoric is something unpleasant, something they would rather avoid or remove in order to get at "the facts." Nevertheless—even for those who deride it—rhetoric seems to be everywhere.

We advance a different understanding. We propose that rhetoric is a necessary part of human interaction. You can neither avoid it nor remove it. If we're right, then rhetorical analysis is essential equipment for daily survival. If rhetoric is everywhere and indispensable, then everyone should learn to understand how it works, and how it could be made to work differently.

If rhetoric is so prevalent, and rhetorical analysis is so useful, then this book is a far cry from the "user's guide to BS" that some might imagine when reading its title. Rhetorical analysis can offer more than X-ray goggles that penetrate bald-faced lies and distortions. So what exactly are we talking about? Allow us to venture a few definitions.

WHAT IS RHETORIC?

Rhetoric is the study and the practice of persuasion. Ancient theorists (such as Aristotle, Isocrates, and Quintilian) pointed out that people are unique among the animals in our ability to form large, complicated societies. Left alone, each of us is in dire straits. In comparison with other creatures, we are not strong or quick, nor do we have furry hides to protect us. We don't even have claws. And our technologies would never exist without sharing, communicating, and building upon other people's discoveries. No one who grows up alone in the wilderness will invent a telephone or a digital camera—probably not even a stone knife or a reliable source of fire. But people can voluntarily organize into cooperative groups. We are, as Aristotle observed, political animals. To paraphrase the great Stagirite himself: Those who live without the company of others are beasts or gods. *People* live in the company of other *people*.

This company, the social quality of human existence, requires persuasion. We must be able to influence one another without destruction or violence. If we can only form societies through force, then we will destroy one another. But if we can find a way to interact without physically damaging or fettering one another, then we can accomplish more than any other species wandering the planet. And so human existence depends upon the study and practice of this interaction, this persuasion. At least, that's what ancient rhetorical theorists have argued, and we are inclined to agree.

If people need rhetoric, then there must be a persuasive dimension to nearly everything that we touch. It would be an overstatement to say that everything is rhetorical, but it seems reasonable to posit that every part of human interaction has a rhetorical dimension. A very famous twentieth-century rhetorical theorist, Kenneth Burke, captured this pervasive domain when he defined rhetoric as "the use of language as a symbolic means of inducing cooperation in beings that by nature respond to symbols" (A Rhetoric of Motives [Berkeley: University of California Press, 1969], p. 43). People need to cooperate, and we do so with symbols. Through rhetoric, we study and practice these symbols and the cooperation that they enjoin.

WHAT IS RHETORICAL ANALYSIS?

Rhetorical analysis is the study of persuasion in order to understand how people have been and can be persuasive. We analyze rhetorically for two reasons: (1) so that we can become better judges, and (2) so that we can become better advocates. The first step toward rhetorical analysis is perhaps the hardest. We have to put off agreement or disagreement. Rhetorically analyzing something requires that we judge its effectiveness. Whether you agree or not, can you see why the argument might or might not appeal to some people? After answering this question, we can use rhetorical analysis to say many other things. We might rhetorically analyze to judge artfulness: Even if an argument failed to convince, was it admirable or useful? We might rhetorically analyze to judge quality: What kind of argument is this? Or decorum and timeliness: Was the argument well suited to the circumstances of its delivery, or would this same argument fare better at another time and in another set of circumstances? Or an argument's effects: Even if the argument was timely, artful, decorous, factually accurate, widely persuasive, and perfectly in line with standards to which all agree, will it encourage people to engage one another in a destructive manner?

Regardless of what you decide to say, rhetorical analysis will not immediately answer the questions that most people would like to ask: Do you agree with the argument? Do you like the film? Are you moved by this piece of music? These will need to be put on hold, though rhetorical analysis can prepare us to answer such questions thoughtfully. After analysis, we're more able to say why we agree (or not), and why others should do likewise. Rhetorical analysis therefore prepares us to be better judges and better advocates. If we understand how we have been persuaded, we can more effectively move others. In the end, rhetorical analysis always points outward. We don't analyze to analyze. We analyze to understand, to judge more justly, to speak more effectively, to behave more responsibly. In general, we analyze to become better people ourselves.

WHAT IS THE RHETORICAL PERSPECTIVE?

Constant rhetorical analysis demonstrates that we are often uncertain about our actions and our beliefs. Appreciating the art, the reason, and the merit of a contrary argument should help you to understand that many of your own convictions have been formed through persuasive actions. Many people might disagree with good reason. This isn't to say that you should abandon all principles, standards, morals, and values. Relativism (the belief that all beliefs are equally good and true) and nihilism (the belief that nothing is good or true) are easy escapes, and they're ultimately unsustainable. We must act, we must believe, and we must believe in our actions. A rhetorical perspective, however, cautions us against absolute conviction. A great deal in our lives is unknown, unknowable, and unpredictable. When we cannot absolutely know something for certain, we must elect the best options, and we must defend the best among a series of good (or possibly bad) choices. In these circumstances, we should learn to see the merit in opposing cases and to see why our own case depends on probabilities, gut reactions, appeals to abstractions (such as freedom or justice), and appeals to pragmatic though not guaranteed effects (such as a balanced budget). Part of the rhetorical perspective, therefore, is an acknowledgment that, however much we may believe an argument, it may be flawed (if not wrong) and, however much we may disapprove of an argument, it may be reasonable (if not right).

Another part of the rhetorical perspective involves the pragmatic search for ways to become more persuasive in the future, or to find better—more ethical, more productive—ways to persuade. While some manners of analysis focus on the beauty of an object, and others focus on its intricacy, rhetorical analysis focuses on an object's function and its potential utility. How did this thing work, and how can it work better? In sum, the lifelong rhetorical analyst will be a cautious believer; a considerate listener; and a careful, effective actor, speaker, or writer.

WHAT CAN YOU FIND IN THIS BOOK?

This book encourages you to develop a rhetorical perspective in three ways. First, we offer a range of rhetorical theories, emphasizing both classical and modern ideas about persuasion. This material is largely presented in the first section of each chapter. Consistently, we emphasize the continuity between modern ideas and classical sources. Chapters 2–5 largely present classical theories, with some explanation of how they influenced twentieth-century thought. Chapters 6–8 present contemporary theories, with reflections back to the classics. The rhetorical tradition is a continuous conversation that is more than two millennia old and still happening today.

Second, we present practical advice about how to use these theories when analyzing. Each chapter, after exploring some theory, gives advice about how to analyze. Each chapter also presents a sample analysis that we have written. We have chosen two classic texts for these long analyses: Martin Luther King, Jr.'s "Letter from Birmingham Jail" and a 1960 print advertisement produced by Volkswagen. In this book's appendices, you can find both of these texts along with a Chrysler ad that we regularly reference. We choose to analyze the VW ad and the "Letter" because these are very rich and very effective arguments. Furthermore, we want to demonstrate how each analytic vocabulary can help you see something new in a familiar argument.

Third, we offer practical instruction about how to write a rhetorical analysis. This book is not only an introduction to rhetorical theory and its analytical application. It is also a guide to writing rhetorical analysis. Each chapter ends with advice about how to come up with and present ideas. Furthermore, Chapters 2–5 present annotated student analysis essays to show you how our students have approached the writing process. We chose not to include sample student works at the ends of Chapters 6–8 because those chapters build on analytic methods addressed earlier in the book. If you can learn to write analyses based on the material presented in Chapters 2–5, you should have no trouble writing analyses based on the material presented thereafter. Finally, throughout the book, we provide additional methods of analysis, topics for further analytical discussion, suggestions about what you can analyze, and questions to help you make analytic observations. This material is located in the segments titled "Methods of Analysis," "For Further Discussion," "Write an Analysis," and "Questions for Analysis."

In addition to our occasional reflections about how classical theory can be used to explain videos, weblogs, and graffiti we offer exemplary student-authored analyses of several nonprint arguments, including a documentary film, a video game, a televised advertisement, and a video public-service announcement. These sample analyses demonstrate that students are quite good at seeing the potential in rhetorical theory—its ability to address a range of media including but not limited to the spoken and the printed word.

By teaching some theory, by modeling a few analyses, by giving advice about writing, and by presenting our own students' work, we aim to help you become a more proficient rhetorical analyst. But we caution you against any expectation of mastery. The ancient Roman rhetorician Quintilian knew that rhetorical education is a lifetime pursuit. Quintilian wanted to teach his students through their childhood, adolescent, and early-adult years. You are likely taking a one-semester course in college. But in that semester you can still learn and accomplish quite a lot. We hope that this brief introduction will get you started.

2

Kairos and the Rhetorical Situation

You tell a joke at a party, and your friends laugh endlessly. The same joke confuses and offends your family. Even the friends you've invited to dinner—friends who guffawed when you initially told the joke—stare solemnly as you repeat the punch line in front of your parents. You load a website on your home computer, and it looks beautifully designed as well as easy to navigate. The same website loaded onto your Smartphone looks cramped and disjointed. You write an essay for your college composition class, and your professor awards you an A. When you send the same essay to the editor of your school newspaper, she says it's stuffy and not appropriate for the opinion section of *The Collegiate Star*. All of these successes and failures have one thing in common. They all depend upon and can be explained by *kairos*.

The rhetorical perspective views discourse—any meaningful use of signs or symbols (words, images, etc.)—as always and inherently *situated*. Any effort to persuade someone involves, in its most basic form, a relationship among the producer of discourse (we'll call this entity the *rhetor*), the discourse produced, and the audience of the discourse. Somebody says something to somebody, with certain motives or purposes, in certain circumstances; the audience interprets and responds, also with motives and purposes of their own. All these things are interrelated: the rhetor's message, audience, and delivery; the audience's interpretation and response; and the circumstances within which this all happens. Thus rhetorical analysis begins with an understanding of the situation. We can ask, "In what ways does a discourse respond to its situation, and how well?" Is the website built for browsing with a Palm, a Blackberry, or an iPhone? Is the joke too blue for an older crowd? Is the essay too "academic" for a school newspaper?

FOR FURTHER DISCUSSION

For further discussion of the motives and purposes in a rhetorical transaction, consider the following scenario: Suppose that you have received in the mail an official-looking envelope (with a window for your address, etc.) from the "National Student Loan Administration," emblazoned with the line, "Urgent: open immediately." Thinking it official government mail, you open the envelope, only to discover that it contains advertising for a nongovernment student loan business. The lender (the rhetor) is perfectly legitimate and acknowledges that you are likely to disregard a lot of solicitous mail. So you are enticed with a vague hook. The rhetor has enticed you by promising to engage an exigence that you, the audience, recognize. You believe that anything the government says deserves attention. But the letter really addresses another exigence—the rhetor wants to sell you something. This situation also raises an ethical question. One must wonder whether it is rhetorically unethical to promise to address a certain exigence but then to talk about something else. If it's unethical in direct-mail advertisement, is it likewise in journalism? If an article promises to address a recent tax cut but only uses this subject to introduce another topic—such as poverty in America— has the rhetor tricked you? Or has s/he changed the *kairos*?

Both classical and modern theories provide some useful conceptual frameworks for thinking about rhetorical situations. The first we will take up, the ancient Greek notion of *kairos*, is perhaps the essence of the matter. After that we will survey some modern refinements on the notions of audience, rhetor, and situation. Then we will turn to practical analysis of a pair of notable examples—Martin Luther King, Jr.'s "Letter from Birmingham Jail" and an advertisement from Volkswagen's revolutionary 1960 "Think Small" ad campaign—with an eye to the situatedness of discourse.

Before we move on, we will define a few key terms that appear throughout this book. The word *rhetor* derives from ancient Greek and originally meant "speaker" or "orator" but later took on broader meanings. Notice that in the paragraphs that follow, we refer to the *practitioner* of rhetoric as the *rhetor*—the speaker, writer, video maker, graphic designer, and so forth—who uses any symbolic means, such as words or images, with communicative and persuasive intent.

We will use the modern word *rhetorician*, in contrast, to mean an *analyst, theorist,* or *teacher* of rhetoric. Finally, you'll notice that we use the term *discourse* to refer to any persuasive effort—a speech, an article, a song, a film. We prefer this term to *text* because discourse does not limit us to words on the page, as text might. We do, however, also use the term *text* to refer to a piece of discourse, as in our discussion of *textualized discourse* in this chapter. An article, such as King's "Letter," can be a text just as a film, such as *The Fog of War,* can be a text.

KAIROS

The ancient word *kairos* basically means time, in the particular sense of a *moment in time,* and especially the *right time* or the *opportune time.* For example, in everyday language one may tell a child that "it's time to go to bed," or speak of "the right person at the right time," or doing or saying "the wrong thing at the wrong time." This is time in the sense of *kairos.*

Further, the moment in time that *kairos* refers to can be any size. It may mean something as short as the fleeting present instant, or as long as a season, a year, or even an historical epoch. "This year, with the economy in recession, is not the time (*kairos*) to be investing in high-risk stocks"; "The year 2008 was a bad time (*kairos*) to unveil websites with Flash animations, since most smartphone browsers could not load Flash"; "Seventeenth-century New England was a time (*kairos*) for witch trials." As these expanded uses make apparent, the idea of *kairos* includes a sense of the *surrounding conditions* (cultural, political, economic, technological, etc.) that make some things more possible and other things less possible. In the early Middle Ages, for example, "the times were not right" for flourishing international trade or vibrant intellectual activity outside the church. The *kairos* was unfavorable. During the 2004 election, the "times were not right" for organizing political campaigns through social networking sites (such as meetup.com or MySpace), though this technology's "time" would come just a few years later.

As a rhetorical term—and hereafter we will use it as an English word, without italics—kairos names both the occasion for discourse and the surrounding conditions that present the rhetor with opportunities and constraints: opportunities or openings to say certain things in certain ways; and constraints that limit what can be said and how. Discourse that responds effectively or appropriately to the opportunities and constraints in its situation may be called *kairotic* or timely. Discourse that fails to do so may be called unkairotic, untimely, inappropriate, or, sometimes, just plain tasteless. For example, parents are expected to smother their children with affection at family gatherings. It's OK for a father to give his teenage son a noogie in front of Uncle Ira. Grandma can pinch cheeks while chirping about her handsome grandchildren. But if Mimi posted "I love you, Pookie-Bear" all over her 15-year-old grand-daughter's Facebook wall, the affection would not only be ill-received but a bit inconsiderate. Much depends, obviously, on the audience and the circumstances.

In addition to the basic occasion for discourse and its surrounding circumstances, kairos also names the immediate, moment-by-moment opportunities and constraints that can arise as the discourse itself progresses. The skillful rhetor will seek to use these moments to his or her advantage. For example, the rhetor may face an audience that is initially hostile or unreceptive to what she wants to say, or simply uninterested or unable to understand. In such a situation the rhetor, if skillful, will first attempt to make the audience more receptive, preparing them for what she wants to say—creating the kairos for it. When the right time has been sufficiently prepared, she can deliver the intended statement more effectively than she could have otherwise.

According to some classical authorities, virtually the whole art of rhetoric boils down to the ability to say what is timely and appropriate to kairos at any moment, and the ability to *create or modify kairos,* and to *set up the moment* when a particular statement can be fitting and persuasive. The process is a little like telling a joke, from setup to punch line. If properly set up, and if delivered at the right moment, the punch line is funny. If delivered without its setup, or if the setup is mishandled, the punch line probably will not be funny and may not even make sense.

What we have said here about kairos may seem fairly obvious and commonsensical. If so, so much the better. It is easier, however, to state and to understand the principle than to do what the principle describes.

ASPECTS OF THE RHETORICAL SITUATION

The modern notion of *rhetorical situation* explores much of what the ancient notion of kairos leaves unsaid. We'll start with the most basic of rhetorical situations—the *oral-aural* situation—and then consider the more complex situation of *textualized* discourse.

The Oral-Aural Situation

Here, someone (orally) says something to someone, who (aurally) listens. Figure 2.1 represents the main components of this situation with a simple graphic:

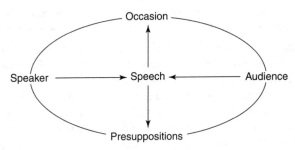

Figure 2.1   The oral-aural rhetorical situation.

As the graphic suggests, the *speaker* produces a *speech* (the speaker's words) for an *audience* (the person or persons to whom the speaker's words are addressed). The speech is produced by the speaker, and interpreted by the audience, in response to some *occasion*. And both the speaker's speech and the audience's interpretation depend on *presuppositions*—ideas (beliefs, values, knowledge, etc.) that make the speech believable. These presuppositions may be overtly stated, as when the Declaration of Independence says "We hold these truths to be self-evident . . .": these self-evident truths are not argued for or defended, but simply *assumed* as the starting-points or givens on which the rest of the Declaration's arguments depend. But presuppositions often are unstated beliefs that go without saying. Presuppositions may not even require conscious thought. An audience or a speaker may hold a deep presupposition without consciously thinking about it. They may *feel* what goes without saying.

Now that we've explained the basics, let's elaborate:

- The *occasion* is typically some event or circumstance that calls for speech. We let many things pass by without comment or remark. Others seem to require some talk. Some require a lot of talk; some require formal public discourse. The *speaker* and *audience*, then, are brought together because they recognize the need for discourse—a rhetorical occasion. This recognition motivates the speaker to speak and the audience to listen. If the speaker's intended audience does not share this recognition, the audience may feel no reason to listen, other than a dutiful politeness. In such a case, the speaker may need to persuade the audience to recognize an occasion for speech. (This is, perhaps, another way of saying that skilled rhetoric not only responds to kairos but also can create and manage it.)

- Within a genuine rhetorical occasion there is an *exigence*—something that the speaker and the audience want to discuss. For example, if the occasion is a funeral, and one of the speakers devotes his time to discussing his feelings about funerals in general, or the clothes worn by the mourners, or a funny thing that happened to him on the way there, he probably has failed to respond to the real exigence that has brought the mourners together. (Unless, of course, he has a clever and persuasive way of connecting these topics to what the audience is really there for.)

- Classical rhetoric typically presents the exigence as an *issue*—a *question* about which people may reasonably disagree ("Should the federal government fund embryonic stem-cell research?"), or a debatable *proposition* ("The federal government should fund embryonic stem-cell research, with certain restrictions."). A *practical issue* requires an immediate decision (as in a trial in a court of law or a Congressional debate over a proposed piece of legislation); a *theoretical* or *general issue* requires more philosophical debate ("At what point is an embryo a human being endowed with human rights?"). A general issue is not necessarily connected to an immediate practical decision or action. However, practical and theoretical/general issues frequently are difficult to separate in practice. (A Congressional debate about funding embryonic stem cell research, a practical issue in itself, may have to confront deeper philosophical issues regarding the question of whether human embryos have human rights. Roommates arguing about an alleged theft may have to address the deeper question of whether or not borrowing with no immediate intention of returning someone's MP3 player is really stealing.)

- Classical rhetoric recognizes three basic kinds—that is, general types—of discourse. These are *judicial, deliberative,* and *epideictic* discourse. Judicial discourse (also called forensic or dicanic) judges the legality or justice of an action in the past. Judicial discourse might occur in a court of law, a college disciplinary hearing for a student accused of plagiarism, or other contexts where authorities will judge and punish. Deliberative discourse (also called symbouleutic or advisory) addresses future actions or policies. Deliberative discourse might occur in a legislature or parliament, a corporate boardroom, a family kitchen table meeting, or in other contexts where decisions will result in actions (such as going to war, raising taxes, launching a product line, or deciding which college to attend). Epideictic discourse is concerned with praise or blame in the present. It does not lead immediately to actions (conviction/punishment, raising taxes); instead it forms attitudes and affirms or critiques values and beliefs. Examples of epideictic discourse include a funeral eulogy, a popular song, a Facebook page, or any discourse that aims at praise/blame and attitude formation. In classical rhetoric the category of epideictic ultimately includes not only ceremonial orations but also history writing, philosophical treatises and dialogues, poetry, fiction, drama, movies, documentaries, and music. The three basic kinds are not completely separate from one another. A particular discourse may include elements of two or more. For example, a movie (epideictic) may include a courtroom scene (forensic), and a political speech (deliberative) may include passages of epideictic praise.

- An aspect of the occasion and its kairos is the *forum* and/or *genre* where speaker and audience meet. By forum, we mean places where people talk, such as a court of law, a legislature, a place of worship, a school, a concert hall, or a TV talk show. Forum can be understood more broadly as the technological medium or the virtual site. Is this a page (discourse) in a website (forum)? Is this a game (genre) played on a tablet computer (forum)? But we also mean informal situations, such as a group of friends meeting for lunch. By *genre*, we mean the recognizable and recurring types of speech that occur in any given forum. In a legislative forum, for example, typical genres include speeches for and against pieces of legislation, debates on policy proposals, ceremonial speeches (e.g., for the Fourth of July, Memorial Day), committee hearings, forensic discussions, and coatroom conversations.

- Surrounding the occasion is the larger *historical and cultural context*. This larger context—events and circumstances—will shape the meaning of a particular occasion, and its specific exigence. Take an example from recent history: A cruise ship docking in Haiti to host a barbecue for its passengers was typically welcomed, but this same activity shortly after a devastating earthquake was met with great disapproval. As we noted with kairos, the historical-cultural context, or what might be called the historical-cultural *horizon*, may be any size. One can speak of a large historical epoch such as the Middle Ages, or a smaller one such as the Sixties, as the historical-cultural horizon (the contextual frame) for a particular occasion.

- The *presuppositions* available in a rhetorical situation are part of the historical-cultural context. They are the systems of ideas—the ways of thinking—that the speaker and audience share, making them a community (more or less). Presuppositions include what they love, hate, fear, admire, yearn for; their sense of what is true, real, normal, likely, and unlikely; what they know as "fact"; their sense of the structure of reality; their sense of what is right and proper; their sense of what the meanings of words are, and what is logical; and their sense of what is proper to the forum and genre. Presuppositions not only determine what the speaker means and what the audience understands; they also determine both the speaker's and the audience's understanding of the occasion. If the speaker and the audience both assume that a disaster calls for mourning and charity, then they will approve of a celebrity's effort at soliciting donations, as long as the celebrity doesn't seem to be self-promoting.

In sum, a shared sense of the occasion and a shared set of presuppositions make it possible for speaker and audience to achieve a "meeting of minds," even when a contentious issue is at stake. The *rhetorical situation* begins from these shared presuppositions and a shared sense of the occasion. The rhetorical situation unfolds (or evolves) as the speaker speaks. A skilled rhetor will shape the speech for the audience by speaking to the audience's presuppositions and by trying to anticipate the audience's likely responses. The speaker will also make adjustments to the audience's actual responses, as the speech goes forward. If the rhetor's assumptions are more or less correct, and if the rhetor makes good adjustments, there is a good chance for a persuasive discourse. But if the rhetor fails, he or she will not speak to the actual audience. Or, to view it from the other end, the audience will not be the person (or kind of person) addressed by the speech.

The Textualized Situation

The rhetorical situation becomes more complex when we are dealing with a printed text—or with any recorded discourse involving a rhetor and an audience, such as an advertisement or a film. A written (or other kind of) text is removed from the basic, oral-aural situation. The rhetor cannot see the actual audience and writes, in essence, for an *imagined audience* whose responses must be anticipated. This is the case even when writing a letter to a friend. Since the writer cannot see the friend, s/he constructs a mental image of the friend and imagines this phantom friend's responses. Unlike a speaker, the writer cannot make adjustments by observing the audience's actual responses. Likewise, a reader cannot see the writer but must construct an image of the person behind the text, and imagine what that person meant. Most importantly, a written (or other kind of) text lasts, possibly for hundreds or thousands of years, whereas an oral-aural communication vanishes once it's spoken and heard (unless it is recorded in some way and can be replayed, in which case it becomes a kind of text). The result is that the written text may be read by readers that the original rhetor never had in mind—readers in very different historical and cultural circumstances. The dialogues of Plato, for example, were written for Greek readers in the fourth century BCE, but are still read by various audiences today.

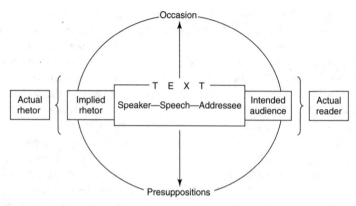

Figure 2.2   The textualized rhetorical situation.

The textualized situation can be represented as shown in Figure 2.2. Once again, this basic description deserves elaboration:

- Here we have a *text*—a written (or other kind of) document—that contains a representation of something said by someone to someone. In Plato's dialogues, for example, we usually find Socrates speaking with one or more characters. In King's "Letter from Birmingham Jail," we find King addressing a group of clergymen who have criticized his actions.

- Associated with the text is the image of its *implied rhetor*, the unseen person behind the text that the reader creates. (This is commonly referred to in literary criticism as the *implied author*.) The implied rhetor *behind* the text and the speaker *in* the text may sometimes be regarded as the same person. That is, the speaker may seem to represent himself or herself, as in King's "Letter." But the speaker may also be a character created by the rhetor, as in Plato's Socrates. The reader typically notices that the text depends on values and beliefs (presuppositions), and the reader also attributes these values and beliefs to the implied rhetor. The text (through the implied rhetor) appears to ask the reader to have certain beliefs, values, and knowledge.

- Outside the text—and outside the bracket in Figure 2.2—is the *actual rhetor* (or the actual writer), the flesh-and-blood person who created the text. What the reader knows about the actual rhetor will be used to interpret the implied rhetor's intentions. To put this another way, knowledge about the actual rhetor becomes part of the reader's imaginative construction of the implied rhetor.

- In some cases the speaker, the implied rhetor, and the actual rhetor appear as more or less the same person. Later, in Analysis 1, we discuss Martin Luther King, Jr.'s "Letter from Birmingham Jail." In this document, King (the implied rhetor) is more or less the same as King, the actual writer. But in other cases these are different roles. For example, in the Volkswagen ad we analyze in Analysis 2 the implied rhetor is Volkswagen, while the actual rhetor is the advertising agency that created the ad.

- Just as a text projects an image of its implied rhetor, it also projects an image of its *intended audience*—or what is also called the *implied audience*, the *implied reader*, or the *ideal* reader or audience of the text. This intended audience may or may not be the same as the addressee within the text. In King's "Letter," for example, the addressee within the text is the group of clergymen he is responding to. But, as we will see, the intended audience beyond the text is white moderates.

- Likewise, just as the implied rhetor and actual rhetor of the text may differ, so too may the intended audience projected by the text differ from the *actual reader* who stands outside of it—and who, in our diagram, is placed outside the right-hand bracket. Since a writer cannot predict what every actual reader of his or her text will be like, the intended audience and the actual reader almost always differ to some degree.

- Just as we develop a sense of the implied rhetor by noticing the kinds of presuppositions the text appears to depend on, so too do we develop a sense of the text's intended audience from those same presuppositions. *The text addresses its intended audience as a person who shares certain kinds of values, beliefs, and knowledge. On the basis of these values, beliefs, and knowledge—or presuppositions—the rhetor and the audience can make certain kinds of judgments.* If, for example, a text asks its audience to make some judgment on the basis of a love for democracy or justice, it apparently addresses its intended audience as the sort of person who holds democracy or justice dear. If a text asks its audience to make judgments on the basis of careful thought, it addresses its audience as an intelligent, intellectually responsible person.

WRITE AN ANALYSIS

Political campaign rhetoric provides some of the best examples for rhetorical analysis. In an effort to explore the quality of the rhetor's (the politician's) relation to the intended audience, we recommend that you discuss and analyze *a specific example (or examples) of campaign rhetoric* (a television ad, a billboard, a speech, a debate performance). What *role* is given to the intended audience—what sort of person is it asked to be—and how does the rhetor treat it? Does the rhetor give the audience an uplifting or degraded role? For example, after Barack Obama gave his nationally televised speech on race and his relationship with the controversial Rev. Jeremiah Wright ("A More Perfect Union") on March 18, 2008, political satirist and comedian Jon Stewart remarked that Obama had spoken to the nation "as if we were adults"; that is, he had given "us," as his intended audience, an "uplifting" or at least a nondegraded role. A rhetorical analysis might respond to that judgment by arguing whether it was justified, and why. (Note: Whether or not one agrees with Obama's speech, one can argue this question either way.)

- If *the reader is willing to be, or become, the sort of person the text addresses*—if the reader responds in the way the rhetor has intended—then s/he will likely be persuaded. You can think of a text's intended audience as a role that the actual reader is invited to step into. Modern readers of Plato's dialogues may become, in some sense, "friends of Plato," although they obviously differ in many ways from fourth-century BCE Greeks. But if the reader refuses the role of intended audience, s/he is likely to resist the rhetor's persuasive efforts.

- Just as shared presuppositions and a shared sense of the *occasion* bring speaker and listener together in an oral-aural situation, they also bring author and audience together in a textualized situation. Here, however, the matter is more complex. Since the original, specific, historical occasion may be long-vanished, the reader must recognize a more generalized version of that occasion—and a generalized version of its exigence—or the reader must be able to step imaginatively into some reconstructed version of the original occasion. A modern reader of a Platonic dialogue may feel that it still speaks to enduring questions and exigent issues in his or her own life, while another may discover a different sense of the dialogue's exigence by relating it to the historical-cultural context of the fourth century BCE, and by imagining (or reconstructing) the probable responses of a fourth-century reader.

METHODS OF ANALYSIS

In this discussion and in Analyses 1 and 2 that appear later in the chapter, we mostly focus on *historical reconstruction* of a discourse's original rhetorical situation and its intended audience. This is a fruitful approach to rhetorical analysis, and it can be further enhanced by *reception study*.

Contemporary rhetorical critic Steven Mailloux, in his 1989 book *Rhetorical Power*, offers both a historical-reconstructive analysis and a reception study of the rhetoric of Mark Twain's (Samuel Clemens') novel, *The Adventures of Huckleberry Finn*. Mailloux shows that the novel was written between 1876 and 1884 in response to what then was called the "Negro Problem"—the question of how the liberated slaves, after the Civil War, were to be assimilated into the national culture. But, as Mailloux points out, literary critics over the decades after *Huckleberry Finn's* publication in 1884 mostly ignored that issue, and commented on other things: the motives and concerns they brought, as literary critics, to their engagement with the text. (We might say that they were involved in "appropriative" analysis.) Further, a new national conversation (a new rhetorical occasion) was emerging in the 1880s over what was termed the "Bad Boy Problem"—juvenile delinquency—just at the time when *Huckleberry Finn* was published. A number of "bad boy books" and editorials on the subject already had appeared, and the actual audiences who read *Huckleberry Finn* at that time tended to view it in the light of that new discussion. Therefore, those who responded to, discussed, criticized, editorialized about, and even banned the book in a few places regarded it as a book about badboyism. Today, *Huckleberry Finn* is still sometimes an object of controversy, though now the controversies usually focus on its use of racist language.

Another possible method of analysis involves positing different audiences, wondering what would happen if someone other than the intended or the actual audience read the work. For example, how might a nineteenth-century or a twenty-first-century African American respond to *Huckleberry Finn*? Positing different audiences often reveals something about the text and the audience itself.

Both the oral-aural and the textualized situations, as we describe them here, assume that the audience and the rhetor are separate. The rhetor designs and delivers a speech, writes a letter, or produces a commercial, and the audience hears, reads, or watches. Many recent technologies, however, make it difficult to separate those producing and those receiving a discourse. The producer and the consumer of rhetoric merge into what industry professionals now call the *prosumer*. One has to wonder who creates a video game like *Second Life* or its predecessors, such as *SimCity*. Surely, the game designers create the space where avatars interact, but the users create the avatars and they manipulate the world. If the video game is an argument, who's the rhetor?

In web design, we have similar trouble separating rhetor and audience. HTML gave readers the ability to link away whenever their fancy struck. People no longer had to march through a determined set of ideas. The most exciting innovation in online media, however, has probably been the arrival of user-created content. Broadcast media follow a one-to-many format, in which content creators disperse information to viewers who either watch or switch channels. Online media make possible a many-to-many format in which users can not only digest content created for them, but also participate in the creation of content. Even HTML's revolutionary linking potential didn't give users this much power. This new format, typically dubbed peer-to-peer or P2P, made the web a forum for many read/write media. It also deeply troubled the division that we assume throughout this chapter. Who is the rhetor on Facebook? The site designers? The users? Who is the audience? The users? Those who simply lurk but never post or friend? How can we differentiate between the audience and the rhetor(s) on Wikipedia (or any wiki) for that matter?

So far we have sketched a number of ideas regarding kairos and the rhetorical situation that are useful for rhetorical analysis. Not all of them will apply to every analysis. As we suggested, the vocabularies introduced in this chapter may need significant amendment (or addition) if they are to address certain new media forums and genres. You should apply whatever seems best to the case in hand. Further, analysis of the rhetorical situation is often part of a larger analysis, providing a frame for the examination of a particular discourse and its strategies. Indeed, that is perhaps what all rhetorical analyses do—consider how a discourse responds to, or manages, kairos in its particular rhetorical situation. But a rhetorical analysis can also focus primarily on developing a description of the situation or particular aspects of that situation.

We now turn to the analysis of situation and kairos in two examples. The first is Martin Luther King, Jr.'s "Letter from Birmingham Jail," a widely recognized masterpiece of modern American rhetoric. Second is an ad from the revolutionary 1960 "Think Small" advertising campaign for the Volkswagen Beetle. (If you are not familiar with these texts, they are available in the book's appendices, pp. 251–269. We suggest that you read each carefully before continuing. We will be returning to both texts in later chapters.)

ANALYSIS 1: KAIROS AND THE RHETORICAL SITUATION IN "LETTER FROM BIRMINGHAM JAIL"

Martin Luther King, Jr.'s "Letter from Birmingham Jail" was written in April 1963. Its basic situation can be summed up as follows: King had been leading protest demonstrations against racial segregation in Birmingham, Alabama, and had been arrested for parading without a permit. Things became unruly. There was some violence in the streets. On the day of King's arrest, the *Birmingham News* ran "A Call for Unity." It was a statement by eight white clergymen expressing general sympathy for the demonstrators' goals, but criticizing King's activities and methods as "unwise and untimely." They urged "Negroes" not to participate in the protest demonstrations, and called for more moderate and "reasonable" approaches to "racial problems," such as the courts and negotiation. King's "Letter" was written in reply, as an *open letter* (genre) to be published in the media, thus addressing not only his ostensible audience, the clergymen themselves, but a wider intended audience as well. He wrote it on scraps of paper and notepads brought to him by his assistants while still in jail. It was first circulated in various excerpted forms in May 1963 and was published in full in June 1963 in *Christian Century, The New Leader,* and *The Atlantic Monthly* (forums). A slightly revised version was published a year later, in King's 1964 book, *Why We Can't Wait.* King's situation, then, included not only the focal exchange between himself and the authors of "A Call for Unity" and its immediate occasion (the demonstrations), but also, as part of the historical-cultural context, the wider national struggle in the 1960s over civil rights and the illegal but still-entrenched practices of racial segregation in many parts of the United States. Racial segregation had been ruled unconstitutional by the Supreme Court's 1954 *Brown v. Board of Education* decision, nine years earlier.

To what sort of audience was King writing? He claims to be addressing the authors of "A Call for Unity," who would of course be part of his wider intended audience, since they presumably would read the "Letter." His wider audience included white Judaeo-Christian liberals who sympathized with the goals of the civil-rights movement and, therefore, with the principles embodied in the *Brown v. Board of Education* decision. Further, we observe that King's "Letter" was published in magazines whose readerships could be described (roughly) as follows:

Christian Century: college-educated, liberal Christians

New Leader: college-educated, left-of-center, moderate liberals

Atlantic Monthly: college-educated, centrist, moderate liberals

It is not certain that King first wrote the "Letter" with those publications specifically in mind. In fact, the idea was first suggested to him by the editor of the *New York Times Magazine*, though in the end it was not published there—so perhaps the readership of the *New York Times Magazine* should be posited as the intended audience, or added to the list. Its readership is roughly similar to that of *Atlantic Monthly*. Probably all these publications and their readerships reflect the kind of audience (or audiences) that King thought he was writing for. (If he had sought to place the "Letter" in a conservative news/opinion magazine like *The National Review*, or a left-wing Marxist publication like the *New Left Review*, that would imply a different intended audience.) Finally, the intended audience probably included people who regarded the clergymen who wrote "A Call for Unity" as religious and moral authorities.

This mostly demographic general impression of King's audience (based on the evidence of publication venues) can be expanded and refined by considering, as well, *the kind of sensibility implied by the presuppositions the "Letter" itself depends on.* What values and beliefs does the "Letter" expect its audience to share? First, one can identify the audience as those who care about the issues under discussion— those for whom those issues matter and who view the debate as worthy. King, as he writes in April 1963, assumes that his readers are genuinely concerned about civil rights and the wisdom of his methods. This could include both liberals and conservatives, and both pro- and anti-segregationists. (The "antis" might be motivated to hear his arguments simply out of a desire to refute and dismiss them.) We have made our case about King's audience using *contextual* evidence, such as historical information, quotes from other publications, and other arguments in the conversation. *Contextual* evidence can include anything not in the *text* (the "Letter") itself.

We can look at the "Letter," however, to learn about the intended audience and its presuppositions. Relying on *textual* evidence, we can focus on the basic values and beliefs that King's arguments appeal to. As many readers of the "Letter" have noted, King frequently appeals to the Judaeo-Christian ethical tradition. He invokes a number of key figures from the biblical prophets and early Christian martyrs to such celebrated thinkers as St. Thomas Aquinas, Martin Buber, and Paul Tillich. Likewise, he invokes at various points such secular hero figures as Socrates and Thomas Jefferson, and identifies himself with the political and philosophical ideals they represent—such as the Enlightenment notion, embodied in Jefferson's words in the Declaration of Independence, that "all men are created equal" and are endowed by their Creator with inalienable rights to "life, liberty, and the pursuit of happiness." One might sum up those ideals as classical Liberalism (though that is not the same thing as the notion of liberal that gets kicked around these days in political sloganeering). King does not defend or try to justify the basic religious and secular ideals that he invokes. Like Jefferson he just *assumes* them as "self-evident" truths, and as the foundations for his arguments. The intended audience of King's "Letter," then, is not only people who care about the basic issues he addresses, but also those who embrace, as good and true, the Judaeo-Christian and liberal ideals that his arguments assume.

The basic occasion for King's "Letter" was, as we have said, the publication of "A Call for Unity" and its criticisms of his actions. The fundamental sources of exigence, however, were the ongoing civil rights protest and the ratcheting up of racial tensions (which sometimes led to violence), not only in Birmingham but in other cities also. When King's "Letter" was published in June 1963, and again in his 1964 book, his readers across the nation would have seen those demonstrations on their televisions, felt those tensions in their lives, and read about those disturbances in their morning newspapers. The audience would recognize the exigence that motivated not only the clergymen's "Call" but King's "Letter" in reply. Behind these immediate sources of exigence, moreover, was the ongoing national conversation and struggle over desegregation (and resistance to it in some states), from the Supreme Court's *Brown v. Board of Education* decision in 1954 to the civil-rights movement of the early 1960s. Beyond that source of exigence was the entire troubled history of race relations in the United States since slavery and abolition, a history that seemed to have reached a moment of crisis.

Here we should note that in the "Letter" itself King says the purpose of the protest demonstrations was to generate a "creative tension" that would spur the so-far unresponsive white power structure of Birmingham to engage in good-faith discussions and negotiations (paragraph 10). In other words, the demonstrations were themselves a rhetorical strategy for creating exigence, and thus for opening genuine occasions for rhetorical exchange. The demonstrations, and the tensions they aroused, created the kairos for the clergymen's "Call," which in turn created the kairos for King's "Letter." This is a good example of the deliberate shaping of kairos—by King. If there had been no demonstrations, there would have been no "Call," and no occasion for King's "Letter" either. If he had simply published the arguments of the "Letter" out of the blue, in response to nothing in particular, would there have been an audience? As it was, in the rhetorical situation that he had in fact provoked, King had the nation's ear, or at least the ear of the white moderates (or Judaeo-Christian moderate liberals) whom he wanted to reach.

What was the initial kairos of King's situation? The great *opportunity* that the clergymen had given him—unwittingly—was an occasion to issue a public statement defending his activities before a wider, indeed a national, audience. Their criticism invited his reply. At the same time, however, King was at a *disadvantage*, since he was being criticized by a group of prominent, respected religious leaders who could influence public opinion, especially among otherwise sympathetic white moderates; and he was, after all, in jail. It is important to remember that, at the time, King was not (yet) the revered figure that he is today. He had not yet delivered his now-iconic "I Have A Dream" speech to a crowd of more than 250,000 at the National Mall in Washington, D.C. That would happen a few months later, on August 28, 1963. If you review the coverage of the Birmingham demonstrations and subsequent events in the *New York Times* between April and June 1963, you will find that, although King is accorded respect as a political leader, he generally is treated simply as one of a number of leaders on the scene and is not necessarily distinguished from others who were more radical. The coverage includes reports that some members of the "Negro" community in Birmingham were not happy with King's tactics and felt he was creating excessive and unnecessary trouble. The *New York Times* "Opinion of the Week" survey for May 5, 1963, includes excerpts from editorials in several southern newspapers, about what the *Times* describes as the raising of "racial tensions [. . .] to a new high." The editorials uniformly condemn King as an "extremist" and "rabble-rouser" whose "abysmal" lack of judgment has produced nothing but "public disorder" and has damaged the cause of "progress toward improved race relations." And the *Times* was sympathetic to the cause of civil rights! It is not hard to imagine that King's image, elsewhere in the national media and in popular opinion, was affected by such portrayals of him as an irresponsible demagogue who had gone too far.

"Letter from Birmingham Jail" begins by respectfully addressing the authors of "A Call for Unity," acknowledging that their criticisms are well-meant and merit a serious response, and then promising to reply "in what I hope will be patient and reasonable terms" (paragraph 1). This reply takes up about half of the "Letter" (paragraphs 2–22, of 50). In the second half, famously, King turns to fairly sharp criticism of the failures of "the white moderate" and "the white church" to live up to their own and the nation's highest ideals (paragraphs 23–47). In essence, he charges his critics with hypocrisy and betrayal—indeed they are worse, he says, than open racists (paragraph 23)—and he ends by resoundingly asserting the complete moral superiority of his own position: "[T]he opposition we now face will surely fail. We will win our freedom because the sacred heritage of our nation and the eternal

METHODS OF ANALYSIS

Our analysis of King's "Letter" invokes one sense of the word *media*. We use the term in its more popular sense—the media consist of the official news and information outlets that discuss topics of general public interest. A topic is "exigent" if it's "in the media." Thus, the *New York Times* is part of the media, and we consult this source to learn about the audience's presuppositions. This is one method of researching and analyzing kairos—consulting the media to learn about the conversation, the audience's presuppositions, and the exigence. At the end of this chapter is Rebecca Reilly's analysis of *The Fog of War*, a documentary. Notice that she did her research using LexisNexis, an academic database, and Google. She found relevant articles in the media, statements about *The Fog of War*, about the director's intentions, and about the audience's presuppositions. This research into the media supports several of her assertions about the kairos and the documentary.

---

will of God are embodied in our echoing demands" (paragraph 44). "The sacred heritage of our nation" refers to the secular ideals and heroes King has been invoking (from Socrates to Jefferson), and the "will of God" refers to the Judaeo-Christian ideals and heroes he also has been invoking. Clearly, the authors of "A Call for Unity" and those who agree with these clergymen are being faulted. According to King, they have failed to live up to the ideals that the intended audience is expected to embrace. Thus we see that King has set up his critics as representatives of a position that his intended audience is asked to reject as morally, politically, and religiously wrong.

Our point is that King cannot *begin* with such arguments, because the initial kairos of his situation is wrong for them. He cannot, at first, respond to criticisms that he is an "extremist" whose methods are "unwise and untimely" by declaring "You hypocrites! God and our nation's heritage are on my side!" He cannot do so because the intended audience likely doubts his own moral standing and the justifiability of his methods. Notably, his opening paragraph does not even suggest that he will turn against his critics in the "Letter's" second half. There is no announcement or forecast of what is to come, probably because such an announcement would be premature and would only provoke resistance in his audience. Since King had ample opportunity to revise the "Letter," and did revise it, one can assume that this nonmention was not an oversight but a deliberate, strategic choice. The kairos, however, has been altered by the time King gets to paragraph 23. At that point, he *can* begin to criticize his critics because his reply has created the conditions for him to do so. This fact is probably why most analyses of "Letter from Birmingham Jail" tend to focus on the first half. It does most of the rhetorical heavy lifting, and not-so-coincidentally contains some of the most memorable passages in modern American literature.

We will look at some of that heavy lifting more closely in later chapters. Our point, for now, is to recognize "Letter from Birmingham Jail" as an exemplary case of a skilled rhetor working with the possibilities that the initial, given kairos makes available, and seizing the opportunities of the new, created kairos that he develops as he goes along.

WRITE AN ANALYSIS

King is obviously unwilling to accept many of his audience's presuppositions, but he is also unwilling to challenge them initially. His effort to slowly change their minds raises a question: What happens when the audience is ignorant or prejudiced, or when the historical-cultural horizon is dominated by a false or vicious belief system? Should the rhetor adapt to bigots by echoing their bigotry? Should the rhetor sometimes challenge or oppose the audience's beliefs? As a case for in-depth analysis, consider Leni Riefenstahl's famous film, *Triumph of the Will*, which is considered one of the most effective pieces of propaganda ever made, as well as a path breaker in cinematic technique. The film is a documentary, commissioned by Adolph Hitler, that brilliantly records and celebrates the Nazi party's spectacular Nuremberg Rally in 1934—with Hitler as the central "hero" figure arriving and parading through town, speaking to the assembled masses, and so forth. One could argue that the film very effectively exploits its kairos, and expresses Nazi ideology with near perfection. How should this film be judged? Is it (as Kenneth Burke might say) a piece of evil "witchcraft"? If evil, does the blame fall on Riefenstahl, or on the rhetorical situation? Should she have resisted the pressures of that situation? Or does her film's technical brilliance redeem it (and her) in some way? Many still watch, study, and admire the film for its technical achievement, so it's difficult to condemn the piece wholly. The same sort of questions can be asked about the 1915 American film *Birth of a Nation*, which positively portrays Klu Klux Klansmen as heroes. Both the *Triumph of the Will* and *Birth of a Nation* speak to their audience's presuppositions very effectively, employing artful cinematography and emotionally moving narratives. Even if we disagree with the presuppositions, shouldn't we admire the rhetoric? Should we acknowledge and study their efforts at appealing to an audience who harbors certain beliefs? Or must we condemn these films as pandering?

You can find the full version of Riefenstahl's film by searching "Triumph of the Will" at YouTube.com. Most of *Birth of a Nation* can be also found on YouTube, but the entire movie does not reside in one location. You can find the first 38 minutes of the film by searching for "birth of a nation part 1" at YouTube.com. The remaining parts can be found with similar searches. You can also search the audio-visual collection of your college library.

ANALYSIS 2: VOLKSWAGEN'S 1960 "WHY" ADVERTISEMENT AND THE HISTORICAL-CULTURAL CONTEXT

We have chosen to analyze two arguments in this chapter because we want to show how versatile this chapter's analytic methods can be. While some of the vocabularies and theories in this book may only be helpful when analyzing certain texts, kairos and the rhetorical situation can illuminate *every argument* because all discourse is situated. Furthermore, we want to explore several dimensions of the rhetorical situation. In our analysis of King's "Letter," we invoke one sense of kairos—the civil rights movement and the situation in Birmingham. In the analysis to follow, we explore another sense of kairos—the historical-cultural context.

To understand the rhetorical situation for the VW "Think Small" ad campaign (and the "Why" ad), we should begin with a bit of history, though we will not focus so closely on the days and weeks before the ad was written and printed as we did with King's "Letter." The rhetorical analyst must decide what historical information best illuminates the exigence. In our analysis of King's "Letter," we focused on the immediate history, but in this analysis of the VW ad, the exigence is better illustrated by a brief history of the corporation's presence in the U.S. market during the decade prior to 1960 (the year "Why" was published). During the 1950s, Americans associated the Volkswagen Beetle (a.k.a. "VW bug") with Germany and with Hitler's fascism. Not only did Hitler himself have a role in the car's design, but the company also flourished under the Nazi government. It would be hard to imagine anything seeming more un-American in the 1950s than a Beetle. Doyle Dane Bernbach (the marketing firm that elected to represent Volkswagen in 1959) had a hard sell. They needed to get people to forget the Beetle's history. Moreover, U.S. auto manufacturers had been producing cars quite different from the Beetle for some time. Throughout the 1950s, American-made automobiles were large, fuel-inefficient, stylish, sleek, and covered in chrome. Cars were even festooned with shark fins and light fixtures that resembled rockets. Car advertisements mimicked what they peddled. (To get a sense of the U.S. car market during the early 1960s, turn to this book's appendices where we have reprinted a 2-page Chrysler ad that appeared in the same issue of *Life* magazine as the VW "Why" ad.) Doyle Dane Bernbach chose to market their product through a series of print ads (*genre*) that appeared in a range of magazines (*forums*). "Why," like many of the ads in the "Think Small" campaign, appeared in *Life* magazine. We can learn a bit about both the intended and the actual audiences for this ad by reflecting on the forum where it appeared (as we did when discussing the magazines that printed King's "Letter").

Some demographic information about *Life*'s readership can shed light on the forum. In 1960, *Life*'s editors proclaimed an average weekly circulation of 6.7 million. By 1969, the magazine's circulation topped 8.5 million. A few other numbers might help us to make sense of *Life*'s reported data. The 1961–1962 U.S. census report estimated the residential population to be just over 179 million. Slightly more than 55 million were less than 15 years old. When we bracket those under 15, we're left with about 123 million people old enough to appreciate the national scope and serious intention of a photojournalistic magazine like *Life*. For every 18 U.S. residents over the age of 15, one issue of *Life* was printed in the week of April 25, 1960. If a single issue were read by more than one person, then it is possible for the magazine to have reached more than 1 of every 18 Americans, aged 15 years or older. (It is wholly reasonable to expect that several readers would pick up each issue of *Life*, and many issues would get read by lots of people. Think of how many times you've perused a worn copy of a magazine while waiting in a doctor's office or an auto-repair shop.) In sum, *Life* offered a very large forum of people who identified as U.S. citizens and who were interested in national political, cultural, and social affairs.

Based on our demographic analysis of the forum, we can make some reasonable arguments about the *intended audience* for the VW "Why" ad. The rhetor wanted to reach a national audience. (In the discussion hereafter, we will use VW [Volkswagen] and DDB [Doyle Dane Bernbach] interchangeably, though we recognize that the "rhetor" in this situation includes both a car manufacturer and a marketing firm.) In today's era of "narrowcasting," "niche marketing," and "micropublishing," it is hard to imagine a magazine that boasts such a broad and varied readership as *Life* did. It is no wonder that VW chose to advertise there. This was their best bet at addressing the majority of Americans. Though circulation data help us to understand this audience's size and scope, they don't tell us much about the audience's interests, their knowledge, or their concerns. King wrote for a series of magazines that addressed a predominantly Christian audience. What can we say about the readers of *Life*?

Looking at the magazine's content might help us to develop a more nuanced picture of both the *intended* and the *actual* audiences. Many of the articles in this issue of *Life* reflect the magazine's national scope. One, for example, discusses an expanded space program proposed by then-senator John F. Kennedy. Another champions the U.S. Olympic swim team. But the magazine's feature article helps us to understand the sort of person who might be most immediately drawn to this particular issue. The April 25, 1960, feature article discusses vacation possibilities for those who would like to tour the southeastern United States by car. The reader is treated to an 18-page discussion of tourist stops, motels, places to eat, and maps to follow. The article is filled with lavish descriptions of America's collective bounty, inviting everyone to enjoy their national treasures. Of course, this enjoyment will happen by way of America's favored mode of transportation—the family car. What could DDB have assumed about their *intended audience*? This was a large and varied group of people all identifying as U.S. residents and probably interested in traveling by car. We can understand why the rhetor chose to feature a car ad in this issue (as did many other car manufacturers).

The occasion for "Why" is more difficult to locate because, unlike King's "Letter," this ad does not reference any immediate context or exigence. Thinking about the forum and the rhetor's purpose, however, gives us some insight into the occasion. Volkswagen (like many firms paying for commercial advertisement) wants to sell. This is their purpose. The forum is likely to attract an audience interested in cars and car travel. The interested reader must be in the market for a new car. If s/he is not, then the ad will not have its intended effect. Thus, even without direct mention in the ad itself, we can use other information to conclude that the occasion (an issue of a national magazine dedicated to car travel) suits the exigence (the intended audience's need to purchase a car). We have relied on *contextual* evidence to make our case about the ad's audience, occasion, forum, and purpose.

We can turn to *textual* evidence—information learned by attending to the ads themselves—to determine the ad's intended audience and their presuppositions. Looking at the "Think Small" campaign, and the *presuppositions* upon which its argument depends, gives us further insight into DDB's *intended* audience. "Why" was one installation in a larger campaign whose principal slogan was "Think Small." This effort included a series of print advertisements in national magazines and a booklet that Volkswagen distributed. The campaign praised the car's quality and affordability, arguing over and over again that substance should trump style. One print advertisement mentioned technical details such as the gas mileage (32 miles to the gallon—exceptionally good by the standards of the day); the unique and dependable engine ("an aluminum, air-cooled rear engine that would go 70 mph all day without strain"); the "sensible size for a family"; and the "sensible price tag." Another print ad titled "Lemon" insisted that Volkswagen had removed all the defective products from its assembly line. The car featured in this ad's principal photograph was rejected simply because of a blemish on the chrome strip above the glove compartment. A third print ad in this same series showcased a photograph of a single Beetle, and claimed to be introducing the "'51, '52, '53, '54, '55, '56, '57, '58, '59, '60, '61 Volkswagen." The text explained that Volkswagen didn't make changes to the car's appearance unless such changes "make it work better." And the customer was assured that a change in body or mechanics would accommodate older models, so any "authorized Volkswagen dealer can repair any year's Volkswagen, even the earliest." These same ads mocked the Beetle's apparent lack of style. One ad featured a picture of the U.S. *Apollo* spacecraft moon-landing module, a hideous contraption. Underneath were the VW logo and the following words: "It's ugly, but it gets you there." Another asked if the VW "fad" had "died out." The answer—yes. The ad's copy explained that some people bought the car because of its quirky appearance but soon discovered its affordability and functionality, so they lost interest in the Beetle as a "cute" car and fell in love all over again. "As a fad," we are told, "the car was a flop." But "as a car, the VW was impressive."

Who would find such ads appealing? What must the audience *presuppose* to find these ads convincing? The "Why" ad, like the others, appeals to an intended audience that values mechanical reliability and affordability. The intended audience does not care about flashy style. They want a cheap car that will run forever, that will rarely break down, and that will be easy to fix when, rarely, necessary. Before we look at the "Why" ad in any detail, let's try to sum up some of our conclusions about the rhetorical situation (with a few comparisons to King's rhetorical situation). Just as King's intended audience must be already concerned about the issues under discussion, Volkswagen's audience must already be in the market for a car. The audience must arrive at the "Why" ad already aware of their exigent need to buy a car. The occasion—a national magazine featuring a lengthy article about road trips—is likely to attract an audience already interested in buying a new car. Just as King's intended audience must harbor presuppositions in line with the liberal political and the Judaeo-Christian religious traditions, so Volkswagen's intended audience must value affordability and reliability rather than style. King's audience arrives with respect for him as a religious leader but worries about his recent direct action campaigns. Volkswagen's audience arrives with concern about the company's and the car's past associations with Nazi Germany. They also know about a flashy style of automobile and showy advertisements (something like the Chrysler ad reprinted on p. 268). They may have even liked these flamboyant ads as well as the cars they peddled.

How does the rhetor address this rhetorical situation? The "Why" ad opens with a question that would probably occur to anyone glancing at three identical cars whose appearance differs so dramatically from what normally would have been seen on an American highway in 1960: Why would I be interested in this small, ugly car? In their chosen title, DDB shows an awareness of and speaks to the audience's presuppositions and their likely reaction. DDB also responds tacitly to the company's and the car's sordid history by redefining the Beetle as an affordable car. They don't mention the company's past because they don't want to invoke a negative association. Rather, they get right to the task of defining the Beetle in terms that will appeal to an audience already concerned with reliability and affordability. Furthermore, the ad acknowledges the Beetle's apparent lack of style by showcasing three identical cars as if they were different. Underneath each picture is a number indicating gas mileage, as if each of the models were unique and thus able to perform differently. The joke here will be evident to any reader familiar with car ads that showcase many different models photographed from a variety of angles (such as the Chrysler spread reprinted at the end of this book).

The ad also demonstrates an awareness of the *genre* and the audience's expectations. DDB knew that the reader would expect a flashy ad with slanted script, exclamation points, dynamic and alluring photographs, and a variety of designs. The ad repeats many of the generic qualities of 1960s car ads. We get multiple pictures of the car and text explaining its unique features. One third of the page is dedicated to text (mostly located at the bottom of the page), while two thirds of the page are dedicated to pictures. But the ad also violates some of the generic qualities, thus catching the audience off-guard and differentiating the Beetle from everything else on the market. The ad speaks in an understated, direct, plain voice. The pictures are small and austere, a grainy black-and-white. The ad itself is simple and inexpensive but (like the product) effective.

We will offer more elaborate discussions of the VW "Why" ad and its kairos in later chapters. For our purposes here, we hope to accomplish two things. First, we want to show how the vocabulary used to analyze King's "Letter" can explain the rhetorical work of another effort at persuasion. Second, we want to show how the notion of an *historical-cultural context* can enrich a rhetorical analysis focused on kairos and the rhetorical situation. Earlier in this chapter, we defined the historical-cultural context as the "events and circumstances" that shape and give meaning to a discourse.

Our analysis so far might lead you to conclude that "Why" persuaded people to buy Beetles by redefining the car, by repeating the generic features of a car ad in a novel way, and above all by catering to people's desire for a mechanically sound and affordable vehicle. This is a reasonable conclusion. But there is another interpretation available once we begin to consider the era's broad cultural developments. In the 1960s, the United States was beginning a dramatic shift in culture, away from 1950s conformity and toward 1960s and 1970s counterculture. "Why" in many ways is a counter-ad, part and parcel of the 1960s counterculture. "Why" repeats the generic qualities of car advertisement while refusing to participate in some of the flashy design and overblown language common to this genre. The ad invites the reader to look skeptically at American advertising in general by conceding that ads often make inflated claims about their products. For example, the body text initially confesses that the Beetle rarely gets the promised 50 miles per gallon. "Why" (and the entire "Think Small" campaign) changed the kairos by telling the audience to be wary of all advertisements, to resist the pressures of U.S. consumer culture, and to look critically at car ads featuring lots of chrome, smiling families, and futuristic dashboard gadgets.

By appealing to the readers' skepticism toward American advertising, DDB drew on and contributed to a broad trend away from the social norms that had dominated American society. The ad tapped into a rip current in the U.S. historical-cultural waters. When the rhetors asked their audience to laugh at automobile advertising, they also asked the audience to separate themselves from all that made America what it was—all that was presented in the April 25, 1960, issue of *Life* magazine. In 1963, Bob Dylan sang, "The times, they are a-changin." "Why" exploited this new kairos. VW became the anti-commercial car and the Beetle thereafter was stamped onto 1960s youth culture. As baby boomers sought to distance themselves from their parents, as youth culture sought to distance itself from what came before it, as counterculture sought to undermine stifling conformity, a series of advertisements positioned a product on the side of the new, the young, the hip, and the deeply skeptical. Interestingly enough, by touting the Beetle as a car that should be bought for its substance, not its style, DDB fashioned a style that attracted young Americans.

Why did "Why" convince readers to buy Beetles? This question can be answered in two ways, each supportable by rhetorical analysis. (1) The ad appealed to readers' presuppositions, particularly their belief that reliability and affordability matter more than style. (2) The ad appealed to a style of nonconformity that suited the historical-cultural developments of a new generation. Which is more likely the case? It all depends on the (rhetorical) situation.

WRITING A KAIROS ANALYSIS

Following is Rebecca Reilly's analysis focused on kairos and the rhetorical situation. We encourage you to notice two things: First, Rebecca thought extensively about the rhetorical situation by answering the questions below. Answering these questions helped Rebecca to see what she had to learn about the rhetorical situation in order to write a kairos analysis. She then set out to do some research. Rebecca consulted LexisNexis to find articles about her topic and the documentary she analyzed. She also consulted several online documents, all listed in her works-cited page.

QUESTIONS FOR ANALYSIS

Occasion and Exigence: What motivating events set the stage for this rhetor's contribution? What conditions or issues affect this discourse's creation or reception? The motivating event for the documentary was the publishing of Robert McNamara's book, *Wilson's Ghost: Reducing the Risk of Conflict, Killing, and Catastrophe in the 21st Century,* in 2001. Conditions and issues affecting the documentary's creation and reception revolve mainly around the Vietnam War and McNamara's involvement. In his book, McNamara apparently claims that he was against the Vietnam War the whole time. Critics of McNamara claim that he was responsible for the war and denounce him for trying to escape this accountability.

Historical and Cultural Context: What recent events affect what the rhetor can say or how the audience will likely respond? What long-term historical, political, or cultural trends does this discourse contribute to or draw upon? Since the release of his book, McNamara has received a lot of criticism for the claims he makes in it. His stances and his critics' responses certainly affect what both Errol Morris (the director of the documentary) and McNamara can say and how the audience responded. The historical/political/cultural trends the documentary draws upon include Ford Motor Company, Kennedy's presidency, Johnson's presidency, the Cuban Missile Crisis, and the Vietnam War.

Forum and Genre: Where did this persuasive effort occur or appear? What kind of discourse is this? What other discourses formally resemble this one? Has another rhetor made a completely different argument that resembles this one in some significant way? What do these arguments share? What are their generic qualities? This documentary appeared in various countries and cities throughout the United States. This symbolic act is a documentary. Other symbolic acts that resemble this one are other documentaries about Kennedy, Johnson, and the Vietnam War.

Kairos: What constraints and opportunities are available to the rhetor? What can or does the rhetor change by intervening in this way? What can the rhetor manage at the beginning, middle, or by the end of this argument? What new opportunities and constraints does the argument create? The constraints on the rhetor, Morris, mainly concern the statement McNamara was making about the Vietnam War and how critics were receiving this statement. The opportunity available to Morris was giving McNamara a chance to explain himself and filming it to show McNamara's side. The book by McNamara wasn't going to speak for itself. Morris may have changed some people's minds about McNamara with this film. At the beginning of the argument, Morris had to be sure that he was presenting McNamara in a way that wouldn't immediately turn off his audience, which would include critics. In the middle of the argument, Morris was laying the groundwork to demonstrate why McNamara felt the way he did about the war (and various other events) and provide evidence to support McNamara's feelings. By the end of the argument, even though McNamara would not commit to saying anything explicitly, Morris succeeded in giving McNamara a chance to explain his actions. This argument certainly opened up more criticism, but it also gave the audience a chance to see how complicated a man's life really is.

Rhetor: Who is the ostensible speaker? Who is the implied rhetor? Who is the actual rhetor? What are both the implied and the actual rhetors' motivations, presuppositions, and intentions? The ostensible speaker is McNamara. The implied rhetor is McNamara. The actual rhetor is Morris. McNamara's motivations and intentions are obvious. He wanted a chance to explain himself in a way that his book could not allow. His presuppositions are mainly that his audience consisted of mostly critics, so he needed to get his point across quickly and clearly. Morris's motivations and intentions are a little less evident. I think he wanted to give McNamara a chance to speak and give his argument more depth.

Audience: Who is the ostensible addressee? Who is the intended audience? Who is the actual audience? What are the intended and the actual audience's motivations, presuppositions, and responses? The ostensible addressees are critics and anyone interested in McNamara's life. The intended audience includes critics, McNamara fans, and Morris fans. The actual audience is really anyone who has access to a computer or a television and a DVD player. The audience's motivations can range from hating McNamara and wanting more ammunition against him to loving Morris's previous work and wanting to see his new documentary. The audience's responses were mostly positive, considering the film won Best Documentary Feature in 2003.

Rebecca's research located *contextual evidence*. As our analyses of King's "Letter" and the Volkswagen ad campaign suggest, to answer some of these questions—such as the questions about audience presuppositions and what they reveal about the rhetor and the intended audience—you should closely examine the text. Rebecca does so, often making observations about what the intended audience believed based on *textual evidence*. Other questions—such as those asking for a description of the historical context—cannot be fully addressed by looking at the text, and often will require some research. In our analysis of King's rhetorical situation, for example, we sampled the opinion pages of the *New York Times* from April to June 1963 to get an index of the national perception of King and his actions at that time. (We were able to access those documents online, through a database in our university's library.) Likewise, we consulted S. Jonathan Bass's book, *Blessed Are the Peacemakers* (2002), for information about the original circumstances in which the "Letter" was composed and its publication venues. (This was found through a library catalogue search for books about King and the civil-rights movement in the 1960s.) We also examined old copies of *Christian Century, New Leader,* and *Atlantic Monthly* from the summer of 1963 (available in our university library) to assess their readerships. Other general background information came from common knowledge about King and the civil-rights movement, for example what is reflected in popular media sources such as the acclaimed PBS documentary, *Eyes on the Prize* (1992).

Our analysis of the VW ad draws on a range of sources, including demographic information about *Life*'s readership in 1960, the U.S. census of the same era, and the actual magazine in which the ad was printed. We found the circulation data in *Life*, the census report online (at www.census .gov), and the magazine in our own university's archives library. In searching our university's library, we also found and consulted a range of books on the history of advertising, each positioning the "Think Small" campaign in a different historical-cultural context. Stephen Fox's *The Mirror*

Makers: A History of American Advertising and its Creators (1997) sets the "Think Small" campaign in the historical-cultural context of mid-century American advertising, exploring the profession, its personnel, and the major firms that shaped U.S. marketing in the twentieth century. Daniel Pope's *The Making of Modern Advertising* (1983) discusses the legal and political context that shaped commercial culture in the twentieth century. Thomas Frank's *The Conquest of Cool: Business Culture, Counterculture, and the Rise of Hip Consumerism* (1998) sets the "Think Small" campaign in the historical-cultural context of 1960s counterculture. These reflections indicate that a range of research skills can contribute to an effective analysis of the kairos, but the research itself should be guided by the terms introduced in this chapter. Before doing any research, we encourage you to think about the text you've chosen to analyze. Try answering the questions listed on pp. 35-37 before going to the library. Your answers should reveal gaps in your knowledge. What do you need to learn about the occasion, the issue, the exigence, the forum, the historical-cultural context, the audience, and the rhetor?

We'll encourage you to notice something else about Rebecca's answers to the questions on pp. 35-37. She generated far more material than she could address in the space of a short, 3–5 page paper, so she had to make some choices. You'll notice in the following analysis that Rebecca chose to focus on only a few important elements—the observations and the terms that explain how the film's argument addressed its rhetorical situation. For example, though the answers to the questions for analysis include observations about the real audience, Rebecca chose not to talk about whether the real audience would actually be convinced. Instead, this question remains open at the paper's conclusion. We encourage you to use these questions in the same way. Answer all of them. Then, read over your answers to determine what is most important. Which answers help you to explain the relationship between the text you're analyzing and its rhetorical situation? Use only the terms, such as *intended audience* and *historical horizon*, and the observations that help you to write your analysis.

STUDENT ANALYSIS OF *KAIROS*
AND A RECENT DOCUMENTARY

Rebecca Reilly
Professor Mark Longaker
RHE 321 Principles of Rhetoric
February 12, 2010

The Kairos of War

Errol Morris's documentary, *The Fog of War* (2005), is an
example of epideictic rhetoric that makes two arguments: one,
the immediate argument about Robert McNamara's reputation;
and two, the broader argument about the difficulty of war, the
responsibilities of the government during war, and all that the
"fog of war" entails. (The entire documentary can be found by
searching for "fog of war" at www.googlevideo.com.) With the
first argument, Morris addresses an intended audience that was
reacting to McNamara's claims about the Vietnam War. With
the second argument, Morris engages a broader conversation,
a larger intended audience that questioned the U.S.'s involvement in the War in Iraq.

The audience of people debating McNamara's reputation
often responded directly by criticizing McNamara himself. In
2001, Robert McNamara published a book entitled *Wilson's
Ghost: Reducing the Risk of Conflict, Killing, and
Catastrophe in the 21st Century,* in which he claimed that he
had been against the Vietnam War from the beginning. The
book received mixed reviews. James Chace of *The New York
Times* called it "a courageous attempt to tackle the most crucial issues of our time" (12) while Chris Bray of *The
Washington Post* called it "an embarrassing failure in every
sense" (T04). <u>Both fans and critics of McNamara were looking
back at his reputation to support and defend their views.</u>

In this passage,
notice Rebecca's
claim (underlined)
about the film's
intended audience
as well as the two
pieces of contextual
evidence (quotes
from book reviews)
that she presents to
support the claim.

In this passage, notice Rebecca's claim (underlined) about the film's intended audience as well as the textual evidence (the quotes) from the film that she presents to support the claim. Look at the next paragraph. What claims does Rebecca make about the film's actual or intended audience, and what kind of evidence—textual or contextual—does she present to support her claim?

Those who lived during the Vietnam War and were old enough to realize that the U.S. was killing a lot of people knew intimately the way Chace and Bray felt about McNamara. Morris's immediate argument regarding McNamara's reputation, then, has an intended audience—an audience comprised of people who knew McNamara firsthand during the 1960s through the 1970s. In the film itself, Morris has clips of American journalist Harry Reasoner telling McNamara what the public thinks of him: "One Congressman called you Mr. I-have-all-the-answers McNamara" and "What about the contention that your attitude is sometimes arrogant, that you never admit that you were wrong?" Reasoner was voicing the opinion of the people.

Morris also showed newspaper clippings about Norman Morrison, who protested U.S. involvement in the Vietnam War. McNamara described the incident saying, "He was opposed to war, the violence of war, the killing. He came to the Pentagon, doused himself with gasoline. Burned himself to death below my office." Americans who lived during those two decades were well aware of how angry some were that the U.S. was fighting in Vietnam, and Morris was more likely to connect with this intended audience by showing events they experienced.

While many in the film's intended audience would have concerns about MacNamara's reputation, many others were concerned with a broader historical development: the U.S. war in Iraq, which began in 2003. McNamara's discussion about the Vietnam War in *The Fog of War* was very relevant to the historical context when it was released in 2004. Morris's film received a lot of attention because his actual audience began having conversations about McNamara's life. The actual audience, which included really anyone with a television and a DVD player, was

In this passage, notice Rebecca's claim (underlined) about the film's relation to its historical context as well as the contextual evidence (the historical information about the war in Iraq) that she presents to support that claim.

Reilly 3

drawing connections between the Vietnam War and the war in Iraq. If one were to search "war in Iraq and Vietnam" in the database LexisNexis® Academic, it returns over 1,900 hits. An editorial published in the *Los Angeles Times* stated, "liberals see the repetitions of Vietnam—they worry that wars fought far from American shores will confront nationalist sentiment, turn Americans into hated invaders and end in morass and humiliation" ("Vietnam" A41). Peter Slevin of *The Washington Post* wrote, "[Rep. Tim] Walz keeps returning to the question of a Vietnam veteran who told him that Obama's dilemma over sending perhaps 40,000 more soldiers to Afghanistan reminded him of another president—Lyndon B. Johnson" (A03). These links were not explicitly made to McNamara's life, but people were definitely talking about it. Helle Dale of *The Washington Times* called the parallels between the two wars "ominous" (A19). Morris's actual audience was showing the same interests harbored by his intended audience.

> In this passage, notice Rebecca's claim (underlined on previous page) about the film's actual audience as well as the contextual evidence (the LexisNexis search and the quotes from selected articles) that she presents to support the claim that the actual audience was talking and concerned about the war in Iraq as it compared to the Vietnam War.

Morris surely intended to speak to those debating McNamara's reputation, but he also intended to speak to this audience of people worried about the Iraq war. In his Academy Award Acceptance Speech, he said, "Forty years ago this country went down a rabbit hole in Vietnam and millions died. I fear we're going down a rabbit hole once again. And if people can stop and think and reflect on some of the ideas and issues in this movie, perhaps I've done some damn good here" (para 3). Morris took the narrow interests of his intended audience about the Vietnam War and applied them to the war in Iraq, in order to engage a broader audience. Morris weaves between the narrow and broad interests, which engages both his intended and actual audiences. In the film itself, McNamara provides general lessons he's learned about war and supports them with specific evidence from his own life.

> In this passage, notice Rebecca's claim (underlined) about the intended audience as well as the contextual evidence (the testimony from the director) that she presents to support this claim.

Reilly 4

Wikipedia describes the "fog of war" as "the level of ambiguity in situational awareness experienced by participants in military operations" ("Fog" para 1). In other words, very few sure decisions are made during war because an all-encompassing view of the situation is impossible. Morris wanted to demonstrate to his audience this ambiguity with the Vietnam War through McNamara's eyes and compel his audience to find the relationships between that war and the war in Iraq. Morris certainly succeeded in addressing his intended and actual audiences with the narrow and broader arguments. Whether or not the audiences were actually persuaded by the rhetor's arguments remains to be seen.

Reilly 5

Works Cited

Bray, Chris. "Damage Control." *Washington Post* 12 Aug
  2001: T04. Print.

Chace, James. "The Future Is a Foreign Country." *New York
  Times* 29 Jul 2001: 7.12. Print.

Dale, Helle. "A Window of Opportunity." *Washington Times*
  1 Mar 2007: A19. Print.

"Fog of War." *Wikipedia.* 2010. 14 Feb 2010.
  < http://en.wikipedia.org/wiki/Fog_of_war>. Web.

McNamara, Robert and James Blight. *Wilson's Ghost:
  Reducing the Risk of Conflict, Killing, and Catastrophe in
  the 21st Century.* New York: PublicAffairs, 2001. Print.

Morris, Errol. "Academy Award Acceptance Speech:
  The Fog of War." Errol Morris. 2004. 16 Feb 2010.
  <http://www.errolmorris.com/film/fow_speech.html>. Web.

Slevin, Peter. "Americans Conflicted over Afghanistan War;
  Voices in a Minnesota Town 'I'm Confused. What Is Our
  Objective?'" *Washington Post* 22 Nov 2009: A03. Print.

"Vietnam to Afghanistan: Obama's Expansion of the War
  Does Not Mean the Nation Is Facing a Rerun of the
  1960s." *Los Angeles Times* 6 Dec 2009: A41. Print.

3

Argumentation

In a popular episode of the 1990s sitcom *Seinfeld* (titled "Comeback"), George Costanza attends an office meeting where boiled shrimp are served as a mid-day snack. As George scarfs down shrimp, an office-mate jokes, "Hey George, the ocean called. They're running out of shrimp." Everyone laughs to George's great embarrassment. Long after the meeting has ended, George invents a comeback: "Oh yeah, Riley, well the jerk-store called, and they're running out of you!" Of course, George failed to deliver the comeback in a timely fashion. For the remainder of the episode, George schemes to recreate the circumstance that elicited Riley's comment. When George finally does get Riley at another meeting, he presents a plate of shrimp and eats them voraciously. Riley gladly voices his clever one-liner, again to boisterous laughter. George triumphantly delivers his comeback to complete silence. George thinks he has a kairos problem—great line, bad timing. He doesn't. As the audience knows, George has an argument problem—bad line, no matter what the timing.

The previous chapter focused on the first part of George's problem, the "when" of discourse. The remainder of this book—and this chapter in particular—focuses on the second part of George's problem, the "what" of discourse. Though kairos is arguably most important, the better part of classical and contemporary rhetorical theory focuses on content and form, not timing. Nevertheless, as we further explore rhetorical theory/analysis, we'll encourage you to remember something George forgot: You need good timing and a good comeback, favorable kairos and an effective argument. You need to analyze the argument in its rhetorical situation.

THE CLASSICAL *PISTEIS*: ETHOS, LOGOS, PATHOS

Before we get too far, let's define some terms. *Argument* is persuasion's engine. An argument seeks to connect a claim to the audience's *presuppositions*: what they already recognize as true, probable, or desirable. A *direct argument* overtly gives reasons and draws conclusions; an *indirect argument* presents a set of ideas and/or images in an effort to get the audience to draw certain conclusions (what we'll call *inferences*). Perhaps the most familiar classical effort to analyze an argument is Aristotle's three-part classification of the *pisteis* (singular *pistis*), or what often are described as the main modes of proof or appeal: ethos as the ethical appeal; logos as the logical appeal; and pathos as the pathetic or emotional appeal. These modern expressions are inexact, unless one keeps in mind the classical notion of *pistis* as a way of correcting and informing what is meant by appeals. *Pistis* means an assurance or guarantee that inspires trust, faith, or belief in something. A *pistis* may be a proof in the modern sense, in which case (if successful) it inspires a high degree of confidence or even certainty. Some *pisteis* fall short of certainty, yet they can be reasons for some degree of faith in an idea.

As Aristotle observed, the three rhetorical *pisteis* derive from the three main aspects of the communicative act: speaker, speech, and audience. We can illustrate by analyzing the parts of a commercial that aired in the United Kingdom during the 1990s. Consider the last scene in an effort to sell the high-performance VW Golf (see Figure 3.1 shown below)

- *Ethos* is the apparent character of the speaker—whatever inspires trust (or the opposite). This includes reputation, credentials, knowledge of the subject, intelligence, fair-mindedness, honesty, goodwill, and general moral quality. In the VW commercial displayed below the logo presents an ethical appeal. The audience is asked to trust the speaker because the logo signifies a recognizable and presumably trustworthy corporation. Aristotle thought that such trust-inspiring qualities were communicated principally through the speaker's self-presentation. A good, effective self-presentation can outweigh a shaky reputation, and in many cases the audience knows little in advance about the rhetor. Other authorities, however, place great emphasis on the rhetor's reputation

Figure 3.1   Closing screenshot of a 1990s VW Golf VR6 commercial that aired in the United Kingdom.

and a good public image. The ethos appeal consists, in essence, of a two-step process. The rhetor petitions the audience for their trust, which, in turn, gives the audience reason to trust the rhetor's statements. The viewer recognizes the logo, trusts VW, and so they have reason to believe the commercial's claims about the Golf VR6.

- *Pathos* is the emotion of the audience. This mood or feeling motivates the audience to believe or do something. It is often said that pathos—desire, fear, anger, love, and so on—moves a person to take action. The VW commercial makes a particularly strong pathos appeal by offering an image of a Golf VR6 driving down a city street at night. Such a vibrant and dynamic scene asks the audience to feel excited about the cityscape and about the car. Like the ethos appeal, the pathos appeal is basically a two-step process. Typically, the speaker must first present *causes for emotion*, or what we'll call *pathemata* (singular *pathema*), to arouse, intensify, or change the audience's emotion. Then the emotion functions as a reason for embracing an idea or taking action. If, as a viewer, you are excited by the image of a lively city street, then you may be motivated to purchase a car associated with that emotion and that place.

- *Logos* is the reasoning itself—in direct argumentation, it is the stated reason or reasons and/or evidence given in support of a conclusion; in indirect argumentation, it is the unspoken relationships between the speakers' statements and the conclusions (inferences) they encourage the audience to draw. (The basic meanings of the word *logos*, in Greek, are "speech, word, statement, reason.") The VW commercial we've discussed so far offers a logos appeal in the text, which reads: "235 Nm torque at 4200 rpm." Since this is an indirect argument, the rhetor does not tell the audience exactly what to conclude, but the viewer is nevertheless encouraged to infer that the Golf VR6 is a high-performance vehicle. We will also say more about logos (and this logos appeal) later in this chapter. The point for now is that the logos appeal consists of reasons for accepting the rhetor's claims; the logical relationships among claim and reason(s); and the audience's presuppositions.

Two additional points should be noted here: First, so far we have discussed the *pisteis* as isolated elements in an argument; we do this to explain concepts. But it probably is better to think of the *pisteis* not as isolated appeals, but as *simultaneous dimensions* of persuasion, though one appeal or another may dominate. A speaker's overt reasoning (logos), no matter how logical it seems, will probably fail to persuade if the audience perceives the speaker as untrustworthy (ethos): "My cousin bought a Volkswagen, and it was not a reliable vehicle." Likewise, a perfectly logical argument may have no effect if the audience just doesn't care about the issue (i.e., *apathetic*, without pathos): "Yes, the Golf VR6 has a powerful engine, but I don't like to drive fast, and my idea of a night out doesn't involve a dirty city street." Correspondingly, an emotional appeal (pathos) may fall flat if what the rhetor says (logos) does not make sense: "Wow, it would be exciting to drive through that city at night! But what do these numbers and letters mean? What's Nm? Are 4,200 rpms a lot?" In a fully persuasive argument, ethos, logos, and pathos support each other.

Second, it is a common mistake to think of logos alone as logical, and ethos and pathos as nonlogical or irrational. All the appeals have a logical dimension, as well as a pathetic dimension. The ethos appeal, for example, arises if *reasons for trust* have been presented—and *trust* is a form of pathos. Likewise, the pathos appeal arises if *reasons for emotion* (or *pathemata*) have been presented. Thus, we can speak of a *reasonable* emotion, and can change how a person feels by showing that the perceived causes for his or her emotion are mistaken or by presenting causes for a different emotion. Moreover, logos itself has a pathetic dimension. The most logical conclusion depends on whether the audience regards the conclusion as a good or bad thing. Indeed, as modern argumentation theorist Chaim Perelman has recognized, all arguments work with natural language—language in its everyday, flexible, common use, as opposed to rigid symbolic logic. Virtually all words in natural language carry a pathetic dimension, as part of their normal meaning. (See Chaim Perelman and Lucie Olbrechts-Tyteca, *The New Rhetoric,* trans. John Wilkinson and Purcell Weaver [Notre Dame: Notre Dame University Press, 1969].)

For these reasons, it usually is insufficient in rhetorical analysis simply to label instances of ethos, logos, or pathos as *appeals.* A more adequate analysis will observe how they work together or interact.

REASONS AND EVIDENCE: THE ARTISTIC AND INARTISTIC *PISTEIS*

Classical theory refers to ethos, logos, and pathos as *artistic* (or *entechnic*) forms of *pistis.* They are created through the rhetor's art (*techne*): the rhetor's self-presentation, the rhetor's reasoning, and the rhetor's handling of the audience's emotions. But there are also *inartistic* (*atechnic*) *pisteis*—forms of evidence that are simply collected and used. These include witness testimony, citations from authorities, documents, contracts, physical evidence (such as, in a criminal trial, crime-scene photographs, ballistics evidence, fingerprints, and DNA), statistics, opinion surveys, and so on. *Inartistic pisteis* are often crucial to an argument. Witnesses or physical evidence, for example, may be necessary to establish or confirm the alleged facts that the rhetor cites as evidence for a claim. Likewise, expert testimony may be invoked as a *pistis*, a source of credibility, for some general principle for an evaluative judgment, or for an interpretation of facts. For example, if Volkswagen wanted to offer inartistic evidence to support its claim about the Golf VR6's high-performance engine, it could cite results generated by engineers in their lab: "According to VW's highly-trained automotive technicians, who tested over 300 new Golf VR6 engines . . ." Or, they could cite an expert, such as *Car and Driver* magazine, which may have reported the Golf VR6 "most powerful in its class" for that year. Of course, the audience's willingness to accept this inartistic proof depends on the credibility (ethos) of the engineers or of *Car and Driver* magazine.

METHODS OF ANALYSIS

To study the interaction among *pisteis* in a single argument—to see the proofs as dimensions of the same persuasive effort—try to isolate one component in a visual or textual argument, and identify the ethical, pathetic, and logical proofs in this same element. For instance, we discuss parts of the VW Golf ad as isolated appeals: ethos in the VW logo, pathos in the image, and logos in the text. But we could identify the ethical, pathetic, and logical dimensions in the text alone. A reader may trust the rhetor because she can see that this speaker knows some technical information about cars: "The speaker must be an expert, since the text includes technical vocabulary such as 'torque' and complex ideas, such as the amount of torque produced when the engine is running at its top end (4,200 rpms)." A reader may feel excited by the promise of a powerful vehicle: "This car must go super-fast!" Finally, a reader may be moved to infer that the car is powerful based upon the evidence presented: "If the engine produces that much torque at 4,200 rpms, the Golf must be a high-performance vehicle." Take another element in the ad—such as the VW logo, the image, or whatever else interests you—and try to identify the ethical, the pathetic, and the logical dimensions to this single component. Or, choose your own argument, and isolate an element in it. What is the ethical appeal here? What is the pathetic appeal? What's the logical appeal? How do they work together?

ARGUMENT AND THE STRUCTURE OF PRACTICAL REASONING

By *practical* reasoning we mean the natural, informal reasoning process involved in everyday human action (*praxis*), from the most mundane to the most momentous—the more or less intuitive process of drawing conclusions. All people engage in practical reasoning, with or without special training. Practical reasoning can be relatively conscious, but much of it can go on subconsciously, as a reflex based on deep presuppositions.

The basic structure and psychology of practical reasoning has been described in different ways by different theorists, including Aristotle. One of the most useful modern theories for rhetorical analysis belongs to philosopher Stephen Toulmin. (see Toulmin, *The Uses of Argument*, 2nd edition [Cambridge: Cambridge University Press, 2003], ch. 3); Toulmin's analysis owes much to Aristotle's account of practical reasoning in the *Nicomachean Ethics, Movement of Animals*, and *Rhetoric*.

Toulmin represents what he calls the basic "layout of arguments" as shown in Figure 3.2.

What Toulmin calls a "datum" we have glossed as an "item of information." By this we mean (as does Toulmin) something fairly broad—in essence, any idea, statement, or perception that enters conscious awareness. When a datum enters consciousness, and is perceived as factual and meaningful, it makes possible an interpretive inference or conclusion, or what Toulmin calls a "claim," but only *if there is a warrant present to justify the inference.* The warrant is what we have been calling a presupposition—an idea already present in the mind, though not necessarily conscious. The relation between the datum and warrant

Figure 3.2   Toulmin's analysis of practical argument.

permits the conclusion or claim. To clarify, let's return to the logos appeal in the VW commercial discussed earlier. Using Toulmin's terms, we can represent its formation in the audience's mind as follows:

Datum (piece of information):	The Golf VR6 produces 235Nm torque at 4,200 rpms
Warrant (presupposition):	[An engine that produced 235Nm torque at 4,200 rpms is very powerful]
Claim (inference/ response):	SO you should buy the Golf VR6.

That is, the datum—if accepted—combines with a warrant that is already available in the consumer's mind. (Note that the warrant has rational as well as emotional components; the audience must rationally understand that the measurement of torque signifies a powerful engine, but they must also feel emotionally excited about driving such a fast car.) Together, the datum and the warrant produce a claim (which, here, may take the form of a conscious thought but may simply be an emotional reaction, a feeling of attraction to the car and its performance). This, then, is the simplest, most basic form of an *argument* in practical reasoning: one datum, one warrant, one claim.

Argumentation

So far we have been discussing practical reasoning—the process of forming arguments—as it occurs in the mind of an audience (a prospective car buyer, in our example). By *argumentation* we mean the process of *presenting arguments* to an audience, in order to guide their practical reasoning. As Toulmin points out, the presentation of an argument like the one just shown typically takes the general form "Datum, SO Claim": "The Golf VR6 produces 235Nm torque at 4,200 rpms, SO you should buy a Golf VR6." (The evidence is presented; then the conclusion is drawn.) But many other surface forms of expression are possible, such as, "You should buy the Golf VR6 because its engine produces 235Nm torque at 4,200 rpms." (The claim is stated; then the reason for it is presented.) In both of these examples, as is common in real-world argumentation, some part remains unstated. In this case, the warrant is left out. The rhetor assumes that the warrant is obvious enough to go without saying and expects the audience to fill it in from their own presuppositions. Sometimes even more may be left out. In the scene we've discussed, the conclusion is left out as well! The viewer must provide the warrant and draw the conclusion. What is stated, what is not, and what can be suggested indirectly, depends greatly on what the rhetor wants or needs to emphasize, and what the rhetor feels can safely be assumed.

The presentation of arguments in real-world argumentation is seldom as bare bones as "Datum, SO Claim." Such one-sentence models only suggest the basic layout. In actual practice, a rhetor might devote hundreds or even thousands of words to the presentation of the datum before drawing the intended conclusion (the claim). The surface expression of an argument and its underlying rational structure are not necessarily the same. A fundamental task of rhetorical analysis is to identify that underlying structure, as well as to assess the surface expression.

The presentation of even simple arguments (like our example) can quickly lead to complications. For example, suppose that upon reading, "235Nm torque at 4,200 rpms," the audience is simply confused: "What's that supposed to mean?" In this case the audience has not presupposed the necessary warrant ("An engine that produced 235Nm torque at 4,200 rpms is very powerful"), so the datum-claim connection is unclear. The argument seems *illogical*. The rhetor must fill in the warrant: "An engine that produces 235Nm torque at 4,200 rpms is very powerful." Such a statement may be sufficient, especially if the audience already believes the idea, and they just need some reminding.

Perhaps, however, the audience simply has no idea what "torque" is, how it's measured, or why it matters. In this case, some *backing* is required—explanation of the technical concepts and terms. (When first viewing this commercial, we were similarly confused and had to consult a Wikipedia article before we could make sense of the datum.) If this backing is sufficient, then the original argument will be persuasive. But perhaps the audience accepts the backing, but only partially. After reading a Wikipedia article about torque and rotations per minute, we agree that an engine producing 235Nm torque at 4,200 rpms is very powerful. But we insist that a high-performance vehicle needs more than a fast engine—it needs all-wheel drive, disc brakes in the front and back, good suspension. In this case the rhetor, to be persuasive with this audience, may need to concede that point by adding what Toulmin calls a "restriction," a qualifier that limits the claim.

Datum:	The Golf VR6 produces 235Nm torque at 4,200 rpms
Claim:	SO you should buy the Golf VR6.
Warrant:	SINCE [An engine that produced 235Nm torque at 4,200 rpms is very powerful]
Backing:	BECAUSE . . . [discussion of how the comparison of torque and rotations per minute can demonstrate the power available in a car engine]
Restriction:	UNLESS you're interested in a car that not only goes fast but also handles well.

Of course, the rhetor might say more about the restriction—"However, VW Golf VR6 has all-wheel drive and disc brakes in the front and the back."

Virtually any part of an argument can be further elaborated. The datum may be established through a complex explanation, which itself consists of numerous datum-warrant-claim structures; the backing may be given further backing, again in the form of numerous subsidiary arguments. Supporting the components of an argument can go on indefinitely. In real practice, however, rhetors and audiences normally have a bottom line of bedrock beliefs and values that they consider nonnegotiable. Without such bottom lines, no argument could ever be resolved and no decision could be made. The viewer may not like fast cars. No amount of talk about suspension, engine performance, or braking capacity will move someone to purchase a Golf VR6 if he harbors certain bedrock beliefs: "High-performance vehicles are expensive; fast cars waste fuel; fast cars are dangerous." Further, there is a limit to how much elaboration can be effective: Depending on the situation, presentation and elaboration of all components can be tedious to an audience; commercials must rely on a brief presentation that leaves most of the reasoning unstated.

This five-part argument scheme, then, is what Toulmin describes as the basic form of all practical reasoning and argumentation. In essence, the core is the datum-warrant-claim structure; the backing and restriction are optional, supplemental elements that the rhetor may develop, as needed, depending on the audience and situation. As we have noted, the surface expression of an argument need not, and often does not, rigidly follow this layout. Arguments can take many forms. Toulmin's scheme represents the underlying reasoning structure that the surface expression can render in different ways. Thus, when *analyzing arguments*, it is necessary to begin by asking questions such as these: What is the rhetor's claim? (i.e., What is the rhetor ultimately asking the audience to believe, feel, and/or do?) What datum (or data) does the rhetor present as reasons for this claim? What warrants (or presuppositions) underlie the datum-claim connection?

CLASSICAL TERMS FOR ARGUMENT: ENTHYMEME AND EPICHEIREME

Enthymeme and *epicheireme* are classical terms for argument. Since we will use them in this book, some discussion is required. These terms refer to the processes of practical reasoning, but they name them in a particularly useful way.

Briefly, *enthymeme* signifies a *simple unit of argument*, consisting of a claim and its main supporting reasons. *Epicheireme*, in contrast, signifies a *complex unit of argument*, consisting of multiple, linked enthymemes. An entire discourse may consist of one or more enthymemes and/or epicheiremes. There is more to say about each.

Enthymeme

The classical notion of the enthymeme (Greek *enthymema*) is actually two related notions. These we will call, for convenience, the *ideational* enthymeme and the *presentational* enthymeme. At the outset, however, we would like to stress an important point: These two notions are really just two ways of looking at the same thing. Every argument has an ideational content and a presentational form. Every enthymeme can be analyzed to emphasize its form and its content. To focus on the presentational quality of an enthymeme, you should look at how the material is presented. What does the reader see or hear first? What does the argument present as its conclusion? To focus on the ideational quality

METHODS OF ANALYSIS

It is often difficult to analyze enthymemes using Toulmin's method because this sort of analysis requires that we translate the "natural" presentation of the argument into an artificial system. Nevertheless, applying Toulmin's categories can help us to understand how the argument works—what the argument asks the audience to presuppose and infer. Take the following selection from a July 21, 2008, entry on jsmooth's video blog illdoctrine.com:

Selection From Video Blog: "When you say, 'I think he's a racist,' that's not a bad move because you might be wrong. That's a bad move because you might be right. Because if that dude really is racist, you want to make sure you hold him accountable and don't let him off easy. And even though intuitively it feels like the hardest way to hit him is just run up on him and say, 'I think your #$@ is racist,' when you handle it that way, you're actually letting him off easy because you're setting up a conversation that's too simple for him to derail and duck out of. Just think about how this plays out every time a politician or celebrity gets caught out there. It always starts out as a 'What they did' conversation, but as soon as the celebrity and their defenders get on camera, they start doing judo flips and switching it into a 'what they are' conversation. [. . .] And then you try to explain that we don't need to see inside their soul to know that they shouldn't have said all that about the watermelon, and you try to focus on the facts of the situation, but by then it's too late because the 'what they are' conversation is a rhetorical Bermuda triangle where everything drowns in a sea of empty posturing until somebody just blames it all on hip-hop, and we forget the whole thing ever happened."

Notice what becomes apparent when we put some of this material into Toulmin's categories:

Datum: Saying to someone "I think your #$@ is racist" lets that person "duck" responsibility for specific actions.

Claim: SO calling someone a racist lets that person "off easy."

Warrant: [stated] SINCE calling someone a racist sets up a "what they are" conversation.

Backing: BECAUSE this accusation allows people to focus on their character, not on their actions, resulting in "a rhetorical Bermuda triangle where everything drowns in a sea of empty posturing."

Backing to the backing: BECAUSE when they talk about what they are, people focus on things they cannot observe or prove, like what's "inside their soul."

Warrant: [unstated] SINCE allowing people to "duck" responsibility is letting them "off easy."

The method of analysis exemplified here is a kind of translation from the natural language of the argument to the artificial language of Toulmin's system. We recommend that you try writing a similar translation to see both an argument's presentational quality and its logical structure.

---

of an enthymeme, you should look at its underlying logic. What does the reader understand as the evidence? What should the reader conclude based on this evidence? Sometimes the presentation and the content of an enthymeme will coincide. Sometimes they won't.

To focus on the ideational quality of an enthymeme, you must consider the argument's structure of ideas (i.e., datum, warrant, claim). You can think of this as the enthymeme's content. This notion of the enthymeme was mainly developed by Aristotle and his philosophical followers. Aristotle's analysis of the enthymeme is based on his much more extensive analysis of the *syllogism*, which is the basic unit of argument in formal logic. (If you take a course in logic from your local Philosophy Department, you will study the forms and rules of syllogisms. This study was in fact pioneered by Aristotle in his treatises on logic, including the *Analytics*, the *Topics*, and *Sophistical Refutations*.) Aristotle thought that the enthymeme and syllogism were *counterparts* and resembled each other, since both were based on the natural human capacity for reasoning. He also thought that the study of syllogisms would enable one to analyze and judge enthymemes more effectively. But, as he recognized, enthymemes and syllogisms differ. The enthymeme is more informal, closer to the structure of everyday practical reasoning. The syllogism formalizes that structure. The syllogism attempts the certainty of a mathematical proof. In contrast, the enthymeme, though more rational, is less rigid. Enthymemes incorporate ethos and pathos. They can be based on opinions (*doxa*) and probabilities (*eikota*) as well as certainties. The enthymeme's ideational content, when successful, produces conclusions that are not necessarily certain truths, but that are sufficiently probable and persuasive to warrant the assent of a reasonable person. One judges syllogisms as true or false, but enthymemes as more or less persuasive, as strong or weak.

To analyze the *presentational* quality of an enthymeme, you must consider inference as a feature of the rhetor's style. The rhetor *caps* a discussion (or a segment of a discussion) by giving its argument a focused, summative, and usually emphatic statement. You can think of this as the enthymeme's *form*, the stylized gesture of *drawing the conclusion*. An example might help to clarify the notion. In a discourse titled *Against the Sophists*, the fourth-century BCE rhetorician and educator Isocrates attempts to distinguish himself from his competitors. He begins with a longish buildup consisting of a review, running for several pages, of the sophists' flaws and inconsistencies. Then he caps the buildup-discussion with a presentational enthymeme:

> So when an ordinary person puts all these things together, and observes that these [self-advertised] teachers of wisdom and transmitters of happiness are themselves in great need and get a mere pittance from their students, that they are on the lookout for contradictions in words but fail to notice contradictions in deeds, and moreover that they pretend to see the future but cannot say anything useful or give any counsel regarding the present—while those who use their own judgment are more consistent and more successful than those who profess to exact knowledge—then that person has, I think, good reason to despise the sorts of things these people teach and to consider them idle talk and foolishness, and not a discipline of the mind. (Isocrates, *Against the Sophists* 7)

In effect, this presentational enthymeme summarizes and pulls together in one emphatic statement the ideational substance of the preceding paragraphs (the data), and configures it in a particular way to generate a particular conclusion (the claim). The argument includes many elements that appear as data and one element that looks like a claim. So far, we've only attended to the presentational form of Isocrates's enthymeme. We can also analyze this enthymeme to notice its ideational content, which can be presented in Toulmin's terms, as follows:

Data: These self-advertised teachers of wisdom are prone to foolish contradictions and are useless in practical affairs [examples . . .]

Warrant: [not stated]

Claim: SO it is reasonable for an ordinary person to consider them ridiculous, and to despise what they teach as worthless.

Isocrates depends on a warrant—a presupposition in his audience's mind—that is hard to summarize, though the basic idea seems to be that people who exhibit incompetence in practical life are generally laughable fools with nothing worthwhile to teach. (He addresses his intended audience as commonsensical people with little patience for flighty intellectuals.) Isocrates might have differently configured the ideational substance, by associating it with a different warrant and drawing a different conclusion. Instead of drawing the conclusion that his competitors' teachings deserve to be rejected and even despised by ordinary people, he could equally well have drawn the more charitable conclusion that his competitors are comical, head-in-the-clouds eccentrics, who can nevertheless prepare young minds for more serious and useful studies. (Isocrates actually does say something like that elsewhere; see *Antidosis* 261–269.) Such a conclusion would not, of course, serve Isocrates' polemical purposes in *Against the Sophists*.

The notion of a presentational enthymeme, however, does not strictly apply to speeches or to printed texts. Another example illustrates how a rhetor can make a presentational enthymeme out of just about anything, including a piece of graffiti carefully placed in an urban landscape. In our own city of Austin, Texas, we have watched an historically underprivileged and Hispanic neighborhood east of I-35 gentrify as wealthier, professional-class, and typically White residents move in. At the edge of East Austin, on a stop sign at Waller and East 4th Streets, one can see graffiti that reads "Yuppies off the EAST SIDE." (See Figure 3.3.) Standing at this location, we can easily see how the surrounding geography serves as data to support this conclusion. Immediately west of I-35 (and behind the stop sign) is the Austin skyline featuring steel-and-glass condominiums filled with professional-class residents. (See Figure 3.4.) Immediately east (and to the viewer's back) is a colorful working-class Hispanic neighborhood peppered with homes that have recently been remodeled and enlarged, the results of "yuppies" moving east. To the right, just one block away opposite the train tracks, is a row of new, trendy, and pricey stores, the kind of retail

Figure 3.3   "Yuppies off the EAST SIDE" graffiti at the corner of Waller and 4th Streets, Austin, Texas.

Figure 3.4   Austin skyline behind "Yuppies off the EAST SIDE" graffiti.

Figure 3.5 Trendy shops to the north of "Yuppies off the EAST SIDE" graffiti.

establishments that only professional-class shoppers can afford. (See Figure 3.5.) (Our brief descriptions and our photographs above attempt to capture the experience of standing at Waller and East 4th Streets. But you may get a better sense of this experience by taking a tour of the neighborhood using the street-view function in Googlemaps.)

Imagine you've driven or biked through this neighborhood. You've encountered all of these geographic elements. And you come upon this stop sign while leaving East Austin and entering Downtown. If you believe already that gentrification destroys the East Side's unique culture, or that "yuppies" migrating east will drive up home prices and drive out working-class families, then you will likely agree with the cap that this graffiti provides to its surrounding geographic data. We can translate this inferential process into Toulmin's schema:

Data: Experience of touring East Austin [examples . . .]

Warrant: [Gentrification destroys local culture and harms working-class families]

Claim: SO "Yuppies off the EAST SIDE!"

But imagine that you have the same experiences yet harbor different presuppositions. Perhaps you're a real-estate investor with properties in East Austin. You may be happy to see new, trendy shops and expensively remodeled homes near your property, since these developments will add to your property's value. You may draw a different conclusion: "Lawyers, Accountants, Consultants! Come to East Austin!" Or, imagine that you feel that gentrification is inevitable. You may conclude that it's best to enjoy this unique neighborhood while it lasts, before gentrification dilutes the local flavor. In fact, a recent Austin blogger drew this last inference when viewing the graffiti at Waller and East 4th Streets: "I say enjoy it now, 'cause change isn't gonna stop coming." (Read the whole blog entry at: http://www.dogcanyon.org/2010/04/30/yuppies-off-the-east-side/)

The rhetor, of course, tries to prevent these latter two conclusions with a few important presentational elements. We've already mentioned the location: On the East Side but in view of downtown, this enthymeme's cap is likely to lead the audience to appreciate East Austin and resent downtown. But there is also an important selection of vocabulary. The rhetor insists that "yuppies" get "off the EAST SIDE." Someone sympathetic to professional-class residents purchasing these homes would not call them "yuppies." (Note that our imagined real-estate investor used more flattering terms, such as "accountants" and "consultants.") Furthermore, the working-class Hispanic population refers to this area as the "EAST SIDE," while the professional-class, White population prefers to call it "East Austin." The "East Side" is associated with the music of the ranchera and the smell of the taquería. By choosing these terms—"yuppies" and "EAST SIDE"—the rhetor asks the audience to remember (and sympathize with) the working-class Hispanic residents. The rhetor also presents this message in a stenciled bit of graffiti on a stop sign. The manner of presentation—lacking polish but certainly alarming—asks the audience to identify with people presumably harmed by gentrification, the same underprivileged population that would likely express themselves with a crude bit of vandalism rather than a televised public-service announcement or a glossy poster.

This, then, is what we mean when we say that the *presentational* enthymeme configures the available ideational *substance* in a particular way. When done effectively, the presentation guides the audience to form, in their own minds, the particular ideational enthymeme that the rhetor intends. Indeed, by filling in the warrant (or other unstated part) for themselves, the audience participates. They come to the conclusion through their own thinking. The presentational enthymeme caps and focuses a discussion by explicitly stating a particular ideational enthymeme.

Validity and Strength of Enthymemes

Aristotle's comparison of enthymemes to the formally logical syllogism provides tools for critiquing the ideational content configured by an enthymeme's presentational form. Such critique involves two main concerns: the *validity* and *strength* of enthymemes. To explain, we'll need to take a brief detour into Aristotle.

Aristotle thought that syllogisms could be judged in terms of their *validity and truth*. Validity is a matter of correct logical form. Consider, for example, the following two arguments, stated in syllogistic form (two premises that combine to generate a conclusion):

Socrates is a man.	Premise 1
All men are mortal.	Premise 2
Therefore, Socrates is mortal.	Conclusion
Socrates is a philosopher.	Premise 1
Socrates has a beard.	Premise 2
Therefore, all philosophers have beards.	Conclusion

In both cases, the premises are clearly true. However, only the first argument yields a true conclusion. Why? According to Aristotle, the first is in correct syllogistic form, while the second is not. (We do not propose to offer a course in logic here, but the problem is the incorrect distribution of the terms in the premises.)

As Aristotle observed, a formally invalid argument cannot be true, or at least cannot be said to prove its conclusion. However, logical validity does not guarantee truth. The truth of a logically valid syllogism depends on the truth of its premises. Consider this example:

The President of the United States is a turtle.

All turtles are fish.

Therefore, the President of the United States is a fish.

This syllogism is formally identical to the Socrates syllogism presented earlier. It is logically valid. However, its premises are false, and they combine to produce a conclusion that necessarily is also false.

Syllogisms, then, can be judged in terms of their validity and truth. Similarly, according to Aristotle, enthymemes can be judged in terms of their *logical validity* and *persuasive strength*. An enthymeme can be formally invalid—in which case it simply makes no rational sense. But a valid enthymeme can still be judged as more or less persuasive, strong or weak, depending on how strongly an audience embraces (or should embrace) its premises. (The modern argumentation theorist Chaim Perelman calls this embrace *adherence*. Arguments that inspire strong adherence are more persuasive than arguments that inspire weak adherence, though both may be valid and reasonable.)

Logic textbooks typically provide lists of *fallacies*, common errors in reasoning that render an argument invalid. These include such things as the *red herring* (an irrelevant point that distracts the audience from the real issue), the *ad hominem* (attacking the character of an opponent instead of the quality of his or her reasoning), the *bandwagon* appeal (taking wide acceptance of an idea as proof of its truth), and so on. Such lists go back to Aristotle's *Sophistical Refutations* and his other treatises on logic. As Chaim Perelman and others have observed, however, in practical enthymematic argument many things that are considered logical fallacies can be both valid and persuasive. In law, for example, questioning the credibility of a witness—undermining his or her ethos, also termed *impeaching* a witness—may be an *ad hominem* attack according to the logic textbooks, but an untrustworthy ethos can indeed be a persuasive reason for doubting a witness's testimony.

As Perelman has pointed out, in practical enthymematic argumentation there are only a few genuine types of formal fallacy, since any argument (any datum-claim connection) appears as valid and rational if there is a perceived warrant to support it. For Perelman, the essential fallacy in practical argumentation is begging the question (*petitio principii*): basing an argument on reasons (either datum or warrant) that the audience does not accept or recognize, or that are more controversial than the claim they are meant to support. You cannot prove a claim with a reason that is more controversial than the claim itself, with a reason widely considered false, or with a reason that does not appear to be a reason at all. This is really not an error of form, but an error of tactics, a type of argument with no strength.

Perhaps the only truly formal fallacy in enthymematic argument is the tautological or *circular* argument, in which the argument's claim and the apparent reason given in support of it are really just restatements of each other. For example, "We need to raise taxes, because an increase in tax revenues is required at this time." This *sounds like* an enthymeme, but it boils down to, "We need to raise taxes because we need to raise taxes." In this case, the presented enthymeme is only an apparent enthymeme, and there is no ideational enthymeme behind it at all—only a single statement. A disputable claim cannot be its own proof.

As we have said, enthymemes that are valid (i.e., that appear to be rational) can still be judged as relatively weak or strong, depending on the audience's degree of commitment (or adherence) to the reasons and presuppositions that support the claim. An audience may judge two competing enthymematic arguments to be reasonable and persuasive, but consider one to be more persuasive than the other.

SIDEBAR: RHETORICAL FALLACIES

Here we present a short selection of commonly recognized *and frequently used* fallacies in reasoning. Logicians regard them as logically illegitimate (though often effective) argumentative moves that a critical thinker should reject. Seen from a rhetorical point of view, most of these fallacies are matters not of formal invalidity, but of problematic reasons or assumptions that an audience (or its notion of a reasonable person) will not accept. Nearly all are versions of *petitio principii*—begging the question (see bulleted list following). Note, too, that in certain circumstances nearly all of these gambits (except circular argument) could be seen as reasonable and persuasive. The determining factor is audience and situation. Consider this sampling of rhetorical fallacies:

- **Circular argument:** presenting, as a reason in support of a disputable claim, some version of the claim itself. "I say we must raise taxes, because an increase in tax revenues is imperative at this time" (= we must raise taxes because we must raise taxes).

- **Petitio principii** (begging the question): basing a disputable conclusion on a reason or assumption that is equally or more disputable, or beyond belief. Varieties:

  - **Non sequitur** (does not follow): no perceivable rational connection between a statement and the inference (claim) drawn from it; no intelligible underlying warrant. "This man keeps chickens in his yard; he surely is a murderer."

  - **Sweeping generalization:** a conclusion that makes broader claims than the presented evidence or premises will support. "Three murders were reported in the local news last weekend; no one should feel safe anywhere."

  - **Faulty (or overextended) analogy:** comparative argument based on things that are not truly comparable; or, incorrectly assuming that two things with some points of resemblance are alike in all respects. "My backyard fence can't keep the neighbor kids off my property, but Smith thinks a border fence will stop adult illegal immigrants from entering our country."

  - **Post hoc ergo propter hoc** (after this, so because of this): incorrectly assuming that, in a sequence of two events, the first caused the second. "After the university raised its tuition fees, average GPA went up; so that is one benefit of the new fee structure."

  - **Ad hominem** (to the person): an irrelevant attack on the person proposing an argument, rather than the argument itself. "Smith says that the new military strategy has turned this war around, but he's a war profiteer, so he'll say anything to keep our troops overseas."

  - **Straw person:** misrepresenting an opponent's argument in a reductive way that makes it seem stupid and easy to refute. "Jones seems to think that taxing everyone to death is a good way to stimulate the economy. Are you kidding me?"

- **Red herring:** an irrelevant distraction from the issue in question, often designed to change the subject, put the opponent on the defensive, and win the argument; often used when the speaker's position on the actual issue is weak. "The widows of the disaster victims have been pressing for more government action; why are the media so focused on all these sob stories?"

- **False dilemma:** reducing an issue to just two alternatives (or a few), when there actually are more. "We must either pass the economic stimulus bill that the President has proposed, or face a catastrophic breakdown in our national economy; so anyone who opposes this bill is speaking against the national interest."

- **Bandwagon:** arguing for an idea on the grounds that everyone (or a large number of people) agrees. "Opinion polls show that 64% of Americans disapprove of this President's policies; those policies therefore need to be changed."

- **Loaded language:** emotionalized or evaluative language that seems out of proportion to the evidence (thus making the judgment implied by the language questionable, or question begging). "This new, devious scheme for national health care is just the latest plot to enslave our medical system to godless socialism!"

Epicheiremes

An epicheireme, as we have said, is an argument made of linked enthymemes. Just as the enthymeme is the rhetorical counterpart of the syllogism in formal logic, the epicheireme is the counterpart of what logicians call a *sorites* (linked syllogisms). There are two main types of epicheireme, which can be described as the *subordinating* and *chain* epicheireme.

Most classical authorities describe the *subordinating* type of epicheireme as follows:

First proposition
   Proof of proposition

Second proposition

   Proof of proposition

   First proposition + Second proposition = Conclusion

The first proposition and its proof are an enthymeme—in essence, a claim and its supporting reason or datum (generally with the warrant left unstated or implied, although it is possible for the warrant and its backing to be discussed). Likewise for the second proposition and its proof. If each of these enthymemes is successful, and if the propositions they have proved can validly be linked, then they combine, like a datum and warrant, to produce the overall conclusion of the epicheireme.

   The subordinating epicheireme, in short, is itself an enthymeme whose premises are enthymemes.

METHODS OF ANALYSIS

Earlier, we analyzed a portion of a video blog as an enthymeme, explaining that the *natural language* may need translation in order to fit into Toulmin's categories. We'll recommend a similar method of analyzing epicheiremes. This time, however, we'll encourage you to chunk a longer text into pieces that individually make particular claims. Summarize and paraphrase in order to diagram each chunk as an enthymeme connected to what precedes or follows. Try to see how the chain of inferences comes together. Take the following chunks of sequential text from jsmooth's "How to Tell People They Sound Racist" (which can be found as a July 21, 2008, entry on illdoctrine.com).

SELECTED TEXT FROM VIDEO BLOG, CHUNKED INTO SECTIONS THAT END WITH PARTICULAR CLAIMS IN AN EPICHEIREME:

Proposition 1: "When you say, 'I think he's a racist,' that's not a bad move because you might be wrong. That's a bad move because you might be right. Because if that dude really is racist, you want to make sure you hold him accountable and don't let him off easy. And even though intuitively it feels like the hardest way to hit him is just run up on him and say, 'I think your #$@ is racist,' when you handle it that way, you're actually letting him off easy because you're setting up a conversation that's too simple for him to derail and duck out of. Just think about how this plays out every time a politician or celebrity gets caught out there. It always starts out as a 'What they did' conversation, but as soon as the celebrity and their defenders get on camera, they start doing judo flips and switching it into a 'what they are' conversation. [. . .] And then you try to explain that we don't need to see inside their soul to know that they shouldn't have said all that about the watermelon, and you try to focus on the facts of the situation, but by then it's too late because the 'what they are' conversation is a rhetorical Bermuda triangle where everything drowns in a sea of empty posturing until somebody just blames it all on hip-hop, and we forget the whole thing ever happened."

Proposition 2: "When somebody picks my pocket, I'm not gonna be chasing them down so I can figure out whether he feels like he's a thief deep down in his heart. I'm gonna be chasing him down so I can get my wallet back. I don't care what he is, but I need to hold him accountable for what he did, and that's how we need to approach these conversations about race. Treat them like they took your wallet, and focus on the part that matters, holding each person accountable for the impact of their words and actions."

Connecting Proposition 1 and 2: "I don't care what you are. I care about what you did."

Notice what becomes evident about the inferential structure when we paraphrase the above text as an epicheireme:

Calling someone a racist allows them to get away with an injustice (prop 1)

> because calling someone a racist allows people to set up a "what they are" conversation
>
> > [stated warrant] "what they are" conversations focus on character, not action, and therefore allow lots of posturing without favoring specific discussions of particular injustices.

Racist speech should be addressed with reference to the actions and not the characters of people who say racist things (prop 2)

> because when treating other injustices (such as theft) we do not focus on the character of the accused but rather on that person's actions
>
> > [unstated warrant] since racist speech is no different from other injustices (such as theft).

So, given prop 1 and prop 2, we should not call people racists but should rather focus on their racist actions.

Try to apply this method. Take an extended argument and break it into chunks, each making an individual claim that is connected to what comes before and what comes after. Diagram these chunks as individual enthymemes in an epicheireme.

In a *chain* epicheireme, the conclusion of one enthymeme becomes a premise for the next:

Premise 1

Premise 2

Conclusion = Premise 3

    Premise 4

    Conclusion = Premise 5

        Premise 6

        Conclusion.

There is, in principle, no limit to these kinds of epicheirematic linkage. In theory, a 500-page book could consist of one enormous, super-complex epicheireme. That would be an impressive logical feat, but it seldom occurs in practice. As Aristotle observed, most audiences have difficulty following a very long and complicated train of reasoning. It's often better to break arguments into shorter units that are easier to take in and remember. Moreover, an extremely elaborate epicheireme is subject to the "house of cards" effect. If the audience rejects one premise, the whole argument collapses. Most rhetors build their arguments with relatively compact, separate enthymemes or epicheiremes that all contribute to an overall conclusion—sequences or bundles of arguments that harmonize with each other but do not all logically depend on one another. That way, if one argument fails, others can still be effective.

Analyzing enthymemes and epicheiremes requires laborious attention to the particular terms and logical connections that an argument requests of its audience. For this reason, we recommend making a textual representation of the argument before trying to analyze its underlying logical structure. Transcribe, paraphrase, or (in the case of a visual or aural argument) describe what you want to analyze. Then try to apply the terms introduced so far. The need for transcription raises an interesting question about technological media and argumentation: Do certain media (such as print text) make certain kinds of logos appeals possible? More particularly, do oral and visual arguments interrupt our ability to draw or analyze complex inferences by preventing a close reconsideration of each element in the argument?

If so, maybe there's something to the old humanities professor's complaint that students don't learn to read print texts. Browsing images and watching videos may keep us from learning to reason in complicated inferential patterns. In a video-dominated world, perhaps we become less critical of the enthymemes and epicheiremes flashing across our screens.

METHODS OF ANALYSIS

Though we imply that complex enthymemes can't be presented in visual media, we do not believe that to be the case. Here's a method for analyzing enthymemes in a visual argument: Pick a photograph or a video, and try to label specific images using Toulmin's terms: datum, warrant, and claim. If you can't find images to label as the claim, put the argument's conclusion in your own words. You can do the same for the warrant. For instance, we chose to look at a campaign commercial aired during the 1968 presidential election. Republican incumbent Richard Nixon aired "Convention" juxtaposing images of the Democratic nominee (Hubert Humphrey), the tumultuous 1969 Democratic National Convention (DNC), the U.S. war in Vietnam, and the riots in cities such as Detroit. The result was an association between Humphrey and turmoil both at home and abroad. (To see the ad, visit www.livingroomcandidate.org/commercials/1968/convention.) We think two enthymemes are presented here, but to understand both, we must label the images as data and we must also paraphrase both the warrant and the claim:

1. **Datum:** Images of Democrats smiling against images of American soldiers and citizens suffering.

   Claim: Democrats don't care about the real problems that America faces.

   Warrant: Only people who don't take problems seriously smile while the country faces poverty and war.

2. **Datum:** Images of Democrats fighting and images of Americans rioting in cities.

   Claim: Democrats are contributing to the violence in America's streets.

   Warrant: Anyone who fights needlessly contributes to the violence that has erupted in recent urban riots.

MORE CLASSICAL TERMS: TOPICS AND STASES OF ARGUMENT

The concepts of *topic* and *stasis* emerged in classical theory as aids to invention. They help a rhetor to discover the things that can be said about an issue, but they are also useful for rhetorical analysis and criticism, for two main reasons. First, they provide a descriptive vocabulary that supplements what we have discussed so far. Second, just as they help the rhetor to come up with arguments, they also help the analyst to discover what the available arguments might be in a given situation.

Topics

The word *topic*—Greek *topos* (plural *topoi*), Latin *locus* (plural *loci*)— originally meant place, and in rhetoric took on the meaning of a place where materials for arguments could be found. Standard theory generally recognizes two kinds of topics: the material and the formal.

Material topics are the warrants or presuppositions on which enthymemes can be based. These include what Chaim Perelman has called "premises of the real" and "premises of the preferable" (though we retain the term *topic*):

- Topics of the real: generally accepted beliefs regarding what is factual, what is true (permanent principles), what is possible and impossible, what is probable (how people usually behave, what usually causes what, etc.), what is feasible (difficult or easy to accomplish), and so on.

- Topics of the preferable: generally accepted values regarding what is advantageous or profitable, legal, just, ethical, honorable, beautiful, enjoyable, necessary, or otherwise desirable or to be chosen.

- Topics for arranging hierarchies of value: quality vs. quantity, unique vs. common, appearance vs. reality, actual vs. possible, ideal vs. practical, easy vs. difficult, old vs. new, personal freedom vs. social constraint, tradition vs. innovation, spiritual vs. material goods, and so on.

These lists are meant to illustrate, not to cover, all possible topics. Material topics are innumerable. They cannot really be listed in any complete way but are learned through education, experience, and social interaction. They constitute the practical wisdom required for good judgment and prudent thought—what is called *phronesis* in Greek, *prudentia* in Latin. When a culture attributes wisdom to its elder members, in effect, it regards them as having acquired a large store of material topics over the course of a long life and deep experience. Our lists, like others in both ancient and modern rhetoric, simply indicate some of the more general headings under which material topics can be organized and searched in a relatively methodical way.

Topics of the real and the preferable can combine, and hierarchies of value can be inverted. For example, in a debate about whether an old, historic building should be preserved or destroyed to make way for new developments (apartments, condominiums, commercial spaces), someone might argue that the uniqueness, historic significance, and authenticity of the building are more valuable than the economic benefit to be derived from the new development (unique vs. common; old vs. new; genuine vs. contrived; unique, old, genuine vs. economic advantage). Another may argue that the new development's economic benefit to the community—the greatest good for the greatest number—outweighs the value of the building's historicity and uniqueness (economic advantage vs. qualities such as uniqueness, age, and authenticity) or that modernization is more important than historic preservation (new vs. old). Still another may concede the desirability of historic preservation, but argue that it will be too difficult and costly (the [dis-]advantageous and the [in-]feasible; the practical vs. the ideal). Another may argue that, as difficult and expensive as preservation may be, "we must not forget our mothers and fathers, the generations before us, and the history that has made us what we are" (ethical necessity; ideal vs. practical; tradition vs. innovation). And on the discussion may go. One can identify many possible lines of argument by consulting topics of the real and the preferable.

In addition to these general categories, there are *field* or *discipline-specific material topics*—in politics, law, business management, medicine, the sciences, engineering, art, architecture, literary studies, and so on. For example, if a plaintiff in a court of law contends that a pharmaceutical product caused him to develop diabetes, he will have to rely on more than commonsense notions of causation. He will have to meet legal and medical-scientific standards of what counts as evidence of causation (field-specific topics of the real).

Material topics also include what traditionally have been called *commonplaces* (Greek *koinos topos*; Latin *locus communis*). A commonplace, in essence, is a frequently used material topic, usually a topic of the preferable, that has become more or less standardized. It is often expressed as a proverb or maxim, or sometimes an expanded set speech, that a speaker can plug in to invoke values that many people hold. These are often encapsulated in common phrases. Take the following two expressions: "A stitch in time saves nine," and "An ounce of prevention is worth a pound of cure." Both invoke the commonplace hierarchy of values: Careful preparation to prevent failure is better than a costly system to manage disaster.

Formal topics, in contrast to material topics, are strategies of argument—moves for relating ideas and drawing inferences from the relation. Aristotle listed many in his *Topics* (a treatise on dialectical logic), and twenty-eight in the *Rhetoric* (2.23). Later theorists streamlined the list, often in different ways. Here we present a streamlined list of our own, which is meant to be illustrative rather than exhaustive:

- Definition (categorical reasoning): invoking a definition in order to place the thing being discussed within the defined category. "Marriage is a union between a man and a woman to encourage procreation and a stable home for raising children. Proposition 214 will destroy marriage by allowing same-sex people to marry."

- Genus and species (whole and parts): dividing a general category into parts or subtypes to discuss the parts or subtypes separately, or to place the thing being discussed in one of them. "There are two kinds of marriage: a religious marriage, which often encourages certain kinds of sexual and family relationships; and a civil marriage, which grants legal rights and privileges. Proposition 214 will ensure the same civil marriage—the same legal rights and privileges—for all people, regardless of sexual orientation or family situation."

- Example (induction): invoking specific instances (either historical or hypothetical) that illustrate a general pattern in how the world works in order to assert that pattern as a topic of the real. "I read about a couple who won the lottery, and were made miserable by their sudden wealth; sudden wealth destroys happiness."

- Analogy (similarity, comparison): drawing inferences based on an asserted equivalence or resemblance between two things. "This war is like Vietnam; we're wasting our blood and treasure."

- Correlative ideas (a variation of analogy): arguments based on assumptions that two ideas are parallel or logically correspond: "If it was right for me to execute the prisoner, it was right for him to be executed."

- Greater and lesser: comparing two similar things of different magnitude to show that what is true for one is even more true for the other (or, conversely, less true): "Babe Ruth hit sixty home runs under much more difficult conditions than batters face in modern baseball, so his achievement is greater than that of those who recently have surpassed his numbers."

- Difference: asserting nonsimilarity between two things, usually to counter analogical arguments based on an assumed equivalence. "This war is not really like Vietnam because we are not fighting a nationalist insurgency, nor is our enemy receiving military support from a superpower."

- Antithesis: drawing inferences from things regarded as opposites: "If an ignorant citizenry is harmful to democracy, then an educated citizenry will strengthen it."

- Contradictories: arguments based on the assumption that two things are mutually exclusive (if X is Y, it can't be Z): "If Mr. Jones has repeatedly cheated on his taxes, he cannot credibly be put in charge of the IRS."

- Causes and effects: making inferences about the probable causes of an effect, or the probable effects of a cause: "Jones was driving erratically; he probably was intoxicated"; "Nation Z has an extremely oppressive government; there must be a resistance movement developing underground." Cause/effect has many variations, all based on assumptions about what sorts of things cause other sorts of things. For example, arguing that something should be chosen (or avoided) for the sake of its effects (consequences): "If an educated citizenry strengthens democracy, let us then seek to make Americans the best-educated people on earth." Or, making judgments about an act (an effect) on the basis of its motivations or causes: "Band X was formed, not so much to make big money, but to open up the possibilities for contemporary music; that alone is a reason for admiring their interestingly quirky art." (There is an antithesis in this argument too.)

- Antecedents: making judgments about an act based on what preceded it: "Is it likely that the defendant stole the painting? Security cameras show him hanging around the museum almost every day for several weeks before the theft."

- Concomitants: making judgments about an act or event based on accompanying circumstances: "The defendant not only killed the victim, but did so slowly, and whistled to the tunes in his iPod while doing it. This is an egregious murder!"

- Association (a variation of concomitants): arguments based on non-causal ideas of what usually goes with what. Advertisements often argue by association—the VW Golf VR6 commercial discussed earlier, for instance, associates the car with a lively urban setting. Association is the most potentially problematic of the formal topics, since it has a built-in tendency toward reasoning based on prejudicial stereotypes, though that is not automatic. The controversial practice of profiling airline passengers to identify potential terrorists relies on this associative form of reasoning. Much of the debate has focused on which methods of profiling are valid and effective, and which are based on mere prejudicial stereotypes. Association also is the basis of the medical notion of syndromes—conditions defined by sets of symptoms that tend to occur together, but do not necessarily all occur, as in AIDS (Acquired Immune Deficiency Syndrome).

As with the material topics, the formal topics provide the rhetor with a range of resources for discovering the possible arguments that can be made on any subject. Not all topics will be relevant to every subject and every situation, but typically several will be relevant to a given case. An experienced rhetor is unlikely to run mechanically through all the *topoi*, but will select from them as needed. You should keep them available as reference points, or as a well-practiced repertoire of discursive moves. For the analyst, they provide a range of descriptive terms and, again, a resource for grasping how well a discourse has developed the arguments that were available in its situation.

WRITE AN ANALYSIS

Choose a short, explicitly argumentative text—ideally one that clearly states the issue and/or its claim, presents reasoning and evidence, and draws conclusions. Possible selections would include the *Declaration of Independence*, Susan B. Anthony's 1873 speech "On Women's Right to Suffrage," a recent op-ed piece, or an argumentative blog exchange. Alternatively, choose a visual text such as a video or an image. Develop a sketch of the rhetorical situation, and run through the previously mentioned material and formal topics. Do you see any assumptions about what should be valued (material topics of the preferable) or what exists (material topics of the real)? Do you see any claims or assumptions about things that tend to cause or be associated with other things (formal topics of cause, antecedents, or association)? You probably will find that some topics are more applicable than others, depending on the text you examine. For instance, at a quick glance, we notice that the jsmooth blog entry discussed earlier depends upon arguments at the formal topics of genus/species (there are two kinds of conversation about racist speech) and analogy (racists speech is like theft). Of course, the argument depends on other formal topics as well as several material topics. The point at first is simply to generate an inventory of analytic observations. Ultimately, you probably will want to focus your analysis on how these topics get woven together into a larger argument. Then develop an argument in which you explicate the argumentation of the text or the topics you have focused on—how they work together and how they engage with the practical reasoning process of the audience.

Stases

The word *stasis* (Greek *stasis*; plural *staseis*) derives from a family of words that generally mean stand or come to a standstill, but that also took on the meaning of strife or disagreement—a standoff, perhaps. (The historian Thucydides, for example, uses *stasis* to refer to a civil war.) In rhetoric, as a technical term, stasis means the crucial question at issue or the main point in dispute in a debate: in essence, the strategic point on which the rhetor takes a stand.

Rhetorical theory recognizes different kinds of stases, each with its characteristic strategies of argument. Recognizing the key stasis of a dispute—or the particular stasis at any given moment in the unfolding of that dispute—enables the rhetor to identify the relevant topics and to discover the best available arguments more effectively. The rhetorical analyst can also observe the rhetor's tactics of argument more precisely. Did the rhetor address the most pressing question at issue?

Traditional theory divides the stases in two main ways. The first divides all issues into *general* and *particular* questions. A general issue, in essence, is a broad philosophical question, either about scientific matters (the laws of nature), or about basic moral, political, economic, or civic principles. Particular issues, in contrast, are questions about specific *cases* with particular circumstances (persons, places, times, actions, etc.). For example, a general issue might be, "How does globalization affect standards of living in developing countries?" (We are asking about a general rule.) In contrast, a specific issue would be, "Will the Central American Free Trade Agreement benefit skilled workers in Honduras?" (We are asking about a specific case.)

General and particular issues resemble each other in a "mirror-image" way. Argumentation on abstract general principles often needs to invoke particular cases as examples or illustrations. Argumentation on concrete, particular cases often needs to invoke abstract general principles as warrants for its claims. When argumentation on particular cases needs to take up and defend a disputable general principle, it commonly leads to something that resembles syllogistic disputation, or what Chaim Perelman has called "quasi-logical" argument.

The second main division of stases originated from the analysis of particular judicial cases, but it can be applied to any kind of issue. Different classical authorities divide these stases in different ways—some say there are four, some five, others more—but the following is a more or less standard modern adaptation:

- Conjecture (question of past, present, or future fact): What has happened, is happening, or will happen? What exists, did exist, or will exist?

- Definition (question of name): What should it be called?

- Quality (question of evaluation): Is it good or bad?

- Policy (question of action): What should we do about it?

- Objection (question of validity of procedure): Should the case be dismissed?

These stases are often thought of as a series of positions (stands) in a sequence of assertions and denials. For example, consider the points of stasis in the following debate about people's influence on climate.

- **Conjecture:** The planet's climate has been steadily changing (particularly getting warmer) for the past century (fact).—The planet's temperature changes regularly but no discernible long-term trend toward global warming can be verified (fact disputed). People have directly caused changes in the planet's temperature by releasing unprecedented amounts of CO_2 into the atmosphere (cause).—No direct causal link can be established between CO_2 emissions and global warming; changes in sunspots might just as likely be the reason for global temperature change (cause disputed).

- **Definition:** CO_2 does cause temperature changes, and these changes can be verified over the past 50 years (facts and causes admitted), but we should call this "climate change," not "global warming" since some parts of the globe seem to be getting cooler or staying more or less the same (definition disputed).

- **Quality:** We can call this "global warming" (definition admitted), but it's not that bad, since warmer periods of human history have typically been periods of progress, improving agriculture and thus contributing to general prosperity (evaluation disputed).

- **Policy:** Global warming is bad (evaluation admitted), but we shouldn't try to dramatically reduce CO_2 emissions, because that would have economic consequences that would far outweigh the minor benefits of reducing global temperatures a few degrees (action disputed).

- **Objection:** The science of climatology is too politically biased and undeveloped to contribute to productive debate or effective policy (validity of procedure disputed).

Procedural objection is not so much a fallback position after policy but an alternative to all the other stases—an escape hatch when the rhetor feels that he or she cannot get a fair hearing, or when the rhetor feels that there is something fundamentally wrong with the debate's setup.

Traditional theory subdivides these stases into *heads* (or *substases*)—subsidiary *topics* that usually are necessary for resolving a question of Conjecture, Definition, Quality, Policy, or Objection. For example:

- *Conjecture* primarily involves questions about what kinds of evidence are available to confirm the alleged facts and how reliable the evidence is. If the evidence is reliable, the next concern is the most probable way to connect the dots in an account of the facts: What happened or will happen or is happening? This will involve the topics of the real—especially the possible and the probable—as well as such formal topics as analogy, cause/effect, antecedents, concomitants, and association.

- *Definition*, as discussed already under the formal topics, involves questions about the defining features of a certain category of things (for example, what are the criteria that define *global warming*) and whether the facts in question fit the definition. Since nearly all words in natural language carry an evaluative (a pathetic) charge, the stasis of definition has an evaluative function; there's a big difference between the portentous-sounding *global warming* and the benign *climate change*.

- *Quality* includes questions about the criteria for evaluative judgment: Is it honorable, just, legal, advantageous, enjoyable, and so on, and to what degree? Such questions involve the topics of the preferable, as well as topics for arranging hierarchies of value, and such formal topics as analogy, correlatives, greater/lesser, antithesis, and contradictories. Further, arguments about legality often involve questions regarding the interpretation of laws or other legal documents (such as contracts), especially in cases of ambiguity, conflicting provisions, the analogical extension of a provision, and the letter and spirit of a document (i.e., the writer's intention vs. a literal reading of the text). Finally, judgments of Quality involve consideration of mitigating factors, such as circumstances and degree of responsibility. An act, whether good or bad, may be less good or bad if the person did it by accident, was forced to do it by circumstances, was mentally impaired, and so on. Last of all, in judicial discourse, a defendant may plead for mercy, if there is no justification available and no mitigating factor.

- *Policy* involves questions about whether a proposed action is necessary, possible, or feasible (easy or difficult); what results it most probably will produce; and whether those results will be desirable. These questions send the argument back to questions of Conjecture, Definition, and Quality, and their related topics. Note that the policy disagreement mentioned earlier turned back to the question of conjecture and quality. Efforts to reduce CO_2 emissions would have dire economic effects (conjecture), so their proposed benefits are not worth the costs (quality).

- *Objection* involves questions about whether a proceeding—a trial, a policy deliberation, a philosophical discussion—is legal, fair, or properly constituted: "There's no point in us discussing climate, since no one—not even the scientists—knows enough about it." Such arguments will generally rely on topics of the preferable (the just, the legal, the correct) and the real (the possible, the feasible), as well as such formal topics as definition, antithesis, and contradictories.

As you can see from this brief outline, the different stases involve different (but overlapping) selections from the material and formal topics. Recognizing the stasis of any given argument gives the rhetorical analyst—as well as any discerning audience—some guidelines regarding what to look for and expect. If the rhetor is proposing an action, has she addressed the necessary topics? Has she discovered the best available arguments?

As our discussion of the Policy stasis shows, argumentation can shift from one stasis to another in complex discourse. Usually, however, there is one primary stasis—the main question the rhetor's arguments mean to settle—with movement to subsidiary stases, depending on the types of supporting arguments the rhetor needs to make. We will observe an example of such stasis-shifting presently in Martin Luther King, Jr.'s "Letter from Birmingham Jail."

It is interesting and often helpful to analyze the stasis of a debate before trying to enter the debate itself. As a topic for a rhetorical analysis, choose a debate that interests you: Is global warming caused by humans? Should homosexuals be given the same ability to marry as heterosexuals? Should public schools teach contraception and abstinence in sex-ed classes? Collect 3–5 recent opinion pieces about this controversy and identify the dominant points of stasis argued in each article. Using these individual analyses, analyze the entire debate. At what point(s) do people tend to disagree? How can a skillful rhetor address these most important points of disagreement persuasively?

SAMPLE ANALYSIS: ENTHYMEMATIC ARGUMENT IN THE FIRST HALF OF "LETTER FROM BIRMINGHAM JAIL"

As we observed in Chapter 2, Martin Luther King, Jr. faces a difficult kairos at the outset of his "Letter from Birmingham Jail." He has a very serious ethos problem. He is in jail and under public criticism from a group of prominent clergymen for being an irresponsible rabble-rouser whose actions have been "unwise and untimely" and have done more harm than good to "race relations." Moreover, his critics have called upon the "Negro" community—and the "white moderate" community—to withdraw their support from King's protest demonstrations. As we also observed, the first half of the "Letter" does most of the rhetorical heavy lifting that changes the kairos and puts King, in the second half, in a position to deliver a scathing critique of his critics and to proclaim the righteousness of his cause. In this analysis, we propose to look at this heavy lifting a little more closely. As we show, King employs ethos, pathos, stasis shifts, and enthymematic argument (logos) in highly compelling ways.

What is the main stasis? The clergymen's critique of King's actions suggests Quality. It involves an evaluative judgment almost in the manner of a trial, with the intended audience functioning as jury and King as the defendant. The clergymen's call to the "Negro" community to withdraw support from the Birmingham demonstrations also suggests Policy, the question of what should be done, as an implicit secondary issue. The clergymen thus have given King a double stasis to address. However, since an evaluation of King's actions is the basis for any Policy decision about whether to support him—and since he begins under accusation, with a problematic ethos—we consider the primary stasis to be Quality, at least through the "Letter's" first half.

From the outset King works hard to establish his credentials and build his ethos. In the very first line, for example, he addresses his critics as "My Dear Fellow Clergymen," thus establishing that he too is a clergyman (or, at least, reminding intended readers who may not be fully aware). In the rest of paragraph 1, he portrays himself as an executive, the leader of a large organization, with a "desk" and "secretaries" to handle the press of daily business and his voluminous correspondence. This information is delivered, moreover, in an emotionally restrained, businesslike style that makes him sound like a reasonable, responsible, professional bureaucrat—not a firebrand rabble-rouser. He appears, in short, as someone his intended audience of "white moderates" can respect. Further, in the paragraph's closing sentence he declares that the clergymen merit what he hopes will be a "patient and reasonable" reply *because* they are well-intentioned and sincere. This statement—itself an enthymematic cap—implies at least two general values (warrants) that bespeak an ethic of civility: Well-intentioned, sincere speech deserves a thoughtful, respectful reply; and "patient and reasonable" speech is a good thing, something one should strive for even in difficult circumstances. These implied values, along with King's credentials, begin to define (or redefine) his ethos. They enhance his credibility and render the implied audience more receptive to his later arguments.

This ethos-building continues, as King responds to the clergymen's charges. In paragraphs 2–11, he responds mainly to the charge of being an "outside agitator." While the primary stasis still is Quality, this section takes on what appears to be a Conjectural issue: What are the true facts about his actions? King corrects the clergymen's (and the nation's) erroneous perceptions by patiently explaining that he was brought to Birmingham by organizational ties. He is president of the Southern

Christian Leadership Conference, which has local affiliates who have called him in (paragraph 2). He then goes on to detail at length the eminently responsible, disciplined, nonviolent way in which the demonstrations were organized and carried out (paragraphs 3–11). In addition to setting the record straight, all of this fact discussion extends King's opening self-portrait as a responsible leader and thus continues to strengthen his ethos appeal.

Early on in this discussion (paragraphs 3–4), King digresses into a sort of commonplace that shifts the issue from the particular case to general principles: "But more basically, I am in Birmingham because injustice is here." The idea that there is a basic moral imperative for him to be there (a topic of the preferable) is amplified and justified through a comparison (analogy) with the biblical prophets and the Apostle Paul: "Just as the prophets . . . left their villages [. . .] and just as the Apostle Paul left his village [. . . to proclaim God's word] so am I compelled to carry the gospel of freedom beyond my home town." This is followed by a series of statements that reach a crescendo with the breathtaking (and frequently quoted) lines, "Injustice anywhere is a threat to justice everywhere. We are caught in an inescapable network of mutuality, tied in a single garment of destiny. What affects one directly, affects all indirectly." The statements made in these passages embody a sort of epicheireme, which might be translated as follows:

There is injustice in Birmingham,

SO I must go to Birmingham

    [SINCE I must go where there is injustice (implied warrant)].

        BECAUSE [backing #1]:

            As a preacher of the Gospel, I must imitate the prophets and Paul.

            The prophets and Paul left their towns to speak God's word wherever it was called for,

            SO I must speak God's word wherever it is called for.

        AND BECAUSE [backing #2]:

            God's word is:

            We all share a transcendental mutuality and destiny,

            SO what affects one affects all,

            SO injustice anywhere threatens justice everywhere.

We are leaving out some parts of this argument, but this translation is enough for present purposes. Note that the memorably stated maxim that "we are caught in an inescapable network of mutuality, tied in a single garment of destiny" is not defended, but presented as a nonnegotiable, bottom-line, transcendent truth (a topic of the real). The rest of the argument develops that idea by adding what appears to be the topic of correlatives.

Paragraphs 2–11 do more than demonstrate the true facts about the demonstrations and King's role therein. These paragraphs also confirm King's ethos as a responsible leader and, moreover, correlate his actions and motives with those of the biblical prophets and the imperatives of transcendent truth—God's word, as reflected in the "garment of destiny" maxim, and God's command to His representatives on earth. King is pursuing a holy calling. A reader who accepts these correlations and views King's ethos in their terms will have difficulty resisting the arguments that follow.

In the next major section (paragraphs 12–14), King responds to the clergymen's criticism that his actions (the demonstrations) are "unwise and untimely." While the principal stasis in King's defense of his actions has been Conjecture, now he shifts to Quality: Are protest demonstrations justifiable at this time? Shouldn't "the Negro" be more patient? In response King develops a large enthymematic unit that clearly follows a build-up-and-cap progression while accomplishing a powerful and memorable pathos appeal.

After some discussion of the circumstances in Birmingham, King remarks that the correction of social injustice seldom happens automatically without pressure from the oppressed (a topic of the real [probability]; paragraph 13), and that African-Americans already have "waited for more than 340 years" (another topic of the real [fact]; paragraph 14). The implicit conclusion from these statements is that African-Americans will not obtain their rights without exerting pressure. That sets up the enthymematic unit that concerns us here. Beginning with, "Perhaps it is easy for those who have never felt the stinging darts of segregation to say, 'Wait,'" King launches into a buildup that consists of a series of insistent "when you have seen" clauses that hammer home the idea: "But when you have seen vicious mobs lynch your mothers and fathers at will and drown your sisters and brothers at whim; when you have seen hate-filled policemen curse, kick, and even kill your black brothers and sisters; when you have seen [. . .]" and so on, for nearly 300 words (about 20 lines of typed text). Most readers find this material overwhelming—a thunderous pathos appeal. A reader who has bought into the "garment of destiny" topos, in particular, is likely to read this passage with great empathy, visualizing the scenarios and imagining how one would feel. It could all be summed up as a "premise" that says, "(When you have seen you will know that) the injustices the Negro suffers are intolerable." The litany of particular, heart-wrenching details builds up an especially rich, and in this case disturbing, bundle of pathemata. This material is then *capped* with:

> —then you will understand why we find it difficult to wait. There comes a time when the cup of endurance runs over, and men are no longer willing to be plunged into the abyss of despair. I hope, sirs, you can understand our legitimate and unavoidable impatience.

The cap proper here consists mainly of the "then you will understand" and the "cup of endurance" statements, which sum up the enthymeme in a pithy and quotable way—with biblical-sounding language that echoes Psalm 23's "my cup runneth over." This makes the enthymematic "cap" an easy-to-remember declaration that echoes, like a proverb, in the mind. The "I hope" statement, in turn, is a sort of epilogue that caps the cap—one that, in its sudden turn from emotionally charged conclusion to cool, dry understatement, creates an emphasis of its own.

Two things should be noted here. First, the cap is a "presentational" enthymeme that summarizes the built-up ideational substance and draws the conclusion in a particular way. The enthymeme's content— its ideational aspect—consists of everything said in both the buildup and the cap. This ideational content *could* be restated—for the purposes of analysis—in abbreviated form, such as:

> The Negro citizens of the United States suffer unendurable injustice [as shown by the "when you have seens"].

> When people suffer unendurable injustice, they may legitimately be impatient for justice [= there comes a time when the cup of endurance runs over].

> SO the Negro citizens of the United States may legitimately be impatient for justice.

Clearly, such a formulation—even if it correctly represents the main gist of the argument, and clarifies its inner logic—falls considerably short of capturing this enthymeme's widely acknowledged power. The ideational cap not only summarizes the enthymeme, it also summarizes the whole passage itself: all its words, all its statements, all the things the audience is asked to see and imagine, and the associations and feelings that those images evoke, or are meant to evoke, in the audience's mind.

Second, we recognize that King could have capped or concluded this enthymeme in other ways. For example, he could have capped the enthymeme with a passionate declaration that "It's time for the Negro to rise up against his oppressors!" That would not have been an unreasonable conclusion to draw from the "when you have seens." And it was being drawn, in fact, by some of King's more militant contemporaries. But it would have turned his argument in a different direction, inconsistent with his rhetorical purposes.

Having demonstrated through pathos that the "Negro" has a right to be impatient for justice, and therefore to engage in public demonstrations that express that impatience, King next responds (in paragraphs 15–22) to the very serious charge that he has encouraged lawbreaking. Even if the demonstrators had a right to express their impatience, did they have a right to express it in illegal ways? The demonstrators had in fact been parading without a permit, and a state court had ordered them to cease. There had been arrests, including King's, as well as scenes of violence and chaos that had appeared on television screens across the nation. King does not dispute those facts, nor even the definition of his and the demonstrators' actions as deliberate lawbreaking. He approaches this issue explicitly at the stasis of Quality: Is this particular act of deliberate lawbreaking, in this particular case, such a bad thing? Is it justifiable or forgivable? He approaches this issue through a logos appeal, which is a good example of quasi-logical argument.

King begins (in paragraph 15) by acknowledging that his promotion of lawbreaking in Birmingham might seem "paradoxical," since he normally urges obedience to the law—especially the Supreme Court's 1954 *Brown v. Board of Education* ruling that outlawed segregation. His solution to this problem starts from a genus/species argument that distinguishes between "just and unjust" laws. This distinction, in turn, permits an argument from antithesis: Just laws should be obeyed, and the unjust resisted or disobeyed. In this way he shifts the debate to a general issue regarding the nature of law and the moral responsibilities of citizens. In paragraph 16, he establishes definitions of "just and unjust laws," derived from the great medieval theologian, St. Thomas Aquinas (expert testimony): A just law is "a man-made code that squares with the moral law or the law of God," and "uplifts human personality," while an unjust law does the opposite (another argument by antithesis). Having established that idea, King then argues—still by definition—that "all segregation statutes are unjust because segregation distorts the soul and damages the personality" (a point established already, in the "when you have seens"). In short, all segregation statutes fit the definition of "unjust law" derived from Aquinas. This idea is further developed through appeals to the thought of the Jewish moral philosopher Martin Buber and the Protestant theologian Paul Tillich (more expert testimony), who argue that racial segregation is dehumanizing and therefore "morally wrong and sinful." All these elements form an essentially philosophical argument at the level of general issue: a Definitional argument that all segregation laws fit the definition of "unjust law"; a Qualitative judgment that such laws are evil; and a Policy argument that all persons have a moral obligation to oppose such laws.

This argument is developed still further (in paragraphs 17–19) with a variety of examples, including the segregation laws of Alabama (paragraph 18). These examples serve to both illustrate and confirm the definitional distinction between just and unjust laws, and thus to establish it not only as an argumentative assertion, but as a topic of the real (a truth) that can be invoked as a foundational premise (a warrant). More pointedly, King argues that the law requiring a parade permit, though reasonable and just in itself, becomes unjust when employed (as it had been) to deny citizens their constitutionally guaranteed civil rights, specifically "the First Amendment privilege of peaceful assembly and protest" (paragraph 19). This argument belongs to the substasis (within Quality) of legal interpretation, specifically the analogical extension of a legal principle. (Look again at our brief discussion of the topics of the Qualitative stasis.) Through these arguments, then, King establishes the ideas that the laws he has deliberately disobeyed are "unjust laws," and that all persons have a moral obligation to resist such laws, so that his action is therefore justified. These ideas put him in position to conclude that principled acts of civil disobedience like his—when "an individual [. . .] breaks a law that conscience tells him is unjust, and [. . .] willingly accepts the penalty of imprisonment in order to rouse the conscience of the community"—actually express "the highest respect for law" (paragraph 20).

In sum, King argues a general thesis about the morality of disobeying unjust laws, and applies it to the specific case of his actions in Birmingham: Those actions may be technically illegal, but they are morally right, fundamentally just, and ultimately more lawful, even, than the segregation-supporting laws that he has violated. This point is further emphasized with comparisons to the technically illegal activities of early Christian martyrs under Roman persecution (paragraph 21) and of those who disobeyed Nazi law during World War II by giving aid and comfort to their Jewish neighbors (paragraph 22). No one (or, at least, no modern-day Christian living in the United States) could assert that those people did wrong when they broke oppressive, unjust, evil laws.

At this point, then, having worked powerful appeals to ethos (paragraphs 2–11 and after), pathos (paragraphs 12–14 and after), and logos (paragraphs 15–22), King has fully justified his actions at the stasis of Quality and is ready to turn to criticism of his critics (in paragraphs 23–47).

Let us examine King's quasi-logical, enthymematic arguments about just and unjust laws a little more closely. King's main argument is, in essence, that his deliberate violation of Birmingham's parade-permit law was justifiable, and even expressed the highest respect for law, because the law was an unjust law. For analytic purposes we can translate (and abbreviate) this enthymeme as follows:

The parade-permit law is an unjust law (in its application) [datum],

SO

deliberate disobedience of that law is morally justified, even required [claim].

The unstated warrant here, the presupposition connecting datum and claim, is something like this: "The citizen has a moral right, even an obligation, to disobey an unjust law." In 1963 that notion already had a certain validity, and emotional resonance, in American culture. It was the subject of Henry David Thoreau's famous 1849 essay, "Civil Disobedience"— which in the early twentieth century had been a major inspiration for Mahatma Gandhi's nonviolent civil-disobedience campaigns against British colonial rule in India (1916–1945). In the 1960s, Thoreau's essay was a standard item in American high school and college English classes, which typically presented it as one of the sacred texts of American culture and identity, a piece of secular scripture. Nevertheless, King felt the need to expand upon and justify (back up) his warrant:

> Deliberate disobedience of unjust laws is morally justified [warrant as claim],
>
> BECAUSE
>
> St. Thomas Aquinas, Martin Buber, and Paul Tillich all agree that an unjust law is invalid and should not be obeyed or enforced [backing as datum].

King goes further, and backs up his backing, by sketching the philosophical justification his authorities provide:

> An unjust law is invalid and should not be obeyed or enforced [backing as claim]
>
> BECAUSE
>
> such a law violates the law of God [2nd backing as datum for 1st backing]
>
> BECAUSE
>
> it degrades the human person [3rd backing as datum for 2nd].

Beneath the argument comprised by backings 3 and 2 lies a further, still more general warrant: "Whatever degrades the human person violates the law of God." Is that true? What warrants that idea? This consideration leads to deep theological waters, but King does not go there. We are at King's bottom line. This is a nonnegotiable article of faith with him and, he assumes, with his intended audience. As such it functions as a topic of the real, a truth.

Notice again, however, that King attributes his backup argument primarily to Saint Thomas Aquinas. Suppose that, instead, he attributed that argument to "my dear old grandfather," or just prefaced it with "it seems to me that. . . ." Clearly Aquinas, seconded by the modern theological/philosophical authorities Buber and Tillich, has been brought in to give the argument more weight. King assumes that his intended audience—while it may not know Aquinas, Buber, or Tillich in any detail—will at least know that Aquinas is one of the greatest philosophers and theologians in the history of Western civilization, will grant some authority to a saint, and will at least recognize Buber and Tillich as important modern thinkers. King's backup argument here relies not only on testimony from authority but also on a still deeper, complex network of ideas (topics of the real) about the truth value of the statements made by great thinkers, the progress of human knowledge, and the resilience of truth across history. All of this material is part of the assumptive bottom line in King's argument, since he does not explain, defend, or even mention it.

By backing up his arguments in this way, King in effect expands his basic enthymeme as a complex epicheireme. One might ask whether he has done this because, despite the popularity of Thoreau's notion of civil disobedience, he has doubts about whether his white moderate intended audience will be willing to apply it to his particular case. After all, his argument for disobeying unjust laws conflicts with another deep assumption in our culture, namely that the law is binding—an idea that King's critics did, in fact, adduce in their "Call for Unity." Further, even for an audience that affirms the right to disobey unjust laws, it is not clear that anyone can simply declare any law they dislike unjust and then ignore it. King has to work to prove that the laws he has disobeyed meet some recognized, authoritative criterion of injustice that morally trumps (in a hierarchy of value) the otherwise powerful belief that what the law says is binding.

Or again, we might ask whether King has resorted to such arguments to frame his particular case (the specific issue) within the context of resonant big ideas (general issues, enduring truths) that will more effectively motivate the audience to identify emotionally as well as intellectually with his position. This is especially important if, in the "Letter's" second half, he intends to turn to Policy arguments about actively supporting his cause. In the first half of King's "Letter," we suspect, both reasons apply. The kairos of his situation both requires and permits him to call upon the philosophy of just and unjust laws—and to derive it from an authority like Saint Thomas Aquinas—to back up his justification of his actions in a way that his audience will find both logically and emotionally compelling.

WRITING AN ARGUMENT ANALYSIS

An analysis focusing on the rhetorical situation differs from an analysis focusing on the argument in one key regard: The analysis that focuses on the argument must speculate about the principal claim. Like Rebecca, whose analysis appeared at the end of our last chapter, you can claim that a film speaks to its audience's worries without stating exactly what the film expects the audience to conclude. But, to analyze the argument, you must present your reader with some summary of the conclusion itself. If you're discussing a piece of direct argumentation, then you may find a moment when the rhetor openly states, "This is what I want you to believe, or see, or do." We are able to find several such moments in King's "Letter." However, you may want to analyze a piece of indirect argumentation. Nearly all of what we have just said applies to the analysis of indirect argumentation—such as the argumentation in advertising, visual art, fiction, drama, films, and music. The most obvious difference is that indirect argumentation often does not provide an explicit statement of the issue. An indirect argument states no claim and draws no stated conclusions. In general, as the name implies, an indirect argument may not appear (on the surface) to make an argument at all. Indirect argumentation produces an *ideational* enthymeme *in the audience's mind* without the appearance (or full appearance) of a *presentational* enthymeme *in the text*. The audience is expected to draw the conclusion for themselves.

David Daniel (one of our students whose argument analysis is presented below), analyzes a piece of indirect argumentation. To do so, David must make explicit the claim and the reasons offered by the video game that he chooses to analyze. Notice his careful effort to present an enthymeme that remains hidden but nonetheless effective. If you've chosen to analyze a piece of indirect argumentation, you might want to begin by answering a few questions:

- What response does the discourse ask from its audience?
- How does the discourse motivate that response?
- What assumptions does the discourse depend on?
- What values, beliefs, or attitudes must the audience implicitly endorse through their response?

Your answers to such questions ultimately will yield a description of an ideational enthymeme, a summary of the principal claim and its reasons even if the rhetor never overtly states the argument.

Whether you're analyzing a piece of indirect or direct argumentation, you should begin by trying to *summarize* the argument. Try to explain in a sentence or two what the piece of discourse wants the audience to believe, to feel, or to do. In fact, we find these three prompts useful, and we think you might productively begin a summary of your argument by completing the following sentences:

- This argument asks the audience to believe . . .
- This argument asks the audience to feel . . .
- This argument asks the audience to do . . .

Once you have written a clear summary, you can begin to label the parts of the argument. Apply the terms we've discussed in this chapter. What are the ethical appeals? The pathetic appeals? The logical appeals? One step toward this effort would involve answering the questions of analysis presented on p. 94–95. If you just want to focus your analysis on the three appeals (logos, ethos, and pathos), then you might try finishing the following sentences:

- The argument tries to get the audience to feel _____ by presenting concrete images that will likely evoke these reactions. These include:
- The argument tries to get the audience to feel _____ by presenting abstract concepts that will likely evoke these reactions. These include:
- The argument asks the audience to trust the implied/actual rhetor by:

- The argument asks the audience to see that the implied/actual rhetor bears them goodwill by:
- The argument demonstrates to the audience that the implied/ actual rhetor is knowledgeable by:
- The argument includes an ideational enthymeme. It can be described in this way:
    - This enthymeme happens at the formal topic of _____.
    - This enthymeme's warrant depends upon a material topic of the real/preferable or a material topic arranging hierarchies of value. The topic can be summarized as:
    - Topic of the real: X is the case.
    - Topic of the preferable: X is good/bad.
    - Topic for arranging hierarchies of value: X is better than Y.
- This enthymeme has a presentational quality. It can be described in this way:
    - The many data are:
    - The concluding cap is:

Summarizing the argument and *labeling* its parts will help you figure out the argument's principal message and the main elements that lead the audience to accept this message. To turn the summary and the labeling of parts into an analysis, however, you must explain how these parts work together to move the audience toward the principal message. You must explain to your reader, for example, how these pathetic appeals fit with this logical appeal to convince these people that they should believe/feel/do this thing. In the sample analysis presented later, notice how David summarizes the argument, labels its parts, and analyzes their interaction with one another. By dedicating portions of his analysis to summary, labeling, and analysis, David explains how the appeals discussed should convince the audience of a particular feeling and a particular belief. In our marginal comments below, we notice the parts of David's essay that *summarize* the argument as well as the parts that *label* the argument's proofs. Most importantly, we label the moments when David shifts from summary to *analysis*.

QUESTIONS FOR ANALYSIS

Before trying to write a rhetorical analysis of an argument, try to answer the following questions to explore the possibilities. What can you notice about this argument? After answering these questions, decide which elements you'd like to emphasize in your analysis and which you'd like to leave alone.

Stasis and claim: What is at issue? What is the central stasis? What is the rhetor's central claim? These questions are all interrelated—the rhetor's central claim is a response to the central stasis, an "answer" to the main question at issue. In direct argumentation, some statement of the central stasis or claim typically appears in the introduction and/or conclusion. Identifying the central stasis and/or claim provides an anchor for the rest of the analysis: How do all other aspects of the discourse relate to the central stasis/claim? Does the stasis shift as the argumentation proceeds? What topics of each stasis are employed?

Argumentation (I): ethos. What does the rhetor (or speaker) do to establish a credible, trustworthy ethos (or the reverse)? What assumptions about credibility/trustworthiness are appealed to? The introduction and the earlier parts of a discourse are typically the place where the rhetor establishes his/her ethos—makes a first impression—though the display of ethos continues throughout.

Argumentation (II): logos. What enthymemes and/or epicheiremes are presented in support of the rhetor's central claim? What is the main argument, and what are the subsidiary (or backup) arguments? Do they form chain or subordinating epicheiremes, or a list of arguments? How are they developed? What kinds of evidence (inartistic proofs) and reasons (premises, topoi) are employed? What assumptions (presuppositions, warrants) do they depend on? Enthymematic analysis requires a detailed close reading of the text, its overall argument and subsidiary arguments, and their relationship to the intended audience.

Argumentation (III): pathos. How do the rhetor's arguments connect with the emotions of the audience, its deepest values, beliefs, desires, hopes, fears? What does the rhetor do specifically to arouse, calm, or modify specific emotions in the audience (such as anger, indignation, pity, or scorn)? What pathemata are deployed, and what sorts of presuppositions do they connect with?

We have chosen to highlight the differences among summary, labeling, and analysis in David's essay, but we would like to emphasize that all rhetorical analysis arguments must include attention to these three elements. As an exercise, you might consider revisiting Rebecca Reilly's analysis of *The Fog of War* in Chapter 2. When does she summarize the argument or label its parts? When does she analyze the interaction between the rhetorical situation and the documentary? Though we have chosen to focus our marginal comments on other aspects of later student papers, as you read the chapters and the student essays to come, we encourage you to continually notice the interplay of summary, labeling, and analysis. When writing your own rhetorical analyses, we likewise encourage you to do more than summarize the argument or label its parts. Explain how the argument works. Analyze the dynamic composition of appeals and their ability to speak to the audience, to address the rhetorical situation, to suit or to create the kairos.

STUDENT ANALYSIS OF ARGUMENT IN A VIDEO GAME

Daniels 1

David Daniels

Professor Carla Praetor

COMM 332 Rhetorical Criticism

March 4, 2010

Building An Electronic Empire with Argument

In 2007, software developer Bioware released an original video game title called *Mass Effect*. It was an instant Blockbuster hit, and its unique draw was the diverse level of control it offered players to shape their gaming experience. By including a deep conversation mechanism that allowed players to engage in fully voiced dialogue with a diverse cast of characters, and offering a cleverly structured tri-fold morality system, the game was able to weave the players into a tapestry of extremism in which they themselves were the epicenter of the action. The sales figures alone, both for the original game and its even more successful sequel, speak for themselves. Literally millions of individuals are living the stories presented by these game worlds.

Now, at times summarizing and illuminating the complicated and oftentimes subtle arguments that are couched within video games can seem daunting. Some games, admittedly, are simple, designed solely for entertainment. Take *Pong* or the sleeper cell phone hit *Bejeweled*. These games have little if any narrative thrust. But some games, like the ones produced by Bioware, become multimedia extravaganza epics, rivaling the elaborate storytelling and narrative drive of any major film. In a world where children are introduced to *Super Mario Brothers* before Aesop's Fables, we need to develop a functional literacy in decoding

Notice that David *summarizes* the general effect of the game here. Later in the analysis, he'll offer more specific summaries of how the game makes the audience feel and what the game asks the audience to believe.

Daniels 2

and engaging with the messages and methods, which video games rely upon. In much the same way that the analysis of film has become second nature to us as consumers, the analysis of electronic gaming media must also become reflexive.

One of the simplest ways to begin decoding games is to look at the way a game is designed to make the player feel. Oftentimes, a game developer's intentions may be difficult to glean. Ostensibly, the developer primarily wants to make the audience feel good enough to continue purchasing products from their company. This involves developing a signature brand styling, and reliably delivering that game style. For instance, developer Team Silent has produced the massively popular *Silent Hill* series, a game world based on the survival horror genre. This game series (which has spawned films, television, and books) relies upon a signature feeling of muted and desolate horror punctuated by sharp bursts of explosive terror. This is an emotional appeal that the developers depend upon repeatedly producing in order to gain the loyalty of a target audience, which can be relied upon to purchase new products. In much the same way, developer Bioware has come to rely upon a certain series of pathos appeals to produce an emotional epoch. By examining the introductory portions of their blockbuster title *Mass Effect*, we can begin to reveal this strategy.

For the sake of this analysis, the set of pathetic appeals that construct the general thrust of the developer's branding can be referred to as the datum. The data in the introductory sequences of *Mass Effect* try to get the audience to feel several emotions that build upon each other. They ask the

David *labels* two component parts of the argument here: the data in an enthymeme and the emotional appeals in the game. He also explains how these two parts interact, thus *analyzing* how the argument works.

Daniels 3

audience to follow an emotional trail through intrigue, awe, and finally involvement.

During the initial sections of the game, the player is invited to create a fully customizable avatar, through facial construction, skill selection, and personal history creation. This is designed to produce both a sense of intrigue, and also the beginnings of ownership. The player may choose to make the avatar (whose last name is always Shepard) male or female, of noble, humble, or dark origins, and of any skill makeup desired. This invites players both to re-imagine themselves or an ideal of themselves within the language of the game world. This allows the players to translate or recreate their identities in a different reality. Also, and crucially, this points the player's view forward to how this particular set of options will shape their gaming experience. They are, in essence, intrigued.

After the process of avatar creation is complete, the game proper opens with a long cinematic, in which the other characters of the game are speaking of the Shepard the player has created. Their dialogue reflects the choices the player made in the initial phases of character creation. However, no matter whether they praise your history as a war hero, or caution each other about your reputation for ruthless efficiency, they conclude that you are humanity's one great hope. The scene is set on a highly advanced space vessel, obviously military, with humans and aliens working side by side. During the course of the introduction, the ship approaches a massive device in space and makes a spectacular high-speed leap, presumably across the galaxy, complete with lightning-like pyrotechnic displays. This serves to move the audience from a sense of

David *summarizes* the parts of the game that contribute to an emotional appeal.

He *labels* the material earlier summarized as a pathetic appeal to make the audience feel intrigue.

David *summarizes* the parts of the game that contribute to another emotional appeal.

Daniels 4

intrigue, into awe, and helps to further solidify the ownership theme, by introducing the audience to their first round of control (the voice actors change what they are saying based on what sort of history the player chose). By moving the audience from intrigue to awe, the developers both fulfill the players' previous feeling of intrigue (I was right to think this was going to be cool) and create a form of ethos which the player can rely upon (if Bioware can do something this impressive I wonder what ELSE they can do?). However, this is only the foundation for the overarching and crucial emotional leap.

Once the opening cinematics end, the players are allowed to wander the halls of the starship themselves, and to speak to crewmen and civilians alike, choosing dynamic and diverse dialogue options that cause people to respond in unique ways and to develop relationships with the player, through their avatar Shepard. This is the final solidifying of a sense of deep involvement that allows players to feel like they own the world. It is the emotional equivalent of taking a 12-year-old boy out to a luxury car lot, asking him which car he likes best, and then offering him the keys. Indeed, this final sense of deep involvement is what a car salesman might call the "hook." By moving the players through intrigue, awe, and finally involvement, the developers weave a tapestry of emotions that draw their arguments close to the player's heart.

However, I promised that this analysis would begin to teach us the methods of decoding those arguments. Earlier, I said that one might think of the various pathetic appeals as data. For the sake of clarity, I'll review the basic parts of an enthymeme. An enthymeme is basically a way of translating an argument into several specific interrelated parts. The first part of an enthymeme is a set of data; something that a rhetor

---

Margin notes:

David *labels* the material earlier summarized as a pathetic appeal to make the audience feel awe.

David *analyzes* how the two pathetic appeals work together and how they also rely upon an ethical appeal.

David *summarizes* the parts of the game that contribute to a third emotional appeal.

David *labels* the material earlier summarized as a pathetic appeal to make the audience feel involved.

David *analyzes* how these three pathetic appeals work together.

Daniels 5

introduces to an audience for consideration. In the case of *Mass Effect's* introduction, the data consist of several carefully crafted pathetic appeals that amount to:

- I can create/translate my own identity into a rich contextual reality presented by the game, which causes me to feel intrigue.
- I am presented with impressive, dynamic, and polished cinematics in which characters within this reality are shown to be dynamically reacting to my choices. This moves me from intrigue to awe.
- I am further allowed to move about freely in this reality, completely immersed by visual and auditory stimuli, as well as deeply engaged by a dynamic system of conversation, combat, and choice that seems to organically respond to my actions. This creates a feeling of deep involvement with the contextual reality of the game world.

> David *labels* the pathetic appeals summarized below as the data in an enthymeme.

The second part of any enthymeme is a claim, what the rhetor is asking the audience ultimately to believe. For the introduction of *Mass Effect,* a fair claim might be: *So* I am in control of the contextual reality of this highly impressive game.

> David *summarizes* the enthymeme's claim. Notice that he must put this in his own words because the implicit argument in *Mass Effect* is never openly presented.

The third part of an enthymeme is the warrant, which moves the audience to accept that the claim derives from the datum. For the introduction of *Mass Effect* the warrant might be paraphrased as: *Since* the complex and dynamic world of *Mass Effect* has been shown to be both responsive and engaged with the choices I make, both in the construction of my personal avatar and in the events that shape the game's over-arching storyline. Another, deeper warrant is also at play—*Since* I must be in control of any reality that responds to and engages my choices (a material topic of the real and a formal topic of causes and effects).

> David *summarizes* the enthymeme's warrant. Notice that he must also put this in his own words because the warrant is left implicit, just like the claim.

Daniels 6

This enthymeme is one of several possible (and likely coexistent) arguments that function in the background of *Mass Effect's* contextual reality. When approaching a complex non-traditional piece of rhetoric like a film or video game, often the process of argument analysis can begin most effectively with the way the rhetoric seems to want the audience to feel. In *Mass Effect* the pathetic appeals of intrigue, awe, and involvement function in concert to produce a logical claim that the player is a vital part of the game world and to support an assumption about the game's responsive nature. And all of it, the pathetic appeals and the enthymeme, induces a lasting sense of ownership on the part of the players.

The ownership is the payoff for the developers. Bioware offers a high-quality piece of storytelling, and convinces the players that they are, in fact, in the driver's seat. The player grants, through being intrigued and then impressed, that the game world is a high-quality product, and then assumes control of that product in dynamic ways. This allows the players to feel, perhaps crucially, effective. This is the emotional foundation for an electronic empire.

David *analyzes* the interaction between the pathetic appeals and the enthymeme that he has labeled and summarized in the previous paragraphs.

David *summarizes* the game's principal message—what the audience should believe.

4

Structure

Why do smokers, who know the consequences to their health, keep lighting up? Why do students (and professors), who know they need to prepare for class, choose to spend another thirty minutes surfing their favorite blogs? Why do citizens, who abhor the politicians in power, stay home on election day? Not surprisingly, Aristotle had an answer to these questions—an answer that describes how arguments interact with human psychology. In his discussion of practical reasoning—the partly conscious, partly subconscious thinking that motivates both animal and human action (*praxis*)—Aristotle notes that, unlike a formal syllogism, an argument in practical reason may be based on not just two premises—a datum and a warrant—but on simultaneous "bundles" of premises—multiple data and/or warrants. (See *Nicomachean Ethics* 1147a and *Movement of Animals* 702b.) Moreover, these premises may be not only conscious propositions but also moods, emotions, and even bodily states (such as hunger, thirst, appetite, sexual desire, fatigue, pain, or fight/flight arousal). Further, some premises may disagree with others. Aristotle illustrates this principle with a simple example, a man looking at a sweetcake and having conflicted feelings about it (our slightly modified rendition is shown in Figure 4.1).

Our hero, upon seeing the sweetcake (and recognizing that it is available for him to eat), associates that input with a number of available warrants already present in his mind: he feels hungry, likes sweets, and believes that they generally are tasty, but he also has a belief that sweets are unhealthy to eat, and his doctor has recently told him he needs to avoid them. In short, his warrants set up two conflicting motivations for action: "eat the sweetcake" and "don't eat the sweetcake." What will he do? According to Aristotle, if he is not simply paralyzed by conflicting ideas (which seems unlikely here), his choice between these competing arguments will be determined by *which premises exert*

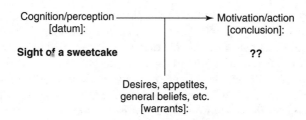

Cognition/perception ────────────➤ Motivation/action
[datum]:   [conclusion]:

Sight of a sweetcake   **??**

Desires, appetites,
general beliefs, etc.
[warrants]:

Feeling of hunger
Belief that "sweets are tasty"
Appetite for sweets (sweet tooth)
Belief that "sweets are bad for you"
Memory of doctor's warning

Figure 4.1   Aristotle's analysis of practical reason.

the most energy in his consciousness. Which ones seem most vivid, most prominent, most urgent? Suppose that, since he is hungry and an inveterate sweet-eater anyway, the pro-sweetcake-eating argument wins the day. We might represent the differential energies of his premises and motives in this way:

SWEETCAKE THERE!
FEEL HUNGRY
SWEETS TASTY
WANT SWEETS
 SO EAT THE SWEETCAKE

but sweets are bad for me
doctor says lay off sweets
 so don't eat the sweetcake

This being the case, our hero says to himself, "I really shouldn't, but it looks so good and I'm hungry!" and he gobbles the dessert. You can think of similar psychological scenarios. Our point is that people's decisions do not always involve complete rejection of an opposing motivation or argument. *Two competing arguments may continue to be regarded as true,* but the larger and more vibrant argument will dominate at the moment of decision. As modern argumentation theorist Chaim Perelman has put it, one argument, or one set of premises, has greater "presence" and therefore exerts more persuasive force.

Why have we brought this up? In this chapter and the next we are concerned primarily with the *presentational* aspects of rhetoric—structure and style—and the role they play in enhancing the *energy* or *presence* of ideas and arguments in an audience's thought. Assuming Aristotle and Perelman are correct (and we think they are), if two competing arguments are more or less equally persuasive, the one that is most effectively presented and exerts the most *energy* in the audience's thought will tend to prevail. Structure and style, then, are not merely matters of superficial ornament or etiquette. They have a necessary role in any argument. They are essential to rhetorical art.

BASIC PRINCIPLES: THE PSYCHOLOGY OF FORM

According to Kenneth Burke, rhetorical "form" or structure is fundamentally a matter of audience psychology. It is a matter not simply of organizing the information (or arguments) conveyed by a discourse—though that is important—but of *organizing the audience's experience* of that information. As Burke puts it, psychologically effective form involves "an arousing and fulfillment of desires." A discourse has effective form, or is perceived to have effective form, if "one part of it leads a reader to anticipate another part, [and] to be gratified by the sequence." (Kenneth Burke, *Counter-Statement* [Berkeley: California, 1968], p. 124.) One can see this principle in action whenever someone sets up an issue ("many people wonder which is more important, earning money or enjoying a career"), works through the relevant evidence and reasons ("while earning more money may lead to greater opportunity and security, enjoying one's career will lead to happiness and a long life"), and ends by drawing a conclusion ("since happiness is best, we should focus on careers that make us happy rather than jobs that make us rich"). Finally, the same principle can be seen in the standard plotline used in many detective dramas: An opening scene displays the aftermath or perpetration of a grisly crime; detectives arrive to investigate; complications arise in the investigation (a difficult witness or a lack of evidence) leading to uncertainty and tension (maybe the killer will get away!); the accused murderer confesses on the stand in a climactic court scene; and a denouement ties up loose ends (while walking down the courthouse steps, the detectives and the prosecuting attorneys trade quips about justice being messy because she's blind).

These examples do not exhaust the possibilities. Burke's basic formula applies to any discourse with a satisfying structure or closure. This principle has three important implications:

- Ideas placed in the forefront of the audience's mind form the interpretive frame and set up the expectations that shape the audience's reception of later ideas. New information is interpreted in light of old information; even, for example, in a discourse consisting simply of a list of arguments or statements. A list may be arranged in an ascending or climactic order of importance, a descending order, or some other order.

- As Burke notes (in "Lexicon Rhetoricae," in *Counter-Statement*), an audience's perception of a specific form or pattern in a discourse, and their anticipation of its completion, leads them to participate— so that, when the form satisfactorily completes itself and fulfills the audience's expectation, it lends emphasis (energy, prominence) and persuasiveness to what is said. An audience may embrace a conclusion, in part, because it fulfills a structural expectation and therefore feels right. This might be called the *formal* or *aesthetic* appeal, in addition to ethos, logos, and pathos appeals. (Alternatively, the formal/aesthetic appeal may be considered a type of pathos appeal.)

- A rhetor also can produce effects by deliberately frustrating but eventually fulfilling the audience's expectations. An audience is often more satisfied by a discourse that does not end in a conventionally expected or obvious way. This is the basic principle of the plot twist or surprise ending in mystery/suspense movies, as well as (in more subtle forms) a great deal of experimental art, film, and literature that deliberately violates the audience's expectations. (It is also a basic principle of comedy.)

In sum, in a rhetorically well-formed discourse, each part—an episode in a story, a unit of argument—sets up the audience for what will follow, elaborates or complicates the setup, or brings the setup to some resolution. (The overall arc of an argument or story can, of course, include other sequences that repeat, in smaller form, the basic setup-to-closure process, just as a complex argument can consist of an overall main enthymeme whose parts are built up as subsidiary enthymemes.)

A major task for rhetorical analysis, then, is to attend to that basic process: to identify the functional parts or units of the discourse in question, and to assess how they guide and shape the audience's desires/expectations and responses.

SOME VARIETIES OF FORM: PROGRESSIVE, REPETITIVE, AND CONVENTIONAL

Burke also offers some general terms for describing structure. (See, again, Burke's "Lexicon Rhetoricae," in *Counter-Statement*.) These terms are not mutually exclusive. More than one can apply to the structural description of any given discourse or its parts. The key terms are *progressive, repetitive,* and *conventional form.* We take these up in turn.

Progressive Form: Syllogistic and Qualitative

As the name implies, *progressive* form involves one thing leading to another. A discourse (or a unit of discourse) with progressive form sustains a feeling of step-by-step forward movement. Further, progressive forms may be *syllogistic* or *qualitative.*

A *syllogistic* progression, as the name implies, embodies a consequential logic in which certain premises lead, or seem to lead, to conclusions. This can be observed in the steps of a chain of arguments or, likewise, in the cause-and-effect logic of a story ("X happened, and in consequence Y happened, leading to Z").

The VW "Why" ad that we analyze in this textbook includes a syllogistic progression that depends upon the presentation of questions and answers as well as claims and evidence. Why does the car seem to get different miles to the gallon? Depends on how you drive it. The car is affordable[claim] because it costs little to insure[evidence], requires little maintenance[evidence], and doesn't lose much value.[evidence] The logical sequence of claim-and-evidence reinforces these formally syllogistic progressions. Since the audience has to read the text from start to finish, as if they were following a line, they must encounter first the question and then the answer, first the issue and then the explanation; or, in the last paragraph, first the claim about affordability ("and you can put these in your bankbook") and then the evidence (low depreciation, low insurance, low maintenance costs).

Note that a syllogistic progression need not always embody a valid or persuasive logic. Any progression that has the form or feeling of a logical sequence is syllogistic. Consider, as a miniature example, this sequence (actually a version of the figure of speech called *anadiplosis*): "He who controls Topeka controls Kansas; he who controls Kansas controls North America; he who controls North America rules the world." There is no particular reason to believe any of these assertions individually; and even if, say, the first is true, the next does not logically follow (what warrants the inference?). Aristotle might call this sequence an *apparent* (as opposed to real) syllogism. Nevertheless it has a syllogistic form, and *feels* syllogistic. For an audience that perceives and participates in the form's unfolding (as we said previously), the formal completion can lend its conclusion a feeling of rightness—or, at least, a feeling of conclusiveness. Not all syllogistic progressions are logically questionable, of course. A logically valid and persuasive argument presented in an effectively syllogistic form will generally have an enhanced persuasiveness. It will seem more forceful, impressive, and memorable than an argument that lacks such form.

A *qualitative* progression, in contrast, depends not on syllogistic logical-consequential or causal necessities (or the feeling of such necessities), but on associative or emotional connections, so that the introduction of one quality, mood, or set of associations evokes another. For example, a short film may consist of a montage that shows, first, a dark and gloomy thunderstorm, then a picture of a mountain standing majestic and serene in the clear sky, then a child playing in a meadow, and so on. There is no consequential or causal necessity to this progression, but there is an associative sequence of moods (e.g., gloom/darkness, to majesty/serenity/brightness, to happy innocence). Each image, with its mood and network of associations, seemingly suggests the next.

Some media theorists argue that print lends itself to syllogistic progression because the audience must read print from start to finish, as if following a line. Print is linear. Since audience members must read from left to right and top to bottom, they're more inclined to expect and appreciate a form that seems to move from one point to another related point, from question to answer or claim to evidence. But another medium, such as television, does not exhibit such a strong linearity. Would an argument in this medium work better with qualitative progression?

In the 1980s, Volkswagen extended their "Think Small" campaign into a television advertisement. See Figure 4.2. (You can watch this entire commercial on YouTube.com. Search for "volkswagen think small commercial.") This commercial includes an image of the Beetle driving across an oversize "Think Small" print ad while a voiceover explains that Volkswagen has been a part of the popular trend toward smaller cars for "21 years."

The commercial depends in part upon a syllogistic progression in the voiceover. The narrator tells us about a great "new idea" that everyone is talking about. He caps the discussion of this "new idea" by explaining that Volkswagen has been "working on it for 21 years." The images parallel this syllogistic progression with a qualitative progression from absence to presence. Initially, the viewer sees a page with a large blank spot where something is apparently missing, leading to questions about what should go in the obviously vacant space. Then, the viewer sees a car fill the void in the center of the screen. The video creates desire in the mind of the audience and then satisfies that desire.

In addition to illustrating the difference between syllogistic and qualitative form, we hope that this brief analysis brings to light an important question for rhetorical analysis: What effect do technological media have on argumentative form? If television lends itself to qualitative progression and print lends itself to syllogistic progression, we must wonder what happens when rhetors engage new media. Do progressive forms lose their persuasiveness when users are no longer required or encouraged to move from left to right and top to bottom?

We can extend such questions to new media as well. Perhaps hyperlinks must create a qualitative progression. A link often creates curiosity in the mind of the web browser about a word or a reference. Clicking on the link may satisfy that curiosity by presenting the word's definition

VW "THINK SMALL" TV COMMERCIAL

WHAT YOU SEE	WHAT YOU HEAR
An image of a "Think Small" VW ad, as printed in a magazine but without the typical graphic in the upper two-thirds of the page. Instead, the top two-thirds of the page are blank, and the bottom one-third is filled with the standard text describing the car and featuring the title "Think Small." Behind the magazine page is a black background.	A deep soothing male voice says, "This year, just about everyone's coming up with a brand new small car, so this year, just about everyone will be telling you about this great new idea. To think small. It is a great idea."
A black Volkswagen Beetle, filmed from above, drives across the page, starting in the upper-left-hand corner and stopping in the middle of the white space where a photo of the car would normally be placed. A man in a white lab coat exits the car and walks towards the top of the page, eventually exiting the scene altogether. Meanwhile, two men, also wearing white lab coats and also filmed from above, enter the scene from the bottom. They carry between them a large VW logo. They leave it on the page near the text where the VW logo would normally be prominently displayed.	The car engine purrs quietly and then ceases shortly after the car stops. The door closes with a soft thud, and audible footsteps are heard as the men enter and exit the scene. We also hear the VW logo strike the page as it is put down.
The VW Beetle sits motionless in the middle of the page. It appears small in comparison to the surrounding white space.	The same deep, soothing male voice says, "We at Volkswagen have been working on it for 21 years."

Figure 4.2   Description of the images and the narration in a 1980s VW "Think Small" commercial.

or the entire source referenced. Imagine how frustrating web browsing would be if links violated the basic qualitative progression from curiosity to informational embellishment. Imagine that, while browsing a Wikipedia page on India, you find an embedded link to Pakistan. When you click on the link, you're whisked to a page about packing sand, as if the link were supposed to create in your mind a desire for words and phrases that nearly rhymed with the words contained in the link. Wouldn't this be frustrating? The frustration arises from the page's inability to follow a certain qualitative form of hyperlinking on Wikipedia.

WRITE AN ANALYSIS

Advertising campaigns present the rhetorical analyst with a unique opportunity to investigate formal differences among arguments trying to achieve (essentially) the same effect. For this reason, we chose to discuss the VW "Think Small" campaign, which appeared in print as well as in televised media. We also notice that the two different media seem to shape the formal differences between two arguments made in this campaign. The print ad appears more syllogistically progressive, while the televised ad seems more qualitatively progressive. You can write a similar analysis that compares form in an ad campaign with print, televised, and online ads. Find another advertising campaign appearing in multiple media. Analyze the form of each instance. If you can stretch this analysis across print, television, and new media, then all the better! Compare the formal differences, and reflect on whether those differences result from the medium or some other factors that we haven't considered here.

Repetitive Form

Unlike progressive forms, repetitive forms involve reiteration of the same thing in different variations. Just as media theorists associate syllogistic and qualitatively progressive forms with print and television, respectively, some media theorists associate repetitive form with oral presentation. Nevertheless, like progressive form, repetitive form can appear in a variety of media. Perhaps the most obvious type of repetitive form occurs in the recurring melodic patterns and repeated refrains of popular songs. Repetitive form can also be seen in familiar fairy tales like "Goldilocks and the Three Bears," which consists of three episodes (Goldilocks tries the chairs, the porridge, and the beds), with the same three steps in every episode (too big/hot/hard, too small/cold/soft, just right).

To illustrate the presence of repetitive form in a moment of oral argumentation, consider the last and most memorable portion of Martin Luther King, Jr.'s "I Have a Dream" speech:

> And if America is to be a great nation this must become true. So let freedom ring from the prodigious hilltops of New Hampshire. Let freedom ring from the mighty mountains of New York. Let freedom ring from the heightening Alleghenies of Pennsylvania! Let freedom ring from the snowcapped Rockies of Colorado! Let freedom ring from the curvaceous slopes of California! But not only that; let freedom ring from Stone Mountain of Georgia! Let freedom ring from Lookout Mountain of Tennessee! Let freedom ring from every hill and molehill of Mississippi. From every mountainside, let freedom ring.
>
> And when this happens, when we allow freedom to ring, when we let it ring from every village and every hamlet, from every state and every city, we will be able to speed up that day when all of God's children, black men and white men, Jews and Gentiles, Protestants and Catholics, will be able to join hands and sing in the words of the old Negro spiritual, "Free at last! free at last! thank God Almighty, we are free at last!"

The last and longest section of King's oration is so moving largely because it elaborates, through a series of repetitions, on an established theme: the movement from a dark and cruel place to a bright and better future, from a low place of segregation to a high place of racial unity. He paints bright images of freedom ringing on hilltops in California and mountaintops in New York, Tennessee, and Georgia.

The repetitive, accumulative restatement of the same argument or idea in different variations can be very powerful, for at least two reasons. First, by dwelling on the same point, the rhetor compels the audience to think about it for a longer time, and therefore gives the basic idea more presence in their thought. An audience easily forgets something that is quickly passed over. But something that is said three times, or ten times, in different ways, generally leaves a larger psychological imprint. Moreover, if the same point can be made in multiple ways, it may seem to be more securely grounded, more massively true.

The risk of repetitive form is that it can become *tediously* repetitive, or can seem arbitrary. Why ten repetitions instead of five, or two? Why *these* ten, and why in this order? In King's speech, each "let freedom ring" passage mentions an area where civil rights would be realized.

King begins in the northeast, moves west, and finally south (where civil rights would presumably be most resisted and last won). But King's repetitive forms combine with his progression across various states, to give a feeling of movement. Another potential source of tediousness in repetitive form is the perception that the repetitions add nothing new. The audience begins to think, "OK, OK, I get it already!" This problem is generally avoided by not letting the list run on too long, by introducing variations that add something and thus expand the audience's sense of what is being repeated, or simply by introducing stylistic variations to keep the repetition from seeming mechanical. King keeps his repetitions from becoming tedious by inserting new geographic details in each instance ("Lookout Mountain," every "hill and molehill," etc.).

Strategies for combining repetitive with qualitative form include arranging the list of items in an ascending order of importance; or, less commonly, in a descending order. Closely related to ascending order is the advice commonly given in writing textbooks—which goes back to the ancient Greeks—to put the strongest point either first or last, but always to begin and end with something strong, and to place the weaker points in the middle. The basic reason is that the first and last positions in a series are generally perceived as more important, and are remembered better, while items buried in the middle seem less important and are more easily forgotten. The traditional advice, in short, aims at making a repetitive list feel like an ascending qualitative progression.

Finally, repetitive forms can be combined with syllogistic forms. Imagine, for example, a story in which a virtuous soldier serves a worthless king. He carries out the king's misguided orders and suffers the catastrophic consequences, yet remains always loyal and does his duty to the end. The episodes of the story may unfold by a cause-effect logic, while each episode reiterates the contrast (in some new way) between the soldier's virtue and the king's worthlessness. One can say that the story's plot develops syllogistically, while its argument develops repetitively. (A version of such form can be seen in the acclaimed 1981 film *Gallipoli*.)

We have focused our analysis of repetitive form on oral arguments, such as King's speech, to illustrate the association often drawn between orality and repetition. But we maintain that repetitive form has many applications. Consider the navigation systems present on any website. These must remain uniform (must be repeated) across all the pages in a site to give the user some sense of uniformity and some ability to find things as she chooses. Likewise, in oral media, repetitive forms help people to remember and to find their place in a discourse ("ah, this is the point in the speech where he repeats that phrase"; "okay, this is the part of the story where she tries different bowls of porridge, just like the earlier part when she tried to sit in a bunch of chairs").

WRITE AN ANALYSIS

Politicians usually make the same argument in a variety of media. They may argue for lower taxes in a stump speech (an oral argument) and then again in an opinion article for a local paper (a print argument). Find two such instances of the same argument in different media: stump speeches, print articles, webpages. Look at the forms adopted in each. Do you find repetitive form in the speech (as might be appropriate)? Do you find the same repetitive form in the web argument, and is the form equally effective there?

Conventional and Minor Forms

Beyond progressive and repetitive forms (and their interactions), Burke recognizes *conventional* and *minor* forms. Conventional forms are regularized genres of discourse that have developed in particular forums or communities where certain kinds of discourses occur repeatedly. These include the State of the Union Address, the business letter, the scientific research report, the judicial opinion, the detective novel, the James Bond movie, and hip-hop music. It is impossible to list and describe all conventional genres of discourse, because they are nearly infinite in number, and new ones are constantly being created. For the most part, conventional forms are learned through experience in particular disciplines, such as business, law, literary criticism, the arts, and the sciences.

It is, however, useful for rhetorical analysis to be aware of conventional forms—for example, to recognize that Martin Luther King, Jr.'s "Letter from Birmingham Jail" is an open letter that is in

FOR FURTHER DISCUSSION

What happens when form *severely* violates, subverts, or complicates conventional expectations? Consider this famous/notorious example: in 1917, the artist Marcel Duchamp took a standard factory-produced urinal, turned it on its back, set it on a pedestal, titled it "Fountain," signed it "R. Mutt," and exhibited it at the Society of Independent Artists annual show in New York City. (Photographs of "Fountain" can easily be found on the Internet: search for "marcel duchamp fountain.") It occasioned much controversy about whether it was "art" or not, and the discussion still continues. In what ways did "Fountain" formally fulfill conventional expectations for a "work of art," and in what ways did it not? How did it shape the viewer's experience, and the viewer's response? What resolution or conclusion could that experience come to? What argument(s) could Duchamp be said to have intended? (Note: In the original event "Fountain" was deemed "not art," removed from the show, and afterwards tossed out as junk; Duchamp resigned from the Society of Independent Artists, which subsequently went into decline and failed. Duchamp made several reproductions of the lost original, which are on permanent display at various museums. He remained unhappy with people who defended "Fountain" as "beautiful" art, and felt that they seriously distorted what he had tried to do.)

---

some sense also a judicial discourse (as he defends himself against accusations)—and to have a sense of what expectations audiences bring to those forms. Likewise, understanding the conventional form of American car ads in the late 1950s enables one to grasp the striking novelty of Volkswagen's 1960 ad campaign. Further, particular conventional genres can themselves be the object of rhetorical analysis and critique. One conventional form, for instance, helps us to understand the VW commercial that we analyzed earlier in this chapter. In our analysis, we posited that when the commercial featured a page with print text at the bottom but a lot of white space at the top, viewers would expect something to be present in the white space. Thus, the first ten seconds of the commercial established the first part of a qualitative progression from absence to presence of an image. By this time (the early 1980s), the audience had been conditioned to expect print advertisements to follow a conventional form, dedicating two-thirds of the ad's space to an image at the top, a headline in the middle, and one-third of the ad's space to print text at the bottom. (Advertising maven David Ogilvy discusses this conventional form in his book *Ogilvy on Advertising*, 1983.) Presented with a print ad missing its dominating top image, the audience would desire to see that image. Since they knew the conventional form of print ads, they would perceive an absence and desire to see it filled.

What Burke calls *minor* forms do not structure whole discourses (or large parts of them) but smaller parts, such as individual sentences or parts of sentences. Minor forms, in other words, are what rhetoric traditionally has called *figures of speech and thought*. These belong to the realm of *style*, to which we will turn in Chapter 5. However, it is worth noting that some figures—such as anadiplosis or accumulation, which we mentioned earlier—can also function as organizing principles for larger units of discourse.

THE FORM OF ARGUMENTATION: THE CLASSICAL TEMPLATE

One important and long-enduring form that rhetorical analysis should be aware of is the classical template for argumentation. Here are the standard parts, with the commonly used names for each (including terms derived from Greek and Latin):

- *Introduction* (prologue, *proemium, exordium*): opening statement meant to announce the subject matter and the issue in question (logos), establish the rhetor's character (ethos), and gain a receptive hearing from the audience (pathos).

- *Narrative* (*diegesis*): exposition of necessary background information, including the facts of the case and/or basic terms and concepts necessary for understanding the issue in question and the arguments to follow.

  - *Partition*: an optional element that may be employed after either the prologue or the narrative (or both or neither). Brief forecast of the main point(s) to be dealt with in what follows.

- *Proofs* (confirmation): the main body of evidence and arguments (enthymemes, epicheiremes) in support of the rhetor's central claim.

  - *Rebuttal*: an optional, floating element that can be placed anywhere, as needed, but often after the proofs. Replies to objections, queries, and counterarguments.

  - *Digression* (prolepsis, anticipation): an optional, floating element that can be placed anywhere, as needed. A strategic turning aside from the main argument to preempt possible questions or objections before they have come up, or to develop extra reflections that enhance the argument.

  - *Summation*: an optional element, used only if the discourse has been long and complex and the audience needs reminding. Concise recapitulation of the argument's main points and central claim.

- *Conclusion* (epilogue, peroration): brief reassertion of the argument's central claim (logos), accompanied by presentation of character (ethos), calls for action (pathos), and/or additional reflections if appropriate.

As this representation suggests, there are four essential parts: introduction, narrative, proofs, and conclusion. The others—partition, rebuttal, digression, and summation—are optional and movable. The floating elements, rebuttal and digression, can be inserted at multiple points in a discourse, wherever needed and as often as needed, or omitted altogether. Even narrative, an essential element, can be omitted if the background information is already familiar to the audience and repetition would be tedious. The absolute core of the structure (as Aristotle noted, *Rhetoric* 3.13.1–2) is the introduction and proofs: Say what you're going to prove (arouse expectation), then prove it (fulfill expectation).

The classical template is not a rigid framework imposed on rhetors by rhetoricians, but a flexible, variable pattern that has emerged and evolved naturally, and that rhetoricians have observed and described, in the real-world practice of rhetors from antiquity to the present. As a form that evolved in real-world practice, it is conventional; but it is also natural because it arises from the psychological necessities of presenting an argument to an audience. As we have suggested already, the introduction establishes and focuses the audience's expectation by declaring the main issue to be resolved. Then the narrative orients that expectation by providing an overview of the issue and preparing the audience for the arguments to follow. The proofs work toward the resolution of the issue, and thus carry the audience's expectation forward (and may also complicate and modify it), by examining the evidence and the reasoning that bear upon the question. The conclusion, if effective, appears as a logical consequence of the proofs and thus fulfills the audience's expectation for a resolution. The optional elements may be inserted or not, depending on what the audience needs in order to follow the argument and stay on board with each step along the way.

The classical template, clearly, is on the whole a progressive and mainly syllogistic form: a progression of four logically related steps from question to resolution. However, its individual parts may manifest different patterns. The narrative, for example, may tell a syllogistic story, but the story may also be told as a qualitative progression, or even as a repetitive collection of episodes in which the same thing repeatedly occurred. Likewise, the proofs may take a syllogistic form, a repetitive form (a list of arguments all supporting the same conclusion), a qualitative form (a list arranged in a climactic order), or some combination of these forms. Moreover, the generally syllogistic character of the whole may be broken up with optional elements serving as qualitative interludes. A rhetor, for example, may insert an amusing digression to give the audience some relief from the mental strain of following a densely argued passage, and to keep them in a friendly, receptive mood.

Conventional Variants of the Classical Template

As we have noted, the *classical template* appears in modern argumentative discourse, including argument produced by rhetors with no training in classical rhetoric, in many specific variations. For example, a judicial opinion (a judge's explanation of his or her ruling on a case) will typically begin with identification of the point at issue (introduction); then offer a review of the background of the case (narrative); then cite the standards for legal judgment established in the relevant case law and conduct a critical examination of the arguments presented in the trial (proofs); and finally declare the ruling that follows from that examination (conclusion). Likewise, the standard scientific research article begins with an overview of earlier research and identification of the specific question to be investigated (introduction); then describes the research methodology used in the study (narrative); then presents and analyzes the data gathered by the research (proofs); and finally offers conclusions and suggestions for further research (conclusion).

Variations of the classical template appear, as well, in many of the conventionalized essay genres commonly taught in college writing classes.

SIDEBAR: THE CLASSICAL TEMPLATE AND ESSAY GENRES:

CLASSICAL TEMPLATE	EXPOSITION	EVALUATION	PROPOSAL
Introduction	*Introduction* (what is X; subject to be explicated and thesis)	*Introduction* (how to judge X)	*Introduction* (what to do about X)
Narrative	*Restriction* (redefine and limit topic)	*Criteria* (present evaluative terms)	*Problem* (describe situation, causes/ effects, etc.)
Proofs	*Illustration* (description, examples, comparison, etc.)	*Application* (relate the thing at issue to the stated criteria)	*Solution* (propose solution, demonstrate probable outcomes, advantages, feasibility)
Conclusion	*Conclusion* (thesis)	*Conclusion* (judgment/ stance)	*Conclusion* (judge proposal, call for action)

Likewise, as we suggested earlier, the classical template also can be seen reflected in the standard plotline used in a lot of popular film and fiction, and commonly taught in creative writing classes.

Our point, again, is that the classical template is not rigid but a flexible and adaptable form that evolves naturally from the Burkean principle and underlies a wide variety of conventional genres of discourse. This makes it a useful heuristic for the rhetorical analysis of form in argumentation, and even in storytelling.

SIDEBAR: THE CLASSICAL TEMPLATE AND THE STORY

INTRODUCTION →	NARRATIVE →	PROOFS →	CONCLUSION
Opening scenario and introduction of conflict/tension	Character-development and further development of scenario	Complication and development of conflict/ tension, leading to climax (solution)	Denouement (wind down and resolution of remaining plot elements)

SPATIAL FORM AND INFORMATION ARCHITECTURE

The notions of rhetorical structure we have discussed so far—Burke's principle, progressive (syllogistic and qualitative) form, repetitive form, conventional form, and the classical template for argumentation (and its variants)—all presuppose a *temporal* experience of discourse. Temporally organized discourse, and the audience's experience of it, unfolds in time, from beginning to end. (As we mentioned earlier, their temporal and linear quality has led many to wonder if these forms can be used in media that do not require a progression from one point to another.)

Of course, not all discourse or all rhetoric or even all argumentation is organized temporally—or at least not obviously so. For example, a mural painted on the side of a downtown building may make a political statement, and may be understood as an argument that intends to persuade. The same may be said about a photograph of beautiful mountains on a Sierra Club poster. How are such visual "texts" and their arguments experienced? Does the audience's experience unfold in time, and, if so, how does the visual text control or guide that experience? Or, does the audience experience the visual text and its argument all at once, or in some arbitrary, unguided sequence of its own choosing?

Something similar may be said about complex informational documents, such as a computer manual or a telephone book, that are not designed to be experienced temporally or to be read straight through from the first to the final page. Likewise for complex websites, in which each page has multiple links that permit readers to navigate through the website in different sequences, and even to navigate out to different websites. The same is true for video games that allow users to construct their own narratives by making choices about what to do and how to interact with the "universe" that the game designers have created. While the computer manual may not have an overtly argumentative function—and therefore may be a borderline case of rhetoric—many websites are not essentially informational but are devoted to advocacy and undoubtedly make arguments. And many video games aim to create a certain kind of experience— exciting, titillating, action-packed—for the players. How is the audience's experience of such arguments organized and guided? Or is it organized at all? If such rhetorical texts have no way of guiding or giving form to the reader's experience, and if the reader's experience is then formless and haphazard, must we conclude that such texts provide their audiences with an inherently unsatisfactory experience?

We intend to leave this question open. It points to a relatively new and unsettled area for rhetorical studies. To a certain extent, it belongs to the discipline of graphic design. To a certain extent, it belongs to the established but rapidly developing field of information science. And to a certain extent, it belongs to the emerging industry of game design. Therefore, just as classical rhetoric encouraged the study of logic and other disciplines as preparations or foundations for rhetoric, we encourage some basic study in a range of disciplines and practices. Here we note just a few considerations:

- Visual rhetorical texts, such as a mural, photograph, or poster with some argumentative (or communicative) intent, can be thought to have *spatial form* rather than temporal form. The visual design can be arranged to define different parts of the image as frame and focus, or background and foreground, guiding the observer's eye to the focal/foreground element and inviting interpretation of it in relation to the frame/background elements. Further, viewers tend to process visual texts from top to bottom and left to right, just as they process written texts, at least in Western culture. The frame/focus and top/down left/right elements (as well as other design elements) can interact to give the viewer an orderly, coherent experience. That experience may even have a temporal element, insofar as the reader/viewer's gaze is encouraged to follow in some sequence. Conversely, visual texts that do not effectively organize the viewer's experience will tend to look chaotic, unfocused, and miscellaneous. (Of course, sometimes the rhetor may *want* to create an impression of chaotic profusion.)

- The examples of computer manuals and advocacy websites suggest the notion of *information architecture*: the design of information for optimal access and use by a community of users. In the late 1980s, Apple Computer gained a great advantage because its user manuals were organized intuitively, according to how and when most users (and especially computer novices) would need to use the information. In contrast, a lot of computer manuals at that time organized their information logically according to technical category, rather than according to the reader's psychology. The result often was that those manuals (and the computers that went with them) were nearly unusable for many. Often the information could only be found by technical experts who already knew how to categorize it. Our point is that the intuitive manuals gave their readers a more satisfactory experience, as well as a *persuasive* experience—that the computer was good and easy to use.

- Something similar could be said about a well-designed advocacy website. Not only would it be visually satisfying (like the visual texts discussed earlier), but it would also provide its viewer/reader with a coherent, formally satisfying experience of its information and arguments. For example, the viewer/reader would first need to know what issue (or set of issues) the site was devoted to (as in a prologue) and probably would need to be provided with some reliable analysis of the facts that the issue arises from (a kind of narrative) to properly experience, assess, and respond to the site's actual arguments (its proofs and conclusions). Many such sites provide a gateway that identifies the sponsoring organization and

WRITE AN ANALYSIS

In the introduction to this book, we argue that classical rhetorical theory can apply to a range of persuasive efforts. In this chapter, and in others, we see how new modes of communication have challenged those invested in tried-and-true concepts, such as the classical template just presented. Write an analysis applying the terms of the classical template to a discourse that seems to defy them. What counts as the exordium in a user's experience with the *Second Life* virtual world? If we call it an exordium, can we also say that this element functions like an exordium in an ancient Greek oration—establishing an ethos, introducing an exigent issue? What part, if any, of the video game *Grand Theft Auto* can we call a digression? The moments when the user can direct her avatar to interact with secondary characters in ways that do not significantly affect the game's missions? The mini-games such as bowling and billiard simulators that the user can play at various places in the game's universe? Are these little persuasive moments to enhance without directly contributing to the game experience? As our brief reflections demonstrate, using a vocabulary that seems inappropriate to the object of analysis will teach you something about the thing you're analyzing and about the vocabulary itself.

You can also write an analysis examining a text that deliberately departs from conventional expectation. Consider, for example, Cicero's speech *For the Poet Aulus Licinius Archias*. Just as in King's "Letter from Birmingham Jail," the latter part of *For Archias*—more than half—consists of a long digression. Cicero remarks at the beginning of the speech that he is going to depart from what is customary in courts of law. How does this deliberate, announced departure shape his audience's (the jury's) experience of the speech and its argumentation, including the digression? For a more extreme case, consider Cicero's *First Catilinarian Oration*, a famous torrent of invective. Is there any trace of the classical template in this speech? (Cicero usually adheres to it, though not mechanically.) If not, is there a recognizable principle of organization, or is audience expectancy constantly disrupted? How is the audience (the Roman senate) meant to experience this speech? We know, by the way, that the speech was a complete success, and that, for the rest of his life, Cicero regarded it as his finest hour.

the particular issues that it is devoted to. Subsequent pages provide links to pdf copies of analysis, opinion, and policy papers on specific topics—at which point, when reading the pdf documents, one is clearly back in the realm of Burke's principle of temporally structured argumentation.

- The notion of guided experience in a complex website also suggests the design of *video games*, which can provide, on one hand, a story line (like the standard plotline discussed above) and a sequenced progress through various levels (or scenarios) to some final scene—but, on the other hand, variable ways to proceed. This raises questions about how their temporal form (in the player's experience) should be described, and how they should (or could) be described as rhetorical documents, or arguments, intending persuasion.

- The website and the video game suggest another kind of information architecture: the actual architecture of, say, a museum building, an exhibit, or some other walk-through structure meant to give the viewer a particular kind of experience. What arguments are conveyed by that experience? What persuasion does it intend? One might, further, apply the same sort of analysis to the structured experience of entering and moving through a building that is not obviously informational, such as an office tower, a four-star hotel, or a shopping mall.

SAMPLE ANALYSIS: STRUCTURE AND THE CLASSICAL TEMPLATE IN "LETTER FROM BIRMINGHAM JAIL"

It is well known that Martin Luther King, Jr. spends roughly the first half of "Letter from Birmingham Jail" defending himself against criticisms, and in the second half turns to criticism of the "white moderate" and the "white church" for failing to actively support his cause. Those are the primary and secondary stases (Quality and Policy) created by the "Call to Unity" that he is responding to. The "Call" condemns his actions as "unwise and untimely" (Quality) and urges the "Negro" citizens of Birmingham (and other people of goodwill) to withdraw their support (Policy). These observations already provide a rough parsing of the "Letter" into its main structural divisions. But more can be said.

First of all, we note that the "Letter" has a clear introduction and conclusion. The introduction is brief, consisting of only paragraph 1. The conclusion (or epilogue) occupies the last three paragraphs (48–50). Its beginning is signaled by the transitional sentence, "Never before have I written so long a letter," which indicates that King is now stepping away from his arguments to offer some closing remarks. Between the introduction and epilogue, the body of the "Letter" appears on the surface to be structured in an episodic way, as King responds to assertions or questions raised by his critics' "Call to Unity." Such a structure is, of course, consistent with conventional expectations for an open letter in response to criticisms, as well as a quasi-judicial defense against a series of charges. This pattern of responding to criticisms is most apparent in the first half of the body (paragraphs 2–22), while the second half (23–47) subordinates such a response to the voicing of "disappointments" with the white moderate, the white church, and his critics.

For these reasons, the "Letter's" overt structure is often described as a point-by-point refutation of the critics—thus implicitly defining it as all rebuttal, and in principle a fundamentally repetitive design. But that is not quite the case. King does not, for example, take up his critics' statements in order. Nor, for that matter, do all his arguments reply to actual statements from those critics (as when he says, "You well may ask . . ."). Further, an all-rebuttal strategy would put him in a constantly defensive and reactive posture, yielding the initiative to his opponents, which generally is a losing strategy. Rather, King's response follows a deeper design, which suits his argumentative purposes. That design, we suggest, reflects the dynamics of the classical template.

Consider, for example, the first main segment of the body, paragraphs 2–11. In this segment, King explains what has brought him to Birmingham (organizational ties and the transcendental call to agitate for justice) and describes the methods and planning of the demonstrations. As we noted in Chapter 3, this segment serves argumentatively to reinforce his ethos and refute the critics' portrayal of him as an irresponsible rabble-rouser, while establishing some key ideas (general truths) that will serve as warrants for later arguments. But this segment also performs the function of a *narrative*—laying out the basic facts of the case that the intended audience (functioning as a "jury") is asked to judge—as King describes the activities for which he has been criticized and explains their rationale. (Note, too, that one traditionally recognized function of narration is the portrayal of ethos.)

This narrative segment is punctuated by King's recital of criticisms and questions, thereby breaking it into three subunits presented as criticism and reply: "I think I should indicate why I am here in Birmingham, since you have been influenced by the view which argues against 'outsiders coming in'" (paragraph 2); "You deplore the demonstrations taking place in Birmingham" (5); "You may well ask, 'Why direct action?'" (10). This repetitive tactic breaks the narrative into shorter subunits, thus making it easier to process, and maintains the feeling of a dialogue with his critics, thus making it more lively.

Following the narrative is what amounts to King's proof segment (paragraphs 12–22). This consists of two main subunits, each marked by an introductory question and each offering an enthymematic (or epicheirematic) argument: first, the question of whether the demonstrations are "untimely," culminating in the famously pathetic "when you have seen" passage and its enthymematic cap (12–14); and then the question of breaking laws (parading without a permit), culminating in quasi-philosophical, epicheirematic argumentation about just and unjust laws (15–22). As we have noted, these arguments effectively complete King's self-defense. The activities described in the narrative are fully justified by the proofs, with great persuasive force.

Why are these subunits in this order? In a repetitive or qualitative sequence, for example, it would seem best to finish with the emotional crescendo of the "when you have seens," rather than the relatively cool (if noble) logic of the argumentation on just and unjust laws. From this point of view, to end with just and unjust laws seems almost anticlimactic—yet few readers (actually none, to our knowledge) have complained. Most find the sequence highly effective. One might argue that King's arrangement forms a syllogistic progression that renders the argument on laws more compelling. After the narrative has portrayed the demonstration as a principled and responsible activity, the next natural (and dialogic) question is whether, even if principled, it should be happening (the charge of untimeliness). When that question is answered with an emotionally force-ful *yes*, the next question is whether, even if the demonstration is princi-pled and timely, it should have license to violate the law. (The question about law breaking would be moot if it were proven that the demonstra-tion was untimely and therefore should not be happening at all.) Further, the emotion created by the timeliness argument disposes the audience to be more receptive to the laws argument, and has established an essential warrant (the truth that the Negro has a fundamental human right to agi-tate for justice) and has endowed it with great energy and presence. So the syllogistic sequence of these arguments is more effective than a qualitative or climactic sequence would have been. Indeed the emotional step down enables the laws argument to capitalize on the emotion already created in the audience. The established emotion flows into the logic and gives it resonance, while the logic reframes the matter in terms of a cool, rational, philosophical objectivity that any "reasonable and intelligent person" (as understood by "white moderates") would assent to.

As we have noted, King's argument is technically complete at this point. He has responded to the focal issue set up in his introduction, and he has effectively made his case. He *could* go straight to a conclu-sion. But, of course, he doesn't. The "Letter" turns to criticisms of the white moderate and the white church for failing to support the cause of civil rights, and continues through twenty-two more paragraphs (23–44). All of that material can be seen as a turn from the primary stasis (Quality) to the secondary stasis (Policy) implied in his critics' "Call to Unity." But structurally, in terms of the classical template, it appears as a long *digression*, or more precisely a pair of digressions (23–32 on the white moderate; 33–44 on the white church). That this material is presented as digression is suggested by the fact that King has not fore-casted it in his introduction, as well as the fact that the argument he overtly promised is functionally complete. Instead, the digressions appear as things that he now feels compelled to say, on the spur of the moment, having made his point, before he turns to final remarks.

Of course, this digressive material is not mere digression—no irrele-vant wandering from the point. Rather, this is a *tactical digression*, bring-ing in additional lines of argument not strictly required for the original, focal issue but nonetheless relevant for King's ultimate rhetorical purpose. His digressions on disappointment are, of course, set up and made possible by the arguments in his narrative and proofs, and they permit him to redouble the force of his fundamental claim by extending it into new (and unforecasted) territory. If his actions are in line with the highest values of the Judaeo-Christian tradition and American political ideals, as he has shown, then his critics are moral failures who have betrayed those values and ideals, as he now goes on to show. King's digressions thus encourage his intended audience to turn away from his critics and to line up with him (Policy).

He throws in a third digression on his critics' praise of the Birmingham police who, as King points out, dealt with the demonstrators rather brutally (45–47). While the first two digressions were introduced as a pair—"I must make two honest confessions to you, my Christian and Jewish brothers" (23)—this one is presented as even more of an afterthought. As King says, "Before closing I feel impelled to mention one other point in your statement that troubled me profoundly" (45). Of course, this third digression works to deepen and confirm his portrayal of his critics as moral failures (who praises police brutality?), gives him an opportunity to add some pathos-inducing description that resonates with the "when you have seens," and enables him to praise those who have struggled for civil rights as the "real heroes" of the South and of America. It is an argumentational *coup de grace*, a finishing blow delivered to a wounded opponent.

Why does King introduce two digressions, then add a third, rather than introducing all three at once? As we have noted regarding King's initial nonforecast of the digressions—if they had been forecast they would not appear as digressions but as part of the plan—here, too, King adopts deliberately the strategy of presenting the third digression as if unplanned. King had ample opportunity to revise the "Letter." The fact that he left this strategy in place suggests that he preferred it. One possible reason for presenting the third digression as an extra may be the fact that the second digression culminates in what is probably the "Letter's" grandest enthymematic cap: "We will win our freedom because the sacred heritage of our nation and the eternal will of God are embodied in our echoing demands" (44). What could anyone add to that? The statement has a highly conclusive feel, and it would be hard to present the third digression as a continuation of the same point. The third digression, moreover, by introducing a new consideration, moves the argument away from critique of the white moderate and church to the Policy question of what good people should praise, support, and do. King thus resolves the seemingly secondary (but really ultimate) stasis while appearing to come to it unplanned.

Another possible reason for preferring the general strategy of unforecasted digression in the second half is the classical rhetorical precept that expressions of indignation or disappointment seem most sincere, and are most effective, when they seem unpremeditated (see Hermogenes of Tarsus, *On Types of Style* 2.7–8). Such expressions should appear as a spontaneous outburst prompted by something that has been said. This is, in essence, what King does. Once he has made his defense with the narrative and proofs in paragraphs 2–22, and with a kairos that now is favorable to him, he digresses in paragraphs 23–47 with seemingly spontaneous sincerity from the ostensible prime issue of the "Letter" to say with maximum effect what he really wants to say.

QUESTIONS FOR ANALYSIS

- What are the main component parts and/or subparts of this text? What does each part or subpart contribute to the audience's experience?

- Do any of these parts or subparts work like the components in the "classical template"? Is there an introduction, a narrative, a partition, a proof, a rebuttal, a digression, a summation, and/or a conclusion?

- Does a particular section in the text set up the reader for an experience delivered later by another part of the text? What expectations are created and then satisfied by these different sections?

- Can you notice a syllogistic or qualitative progression or a repetitive series in the text? What does this progression or repetition contribute to the audience's experience?

- If the rhetorical artifact in question is a primarily visual or multimedia text, how do the spatial elements of its design organize the viewer's experience? Do spatial and temporal forms interact?

- Finally, what conventional forms are at work? If the audience recognizes the discourse as an instance of some conventional genre, what expectations is the audience likely to have? Does the text meet those expectations, or subvert or complicate them for particular effects?

He then devotes his conclusion (48–50) to some final reflections and conciliatory gestures, returning to the respectful tone (and ethos) of the introduction.

In sum, King initially sets up the "Letter" as a defensive response to the "Call for Unity's" criticisms—and seems to answer them point-by-point—but actually first works through a narrative and proofs that persuasively justify his actions. He then digresses at length in the second half concerning his disappointments, in order to offer a devastating critique of his critics while redoubling his own claims to represent values that are sacred to all Americans. Structurally, the "Letter's" deeper strategy for shaping the audience's experience is a subtle and highly effective variation on the classical template for argumentation.

WRITING A STRUCTURE ANALYSIS

To analyze the structure of a discourse, you must first describe that structure to yourself. We recommend that you begin by simply chunking the text into pieces that seem coherent by themselves and that appear in an order you can recognize. Try to write a play-by-play description of the typical audience's experience. Ask yourself what the reader/viewer/user is likely to experience first. What comes second, third, and so on? If you're dealing with a print text or an oral speech, you can do this by marking (circling, drawing lines between) the major units in the discourse. If you're dealing with a video, you can write down the time when the viewer is likely to notice major transitions (for example, 1 minute, 13 seconds into the video). If you're dealing with a static visual (such as a photograph or a piece of graphic design), you can mark (circle, number, etc.) the elements that the viewer is likely to notice first, then second, then third. When chunking a static piece of visual rhetoric, it's a good idea to have reasons why you think the viewer would be likely to look at something first, such as "it's in the center of the page," or "it's the largest element on the page." Once you have the discourse segmented into units, you're ready to label these parts.

We've introduced three basic terminologies in this chapter that you can use to label the component parts of a persuasive effort. You can use the classical template—"this image functions as an introduction" or "this segment of video functions as a narrative." You can use the notion of progressive form—"this segment of video progresses syllogistically from examples to a conclusion" or "this piece of music progresses qualitatively from tension to rapturous release." Or you can use the notion of repetitive form—"this video game repeats a pattern of increasing difficulty within each level of play." Once you find a vocabulary that seems to adequately describe the text's structure, you'll have to explain how this form contributes to the rhetorical effect. Does the structure set up an expectation in the reader's mind and then fulfill that expectation? If so, what does the structure ask the reader to expect, and how does the discourse fulfill that expectation? Does the structure make the reader feel something in particular? Does the structure reinforce a logical inference?

When writing a structure analysis, you can try to reproduce the play-by-play effect by telling *your* reader what comes first, what effect this initial effort has on the reader, and how that effect contributes to the discourse. Then, you can tell your reader what comes second, how that follows from what comes first, what this second effort has on the reader, and how that effect contributes to the discourse. We've adopted that strategy in our analysis of King's "Letter." But that play-by-play strategy often doesn't allow statements about the entire structure or how the entire structure affects the audience's experience of the entire discourse. So, at times, we have to back away for a paragraph or two, to give an overview. In our analysis of King's "Letter" for instance, we must step back to give general statements that describe the overall structure of King's argument and this structure's rhetorical purpose:

- "King's response follows a deeper design, which suits his argumentative purposes. That design, we suggest, reflects the dynamics of the classical template."

- "King's arrangement forms a syllogistic progression that renders the argument on laws more compelling [. . .] So the syllogistic sequence of these arguments is more effective than a qualitative or climactic sequence would have been."

- "In sum, King initially sets up the 'Letter' as a defensive response to the 'Call for Unity's' criticisms—and seems to answer them point-by-point—but actually first works through a narrative and proofs that persuasively justify his actions, and then digresses at length in the second half on his disappointments, in order to offer a devastating critique of his critics while redoubling his own claims to represent values that are sacred to all Americans."

Our point is that a play-by-play arrangement that mirrors the structure of the text you're analyzing is very useful. Such a play-by-play account can recreate the audience's psychological experience while explaining why the elements are arranged in this particular manner. But the play-by-play arrangement has potential pitfalls as well. In the midst of an analysis that tells us first this, then this, then this, your reader may have trouble understanding why the elements appear in this order and how the entire structure fits together. Broader descriptions and explanations of the entire structure are therefore a welcome supplement.

Another option for arranging your structure analysis is to describe the entire structure first and to focus your attention on this entire structure. One of our students, Haley Faulkner, adopted just such a strategy for arranging her analysis of a Dove commercial. Haley's analysis (reprinted here) begins with a general description of the ad's structure. She explains how this overall structural principle (syllogistic progression) functions in the discourse. Only after describing the commercial's entire structure and explaining what this structure contributes to the commercial, does Haley give her reader (in this case, you) a play-by-play account of the introduction and the progressive form in the commercial's proof. Whichever strategy you choose to adopt—whether you emphasize the play-by-play or the general description of the text's structure—it's important to tell your reader both how an audience is likely to experience the text sequentially *and* how the overall structure appears. Finally, it is important to explain how the individual units and the overall structure contribute to the discourse. (At the end of Chapter 3, while setting up David Daniel's analysis of *Mass Effect*, we explained the importance of offering both *summary* of a discourse and *analysis* of how the discourse works. Our point here is similar. You must not only *summarize* the argument, including its structure, you must also *label* the structure—syllogistic, qualitative, classical—and you must *analyze* how that structure contributes to the overall effect on the audience.)

STUDENT ANALYSIS OF STRUCTURE IN A COMMERCIAL

Faulkner 1

Haley Faulkner
Professor Jeffrey Walker
WRIT 307 The Rhetoric of Advertising
April 24, 2010

Real Beauty, Real Form: An Analysis of Structure
in the Dove "Onslaught" Video

The structure or arrangement of an argument functions to
enhance the energy of its discourse by drawing on logical,
ethical, or pathetic appeals. Depending on how the argument
is presented (book, speech, video, etc.) and what claims the
rhetor is trying to convey, certain arrangements can better supplement the persuasiveness and effectiveness of the presented
arguments. From Dove's Real Beauty campaign, the
"Onslaught" video utilizes syllogistic progression to help the
audience follow and hopefully understand its claims. (The
entire commercial can be found, with some navigation, at the
Dove site [www.dove.us] or on YouTube.com. Search
YouTube for "dove onslaught commercial.") With the assis-
tance of this progressive form, the video argues the media
has distorted the definition of beauty; furthermore, the
indirect, yet influential voice of the media negatively affects
its viewers. As opposed to books or speeches, videos allow
the argument to visually unfold. They make the audience
read not between the lines, but between the images.

At the beginning of the "Onslaught" video, a young
girl stands and gazes innocently into the camera while a
song plays in the background. As the tempo of the song
increases, the intensity of the singer's voice swells
("Here it comes...here it comes...here it comes"). This

Haley labels the
form that she'll
analyze in
greater detail
later, and she
explains what
this form
contributes
to the
commercial's
rhetorical effect.

Faulkner 2

crescendo helps to create an expectation in the audience that something is about to happen, and this buildup of expectation sets up the audience for the subsequent progressive form. Moreover, the opening arrangement leads—or eases—the audience into the video's central argument, which is presented and arranged in a way that may appear overwhelming.

In the previous paragraph. Haley offers a play-by-play account of the commercial's opening segment. She describes the psychological effect of this structural unit. In the paragraph to follow, she explains how the video fulfills the psychological expectations created by the introduction.

More often than not, a syllogistic progression is observed in a chain of arguments, but for the "Onslaught" video the syllogistic progression is portrayed in a chain of images. As the rhythm of the song culminates, the series of images begin, and arguably the climax of the song purposefully parallels the presentation of the progressive form, fulfilling the expectation in the audience.

The next three paragraphs describe segments of the commercial while also explaining what these segments contribute to the discourse. Thus, Haley offers a play-by-play description of the commercial while also analyzing what each segment rhetorically contributes.

The first sequence of images depicts several advertisements with the following: half-naked models, half-naked women dancing in music videos, magazine articles featuring models accompanied with suggestive headlines (HOT!, Lose Inches, Diet Diaries), and unrealistically thin mannequins showcased in front windows of boutiques. Basically, images of female bodies are virtually everywhere, and this first sequence is only a glimpse of their pervasiveness. These images are idealized and serve to create unattainable, unrealistic standards. Because of this, they conjure up feelings of insecurity and apprehension, leading women to think they are not thin enough, pretty enough, etc. As these negative thoughts convene, they plant the seeds that will eventually grow into grossly distorted perceptions. And, this is the first part of the video's syllogistic progression—generating negative feelings and thoughts, and creating a distorted perception of beauty.

So, the media has planted a seed, and in order for it to grow, the media needs to cultivate it. The "Onslaught" video

Faulkner 3

presents this idea in the next sequence of images, which include commercials advertising various diet pills (one actually says, "Starve Now"), these same diet pills in the homes of consumers, someone on a restrictive diet, and someone running on a treadmill. These images provide ways for people to act on the negative thoughts and feelings created by the first sequence of images. They are basically saying, if you're not happy with your body, do something to change it. But, change it to look like what? Women, even young girls, believe they should change their appearance to resemble the women shown in the ads or commercials. So, the first sequence of images generates body dissatisfaction, whereas the second sequence motivates women to change their bodies according to the media's unrealistic, ideal standards.

If fad, restrictive diets and exercise don't give you the results you want, there are more extreme measures like the ones presented near the end of the video: bulimia and cosmetic surgery. These images are the most shocking and disturbing, and they show the power of influence. It's important to keep the young girl in mind as the video unfolds. The media constructs the definition of beauty for her, and then shows her the different steps to achieving the media's idea of beautiful, even if it means taking drastic measures.

In this last paragraph, Haley returns to her overall description of the commercial's entire structure, explaining in greater detail what this syllogistic progression contributes to the commercial's argument.

The arrangement of the video, specifically the series of images, has the feeling of a logical sequence, which evaluates how exposure to certain ideas can shape and distort our perceptions of reality, and in this case, beauty. The arrangement also shows the audience how our distorted perception of beauty came to be, in a step-by-step syllogistic progression. In addition, this process begins at such a young age when a pre-adolescent becomes increasingly aware of society's standards. The importance of the

Faulkner 4

"Onslaught" video is expressed when it says, "Talk to your daughter before the beauty industry does." The video understands the media's power of influence by showing how it operates, and then the video advises viewers to pass the word along.

5

Style

Would a reasonable and intelligent person agree to an argument that sounds good but has no real substance? To the long-winded politician who's short on ideas? To the silver-tongued salesman who sells swampland? Maybe. Not surprisingly, Aristotle recognized the problem about 2,300 years ago, and rhetoricians have discussed it ever since. Aristotle contended that, ideally, rhetors should present factual evidence and logical proof alone; they should treat presentational matters as irrelevant. But, Aristotle conceded, presentation actually "has great power [. . .] due to the audience's defects," and therefore it must be practiced (*Rhetoric* 3.1.5). By "defective" audiences, Aristotle meant audiences of common people, non-philosophers, in democratic assemblies. He feared that such audiences were poorly educated and weak in judgment. Unscrupulous demagogues could manipulate them. Because of people's shortcomings, Aristotle considered stylistic persuasion to be an unfortunate necessity for the advocates of the good and true.

In contrast to Aristotle, many have cheerfully regarded presentation—style especially—as the very essence of rhetoric. For many, rhetoric is an art of emphasis, of style. Eloquence consists of impressive verbal effects, flourishes, and "flowers of rhetoric" that charm, beguile, and move the passions of the audience. The sophist and rhetor Gorgias of Leontini, for example, compared style (especially rhythmic style) to drugs and witchcraft in its power to "mix with opinion in the soul" and cast a spell upon the listener ("Encomium of Helen" 9–10, 14). Following Gorgias, rhetoricians over the centuries have developed a mass of stylistic lore, complete with catalogues of dozens to hundreds of figures of speech with strange-sounding names in Greek, Latin, English, and other languages. The descendants of those catalogues still can be seen today in handbooks of rhetorical terminology.

Both of these ancient viewpoints represent different attitudes toward the same notion. Whether one likes the fact or not, style has great impact. But the followers of Aristotle and Gorgias are missing something too, if they consider style to be separate from and added to the substance of the argument itself. In previous chapters, as a convenience for analysis, we distinguish between an argument's substance and its presentation. But we are presenting, of course, an interpretive abstraction from the actual discourse. Our idea of the argument itself (as a thing apart from its structural and stylistic presentation) is an interpretive fiction, a convenience generated for the purposes of understanding, analysis, and critique. But what the rhetor composes, and what the audience experiences, is always the structural and stylistic presentation with its full texture of meaning. Style is not something added to the argument. It is the argument embodied.

Style, as a rhetorical term, traditionally is a name for the specific texture of the sentences, phrases, words, and even syllables of which a discourse is composed. Traditionally the study and analysis of style divides into five main concerns:

- Virtues of style
- Diction
- Figures of speech and thought
- Rhythm
- Types of style

To these can be added a sixth concern, *delivery*—the actual performance of the discourse. Classically, delivery is not considered part of style, but a separate *canon* of rhetoric. (The traditional five canons are invention, arrangement, style, memory, and delivery; the first three have always gotten the most discussion.) Since delivery is closely related to style, we will discuss it briefly in this chapter. But first we turn to the stylistic virtues.

THE VIRTUES OF STYLE

The *virtues* are the main elements of effective style. In traditional theory, there are four: *clarity*, *correctness*, *appropriateness*, and what we will call *distinction* (which classical tradition calls by various names, such as *urbanity* and *ornament*). These serve as touchstones for stylistic analysis and criticism. Is the rhetor's language clear, correct, appropriate, and distinctive? In what ways, and to what effects? We will treat the first three virtues quickly; the fourth—the source of all those catalogues of figures—requires more time.

Clarity

This is, as Aristotle said, the first requirement of style. Quite simply, the audience must understand what the rhetor says (*Rhetoric* 3.2). Rhetorical analysis or critique of style may focus on the features of a discourse that contribute to its *clarity*, or lack thereof, for a particular audience. Features typically ascribed to clarity include the following:

- Directness: using precise, familiar language; accessibility
- Economy: avoiding both filler language that pads expression without adding anything significant to the meaning and convoluted, clumsy sentence structures that obscure meaning or bury key ideas
- Vividness: using concrete language that brings what is described before the eyes (where possible); avoiding unnecessary abstraction
- Energy: using compact, emphatic sentence structures, phrasings, and rhythms that mimic lively speech

Note that these features do not necessarily add up to plain style (meaning a style with little ornate speech). A plain style can be clear, but it also can be imprecise, inaccessible, bloated, abstract, and dull. Similarly, clarity and grammatical correctness are not the same. Grammatically correct discourse can be unclear. Likewise, while grammatical incorrectness can hamper clarity, it don't always.

The stylistic virtue of clarity in oral and print discourse will manifest itself in the features that we have discussed so far, but they will appear different in other forms of discourse. Take photographs, for instance. In technical manuals, it is common to photograph an object (such as a tool or a microprocessor) next to a ruler or a dime to clearly convey the object's size. In landscapes, like those of the nineteenth-century Hudson River School, large scenic pictures often include a few people to demonstrate the painting's vast subject matter. In video games, it is common to include a small map in one corner of the screen (or on an easily accessible but separate screen) to show the player's location within the game's virtual space. All such techniques embody clarity of a sort. The rhetor speaks efficiently to the audience in a language that they are likely to understand.

Correctness

We need some history to properly grasp this notion. In the classical tradition, *correctness* originally meant speaking Greek like a well-educated Greek, or speaking Latin like a well-educated Roman. The terms for this were *Hellenismos*, Hellenism (i.e., Greek-ness), and *Latinitas*, Latinity (Roman-ness). Both terms meant using the language of the *literate dialect*, the language of the most esteemed authors.

The literate dialect was an idealized, purified, artificial construct based on books and acquired through an arduous education. It served as the language of public affairs, politics, law, philosophy, scholarship, and fine literature in what was otherwise a multilingual, multicultural empire. Members of the governing class might have different origins— some from Syria, some from Spain, some from Italy, some from Africa, and so on—but they all shared the literate dialect. (We find very similar phenomena in ancient China, India, Egypt, and elsewhere.) As centuries passed, the literate dialect changed very little because it was fixed in books and formal education, but it became increasingly remote from the vulgar (common) and evolving Greek or Latin spoken in the street. Consequently, the literate dialect became increasingly the special, distinguishing possession of well-educated, upper-class insiders. It signified their right to be in charge.

We moderns like to think we're more enlightened than the ancients. In truth, however, the ideal of stylistic correctness remains much the same. Today it usually means writing and speaking the literate dialect known as Standard Written English—the language of newspapers and magazines, TV news anchors, congressional debates, business documents, scientific reports, scholarly books, fictive literature, the sentence you now are reading, and public discourse generally. Much as in antiquity, the literate dialect is a publicly shared language learned in school. It does not differ as obviously as classical Greek or Latin did from the common language spoken in the street (though it does in fact differ), and it is less rigidly conservative. If modern Standard English were as conservative as ancient classical Greek or Latin, today we would expect all educated people to talk and write like Shakespeare, forsooth. Standard English also is more (though not perfectly) democratically dispersed through public education.

We would further contend that any established form of communication eventually develops a standard of correctness. How could we identify "outsider art" if there were not "insiders" making a recognized and generally accepted form of visual persuasion? Why would we marvel at a self-taught director whose films show technical merit if there were no standards for correctness in film production? Even the computer programmer whose code appears amateurish to professionals is judged by a standard of correctness. Correctness will get established anytime a group of people agrees upon, formalizes, and trains others to master a form of communication.

In modernity as in antiquity, correctness rhetorically signifies education, and therefore is an element of ethos, or the rhetor's credentials. Both classical and modern culture view the occasional use of nonstandard or colloquial locutions as a way of adding "salt" or "earthiness" to a discourse that otherwise displays mastery of Standard Written English. But again, in both modernity and antiquity, an evident lack of such mastery—usually revealed by unconscious, nondeliberate deviations from the rules—signifies not wit but outsider status. The error-prone writer or speaker may be perceived (fairly or not) as poorly educated, unsophisticated, unfamiliar with the world of public or professional discourse, and lacking authority.

Appropriateness

The stylistic virtue of *appropriateness*, also called *decorum*, involves language that is not only clear and correct, but also appropriate to the rhetorical situation. Formal language in an informal situation is usually inappropriate; so is informal language in a formal situation. A sixtyish public speaker who tries to "talk like the kids" usually seems to violate decorum, especially if he gets it wrong. (That's like totally whack, dude!) Using pompous language for a trivial topic (magniloquent verbiage for a silly subject), jokey language for a solemn concern, poetic language for a scientific report, are likely to be seen as inappropriate. And we can extend this principle beyond verbal and textual discourses as well. A sunny and light-hearted film that addresses a somber subject (such as cancer) will strike many as inappropriate. A Halloween costume that jokingly depicts racist stereotypes will not be happily received at a party. Of course, as with correctness, it is sometimes possible for a rhetor to deliberately violate decorum for effect, if the kairos is right.

Distinction (Urbanity, Ornament)

We have chosen the term *distinction* as an adaptation of the Greek and Latin terms *asteia* (urbanity) and *ornamentum* (ornament) for this virtue of style. *Asteia* originally derived from *asty*, meaning town or city, and signified speech that was citified—witty, clever, sophisticated, and distinguished. The Latin equivalent of *asty* is *urbs*, from which we likewise get *urbanitas* and urbanity, or the notion of urbane style. The Latin term *ornamentum* originally did not mean what *ornament* means today. It derived from *orno*, meaning equip, furnish, set apart, dignify, and from *ornatus*, meaning equipped, distinguished. A soldier was *ornatus* with his weapons and armor on. The soldier's ornaments equipped him, distinguished him, and dignified him as a soldier.

A discourse is distinctive when it stands apart from the ordinary and the bland. Distinctive discourse exhibits such qualities as individuality, variety, wittiness, expressiveness, impressiveness, charm, memorability, pathos, emphasis, sophistication, even beauty. Distinction involves the main traditional devices of style, requiring a range of stylistic qualities but not depending upon any single effect. Distinction, like all the other stylistic virtues, can be used to describe nonoral and nontextual discourses. A film with lots of camera tricks and special effects can be described as ornamented. So can a video game with stunning (and perhaps distracting) graphics. A style of dress or architecture that incorporates the latest fashion, without overdoing it, can be discussed in terms of urbanity.

WRITE AN ANALYSIS

Following the basic direction of classical rhetoric, we have focused our discussion of the stylistic virtues on oral and print arguments. However, we have also indicated that these terms (clarity, correctness, appropriateness, and distinction) can be applied to a variety of discourses. Select a nonprint/oral text that interests you and that you think embodies all of these virtues. Using examples from this text, write an analysis that explains what clear rhetoric looks like in this form of persuasion. (For a student-authored example of such an analysis, turn to Tara Hall's essay at the end of this chapter.) What does an appropriate style of rhetoric look like in wildlife photography? What are its features? What qualities must a "correct" website exhibit? What would a distinctive Facebook, MySpace, or blog page do to set itself apart from the rest? Alternatively, you can analyze an atrocious example of a particular discourse to demonstrate how these virtues get violated. What elements of this weblog's style are incorrect, unclear, or inappropriate? Make sure to include reflections on the audience in your analysis. Why would the audience find a blue hyperlink clear but not a grey one? Why would the audience think it incorrect to wear suspenders with cheer shorts?

DICTION: WORD CHOICE

As we briefly noted in Chapter 3, in natural language nearly every word carries a range of possible meanings and associations, including an evaluative or attitudinal component. Virtually every word is *polyvocal* (many-voiced). Any particular use of a word will activate some part of its potential meaning depending on the verbal and situational context in which it is used. For example, if your colleague at work says, "This project is a real dog," you probably will not assume that she's talking about a furry animal. *Project* influences what *dog* means, and vice-versa, while the situation ensures that you probably will take it to mean a work-related matter. The particular expression chosen to name a particular thing configures and interprets it within a particular network of ideas and feelings.

Diction, then, is *word choice* and the texture of meaning it creates. Classical theory divides diction into *proper expression* and *figured expression*. Modern theory has questioned that division. The rhetorician I.A. Richards and others have remarked on the fundamentally metaphorical character of all language. What we call proper (or literal) expression is simply habitual, even centuries-old usage whose metaphoricity we no longer notice. Some call it a dead or fossil metaphor. The expression *leg of a table* is an obvious example. The thing that holds the table up is not really a leg—*table leg* is a metaphor based on resemblance—but it long ago became habitual. We now experience it as a literal expression, forgetting its metaphoricity. Or so the argument goes.

We do not reject that analysis. Nevertheless we also find the classical distinction useful because it is *rhetorically relevant*. The point is that audiences *experience* particular word uses as proper or figural. There are old, fossil metaphors and there are lively new metaphors. But there is more to say about proper expression. First, the modern analysis of meaning is in fact recognized in the classical account of proper diction. For example, a Greek rhetorician of the eleventh century remarks, with a racy example, that "if you call a prostitute [*porne*] a courtesan [*hetaira*] you transform her; you dignify what she is called" (Michael Psellos, *Synopsis of Rhetoric* lines 341–342). The root meaning of *hetaira* was [female] companion, suggesting a high-class escort or mistress. Psellos recognizes how the two words *porne* and *hetaira*—both proper—bear with them different networks of ideas, differently configure and transform the thing they are employed to name, and imply different attitudes and judgments.

Further, proper diction comes from what linguists call different *registers*: different fields of discourse with distinctive vocabularies or phraseologies. There is the common register—the core vocabulary shared by more or less all varieties of English, and specific to none of them, like *tree, mother, perhaps*—as well as more specialized registers, such as legal language. Shifts of register, or what literary critics sometimes call *code-switching*, can be employed for a wide range of effects. For example, a journalist or lawyer may resort to clinical language to describe a particularly revolting murder, substituting scientific-sounding abstractions for more graphic common language, in order to view it more objectively, that is, with emotional distance or neutrality.

In addition to specialized registers, there are also formal and informal registers. Colloquial speech is generally regarded as informal. Standard Written English can be used with varying degrees of formality both to make a discourse appropriate and to achieve a variety of effects. A widely used register is *archaism,* or antique language, derived from a variety of literary sources and the Bible (particularly the 1611 King James Bible, which remained the standard English version until quite recently). We hear archaism when people say things like "lo and behold." Until fairly recently, archaism was a standard resource for poetic language. Nineteenth-century poets were fond of antique usages like "thee" and "thou," which had long since dropped out of English speech. Such expressions made their language sound like an echo of centuries-old tradition. One of the more famous archaisms in American literature is the opening line of Abraham Lincoln's Gettysburg Address: "Four score and seven years ago, our fathers brought forth on this continent, a new nation . . ." *Four score and seven* is an antique way to say eighty-seven (and it was antique in Lincoln's day, too). Most readers, if asked to comment, will say that the locution seems biblical, and that it invests what Lincoln is saying with a special solemnity and dignity. The founding of the nation is, in effect, presented as an event in sacred history.

FIGURES OF SPEECH AND THOUGHT

Classical theory divides rhetorical figures into *figures of speech* and *figures of thought.* Figures of speech, also called *figures of words,* involve manipulations of language—alterations of meaning or form—and are in essence special types of diction. Figures of thought, in contrast, are gestures or poses that dramatize the speaker's thought process or attitude.

Further, figures of speech are divided into *tropes* and *schemes.* The word *trope* derives from a Greek word that means turn or twist (*tropos*), and in rhetoric indicates twisted *word meaning;* that is, using a word in a way different from its normal, habitual, or proper use. "Stop *dogging* me" is a trope (though perhaps a fossilized one). The word *scheme* derives from Greek *schema,* which signifies a shape or configuration. A scheme is a notable *arrangement* of linguistic form. For example, "Empire breeds *arrogance; arrogance* breeds *ignorance; ignorance* breeds misjudgment and disaster" is a scheme (linked repetitions, as well as the repeated phrase-structure "X breeds Y" and a syllogistic/climactic progression). The classification of figures thus breaks down as shown in Figure 5.1.

We should note that some modern rhetoricians have classified figures of speech differently, as figures of addition, omission, rearrangement,

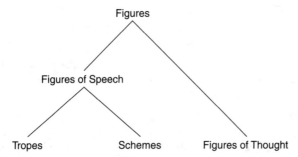

Figure 5.1 Types of figures.

and substitution—though they do not address the figures of thought. (See, for example, Arthur Quinn's *Figures of Speech: 60 Ways to Turn a Phrase*; or the *General Rhetoric* of "Groupe μ" [mu].) Admittedly, the classical approach is not perfect. Different authorities give different definitions, and the boundaries between schemes and tropes, and between figures of speech and figures of thought, are not always clear. Nevertheless, we'll stick with the classical approach. We begin with figures of speech.

Figures of Speech: A Sampler

What follows is not an exhaustive catalogue. You may even want to skim the short list that follows. Come back to it later as a reference. The essential thing is to grasp the basic types, recognize a figure when it occurs (even if you don't have a name for it), and analyze its effects. Following, then, are the more common tropes and schemes.

Tropes

Figures that use a word in a twisted sense, or substitute an expression for the proper one in a given context.

- **Metaphor.** From the Greek word *metaphora*, or transfer. Often used as a name for tropes in general. More specifically, the substitution of one word for another on the basis of *resemblance* or analogy: "[You see] ominous *clouds of inferiority* begin to form in *her little mental sky*" (King, "Letter" paragraph 14).

- **Simile.** The insertion of *like* transforms a metaphor into a simile by making the comparison explicit: "Feelings of inferiority formed in her mind, *like clouds.*"

- **Allegory.** The expansion of a metaphor as the governing concept for an extended piece of discourse. For example, George Orwell's *Animal Farm* portrays the Russian Revolution through a story about animals who overthrow their human masters.

- **Metonymy.** A substitution based not on resemblance, but *on logical relationship*, such as cause/effect or container/contained. A familiar example of cause-for-effect (or instrument/act) is, "The *pen* is mightier than the *sword*," originally penned by the Victorian playwright Edward Bulwer-Lytton in 1839 (*Richelieu* 2.2). Container-for-contained: "*The fourteenth century* sent European thought in a new direction."

- **Synecdoche.** Regarded by some as a type of metonymy. Substitution based on part/whole (or attribute/essence) relations. Part-for-whole: "The theater manager's only concern was putting *butts* in seats." Whole-for-part: "*The court* delivered its opinion."

- **Catachresis.** Greek for abuse (the Latin name is *abusio*); sometimes also called *oxymoron* (literally sharp stupidity). A trope in which the implied relation between two words violates or abuses their normal range of meaning, or involves an apparent contradiction in terms. For example: "I stood on a *dizzy precipice.*" At an extreme: "She gazed through the *elephant windows* into the *infected sky.*"

- **Irony.** Verbal irony occurs when there is *opposition or contrast* between what is said and what is meant: "I'm *afraid [this letter] is much too long to take your precious time*" (King, "Letter" paragraph 48).

- **Litotes and Hyperbole.** Similar to irony are *litotes* (understatement) and *hyperbole* (overstatement, exaggeration). Litotes: "The prisoner *explained that he rather preferred* not to be executed." Hyperbole: "He's a veteran of *a thousand first dates.*" Both tend to work well when used for humorous effect.

- **Pun.** Another relative of irony. There are two main kinds: words that sound alike but have different meanings (*paronomasia*) and repetitions of the same word in different senses (*antanaclasis*). Paronomasia: "This author has the *write* stuff." Antanaclasis: "We must all *hang* together, gentlemen; else we shall all *hang* separately" (Benjamin Franklin, after signing the Declaration of Independence).

- **Periphrasis (circumlocution).** The substitution of many words for one: "Now he is *going down that dark road from which they say no-one returns*" (Catullus, Song 3, speaking of the death of his mistress's pet sparrow; there is a humorous irony, too, in this example).

- **Enallage.** A deliberate grammatical mistake, or the substitution of a nonstandard grammatical form. It is perhaps the prototype of all other tropes—if a trope is defined as a departure from proper usage. The Rolling Stones' line, "I *can't get no* satisfaction," is an enallage (from the viewpoint of Standard English), as well as a register shift (to colloquial lower-class speech). One type of enallage (called *anthimeria*, or abnormality) involves the substitution of one part of speech for another, such as using a verb in place of a noun: "he sang his *didn't* he danced his *did*" (e.e. cummings, "anyone lived in a pretty how town").

Schemes

Schemes involve not twisted word usages or substitutions, but distinctive word arrangements (or additions, subtractions, and/or rearrangements). Schemes create a wide range of effects, depending on what's being said, the situation, and so on. We begin with figures of *parallelism* and *accumulation*, each of which has several subtypes, and then we continue with an assortment of common others.

Schemes of Parallelism

Repeating words or grammatical structures, usually for emphatic effects or for a sense of elegance and balance. The latter is why schoolteachers tell students to put a sequence of parallel ideas in parallel form: "The issues are urbaniz*ation*, tax*ation*, and represent*ation*," rather than "The issues are urbanization, taxes, and who our representatives are." Both sentences, in fact, are grammatically correct, but the first is more elegant—though sometimes a rhetor might prefer the looser form, to sound more informal. The more notable schemes of parallelism are *anaphora, homoioteleuton, isocolon, chiasmus, anadiplosis, zeugma,* and *polyptoton.*

- **Anaphora (taking up).** The *repetition of beginnings* in a sequence of clauses or phrases, as in King's "when you have seen" passage ("Letter," paragraph 14). Anaphoras like these tend to create a sense of emphasis, urgency, or pathos. They can also be used to enhance memorability.

- **Homoioteleuton (same ending).** The *repetition of endings.* This includes rhyme in poetry, as well as rhyme-like effects in poetry or prose, such as, "onward I sped in the *battle*, the even-contested *battle*" (Walt Whitman, "Vigil Strange I Kept on the Field One Night"). The ancient rhetor Gorgias of Leontini wrote, "Telling the knowing what they know seems *right*, but it gives no de*light*" ("Encomium of Helen"; it rhymes in Greek, too). Whitman's homoioteleuton seems emotive, and expresses a sense of urgency and stress—he can't stop to help a fallen soldier because of the battle, the battle—while Gorgias's seems elegant and witty.

- **Isocolon (equivalent sentence-part).** The *repetition of equivalent phrase or clause structures.* A famous use of isocolon is Abraham Lincoln's "government *of the people, by the people, for the people*" in the Gettysburg Address—a triad of <preposition+the+noun> phrases, reinforced by homoioteleuton. Its stately cadence gives the idea a solemnity and grandeur that it would lack if Lincoln had written "government of, by, and for the people" (though that is correct, clear, and economical). Isocolon also can be produced simply from parallel grammatical forms, without repeating any word: "We *slept miserably on the ground, afraid for our lives,* while they *lay comfortably in their beds, secure in their plans.*" Here the isocolon serves to heighten the contrast by making it seem entirely point-for-point.

- **Chiasmus.** *Crossover parallelism.* The name derives from the Greek letter Χ (chi), which visually illustrates the idea. A well-known example is John F. Kennedy's line from his 1961 inaugural address:

Ask not what *your country* can do for *you,*

ask what *you* can do for *your country.*

As this example suggests, chiasmus lends itself well to antithetical expressions and makes them more pointed, as well as more memorable. But it can also be used for other purposes, as in: "I finished the work, and the work finished me."

- **Anadiplosis (doubling up).** The *repetition of endings as beginnings*: "Empire breeds *arrogance; arrogance* breeds *ignorance; ignorance* breeds misjudgment and disaster." Here the anadiplosis creates the feeling of a syllogistic (as well as climactic) progression, as if empire leads inevitably to disaster. Or again: "I made a lot of *money;* the *money* bought *good times;* the *good times* left me broke: so here I am." Here the sequence seems more comical and portrays the speaker as an improvident fool wandering down the path to failure.

- **Zeugma (yoke).** The *yoking-together of parallel phrases or elements with a common word.* For example, the poet Alexander Pope, satirizing the dangers that party girls faced at high-society soirées in the eighteenth century, wrote that a young woman might "stain her honour [phrase 1] or her new brocade [phrase 2]" (*The Rape of the Lock*). The two phrases are yoked to "stain." There is a punlike effect here, since staining one's honor and staining one's fancy new dress are not equivalent—though to the young women Pope is satirizing, they are. But not all zeugmas are punny or satirical. Lincoln's "government of the people, by the people, for the people" is triple zeugma, with three parallel phrases (isocola) yoked to "government."

- **Polyptoton (many changes).** The *repetition of the same word in different forms*: "She went to *school* to be *schooled,* and *schooled* the *schoolmen*"; "How can we know the *dancer* from the *dance*?" (W.B. Yeats, "Among School Children").

Schemes of Accumulation

Accumulation involves *repeating, augmenting, and emphasizing an idea by restating it in different ways*. Accumulation is often reinforced by parallelism, and indeed both fall under what Burke would call repetitive form. But they are not the same. Parallelism involves the repetition of structures or words, while accumulation involves the repetition of ideas. Some major variants of accumulation are *climax, antithesis, analogy, enumeration,* and *correctio*.

- **Climax.** A series of *reiterations in ascending order of importance.* (The Greek word *klimax* means steps or staircase; the Latin word *gradatio,* another name for this figure, means the same thing.) For example, "It is a crime to bind a Roman citizen, an outrage to scourge him, almost an unnatural act to put him to death: what then shall I call this crucifixion?" (Cicero, *Against Verres* 170). The overall effect of this climax is to make the provincial governor Verres' illegal crucifixion of the citizen Gavius seem to be a crime of unspeakable depravity.

- **Antithesis (as a figure of speech).** The repetition of an idea *by restating it in opposite terms.* Here are two examples from Abraham Lincoln: "with *malice* toward *none,* with *charity* for *all*" (Second Inaugural Address) and "The world will *little note, nor long remember, what we say here,* but it *can never forget what they did here*" (Gettysburg Address). Note also the homoioteleuton and isocolon in the ending phrases, which reinforce the antithesis.

- **Analogy (as a figure of speech).** The repetition and enhancement of an idea by *re-stating it in terms of comparisons*: "I was left shocked and speechless by this new information. It was as if an earthquake had suddenly undone the familiar structure of my world, and left my points of reference like so many pieces of broken architecture tumbled on the ground. I was a ship adrift on an open sea, without sail or compass, without wind or current to guide me on my way. I was blind and groping in an endless darkness, alone" . . . and so on. While each of these comparisons is saying more or less the same thing, each highlights different aspects of the experience.

- **Enumeration.** Restating and amplifying an idea by *dividing it into parts*. For example, the sentence "He ruined himself in riotous living" can be enumeratively restated by listing the various ways he ruined himself. "He ruined himself in riotous living: he became addicted to amusements, spectacles, and parties; he drowned himself in drink and drugs; he let his mind decay; he alienated his better friends and attracted worse; he got lost in a whirl of women of questionable virtue; he exhausted his body and wrecked his health; he became obsessed with gambling; and he wasted all his money."

- **Correctio (self-correction).** The speaker repeats an idea by *revising or correcting what has just been said*: "We were poor—no, not poor, but penniless." Correctio is not only a figure of speech (a scheme of accumulation) but also, in part, a figure of thought (a pose that dramatizes the speaker's state of mind).

FOR FURTHER DISCUSSION

We have listed and exemplified numerous schemes in this section, but we categorize them all under two headings to emphasize a simple point. Two basic principles drive these schemes—parallelism and accumulation. Or, to put this another way, local elements that resemble or build upon one another exhibit a stylistic felicity and often achieve important rhetorical effects. The schemes themselves may have no application beyond print or oral arguments. What would a zeugma look like in a photograph or a film? But the principles apply across a range of persuasive efforts. One can find parallel construction in film (as we did in Chapter 4 when noting repeated qualitative progression). And one can find accumulation as well. (Again, accumulation is a kind of qualitative progression.) The questions for the rhetorical analyst, in this case, are: What local elements in this argument contribute to the parallelism or the accumulation? Is the musical score repeated in several scenes, thus achieving a kind of dramatic parallelism? Or does the musical score slowly intensify as the dialogue becomes more heated, thus achieving a kind of climax? Does the proliferation of detail in a video game's universe have the same effect as enumeration? Do all the characters, plots, places, and cleverly placed minutiae amplify the player's sense that this is a real world?

Other Schemes

Beyond the schemes of parallelism and accumulation, a few more should be mentioned. We'll take up *polysyndeton, asyndeton, ellipsis, parenthesis, metaplasm,* and *hyperbaton.*

- **Polysyndeton (many connectives).** The *insertion of extra conjunctions,* such as *and* or *but,* where they normally would not be used. For example, Standard English requires that a list of nouns be separated by commas, with an *and* or *or* for the last item: "The issues are urbanization, taxation, and representation." With polysyndeton this becomes, "The issues are urbanization *and* taxation *and* representation." Polysyndeton seems to emphasize each item as equally important. A version of polysyndeton is the use of a conjunction (usually *and*) at the beginning of a series of phrases, clauses, or sentences: "And the earth was without form, and void; and darkness was upon the face of the deep. And the spirit of God moved on the face of the waters. And God said, Let there be light: and there was light" (Genesis 1:2–3, King James Version).

- **Asyndeton (without connectives).** The *omission of conjunctions* where they might be expected. Rather than "The issues are urbanization, taxation, and representation," asyndeton produces "The issues are urbanization, taxation, representation." Lincoln's "of the people, by the people, for the people" may be regarded as asyndetic, since he could have written, "of the people, by the people, and for the people."

- **Ellipsis (taking out).** The *omission (elision) of elements* that are meant to be understood, for the sake of emphasis or effect. Asyndeton is one type of ellipsis—ellipsis of conjunctions. There also may be ellipsis of verbs or nouns, for example, "John loves Mary, and Mary John."

- **Parenthesis (set-aside).** Perhaps the most familiar type of a series of figures that involve the *insertion of elements, or the interruption* of a unit of discourse. The stylistic equivalent of *digression.* For example, "Everyone who cares about this issue (and I believe that includes everyone in this room) should turn out to vote." The parenthetical insertion interrupts the sentence to add a side remark. Note that parenthetical insertions can be punctuated in different ways; we could replace the parentheses above with hyphens or commas. The parenthesis, like digression, is a favorite figure in academic rhetoric, because it permits all sorts of qualifications, reservations, and corrections. When done well, parenthesis gives the impression of a careful, thoughtful, and complex thinking process. When overdone, it ruins clarity.

- **Metaplasm (transformation).** This is the general name for an odd group of figures that involve the alteration of single words in various ways. Examples include "dumb and *dumberer*" (addition to the end); "Let's *par-tay!*" (lengthening of the last syllable); "I have two words to say about that—*im possible*" (cutting); "*intoxificated*" (addition to the middle); and "the *fed'ral gov'ment*" (elision from the middle).

- **Hyperbaton (transposition; also called inversion).** The *rearrangement of normal sentence structure* by transposing words or sentence parts. For example, "About suffering they were never wrong, the old masters" (W.H. Auden, "Musée des Beaux Arts"). Compare "the old masters were never wrong about suffering" (the normal arrangement). The hyperbaton serves to emphasize particular words/ideas by foregrounding them.

Figures of Thought: Another Sampler

As we have said, figures of thought involve the striking of poses, or the dramatization of the speaker's thought process or state of feeling, whereas figures of speech involve the manipulation of word meaning or linguistic form. For example, the traditional lexicon for figures of thought includes such terms as *indignatio*, the striking of an indignant pose (harrumph); or *ratiocinatio* (ratiocination), which involves making a show of going through a logical reasoning process. King's argument about just and unjust laws in "Letter from Birmingham Jail" is presented ratiocinatively.

As the examples of indignatio and ratiocinatio suggest, almost any mental process, mood, or attitude that can be dramatized in speech can be identified and named as a figure of thought. This observation opens up an almost infinite range of such figures—cheerfulness, solemnity, puzzlement, scorn, confidence, and so on, but our list cannot go on forever. We will limit ourselves to briefly mentioning some of the more common and striking figures of thought. These include *apostrophe, prosopopoeia, dialogism, sententia, enthymeme, erotema, paradox, praeteritio, aporia, aposiopesis,* and *praecisio.*

- **Apostrophe (turn away).** The *interruption of an ongoing discourse to deliver an aside*—an oath, an exclamation, a declaration, a short speech—ostensibly to another audience, to God, or to oneself. It is a discourse-level version of parenthesis. For example, a rhetor, in the process of arguing that some political development undermines the founding principles of the Declaration of Independence and the Constitution, might turn aside to declare, "Are you spinning in your grave yet, Thomas Jefferson? What has happened to your vision of America?"

- **Prosopopoeia (impersonation or personification).** Also called *ethopoeia.* Closely related to apostrophe. *Adopting the voice of some character,* either historical or imaginary. In the apostrophe to Jefferson, the rhetor might follow up with a *prosopopoeia,* adopting the voice of Jefferson in answer: "And now that I have asked that, I think that Jefferson might say . . ."

- **Dialogism** (from the Latin name, *dialogismus*) resembles prosopopoeia, in that the speaker adopts both voices in a dialogue or conversation. One use of dialogism is to set up a tactical digression by framing it as a reply to an anticipated question from the audience or an opponent, thus presenting the argument as a conversational exchange. As we have seen, King does this in "Letter from Birmingham Jail." Dialogism also can be used for a meditative "conversation with oneself."

- **Sententia (Greek *gnome,* maxim).** The *resonant, proverb-like declaration* of an idea as if it were deep wisdom, fundamental truth, or traditional belief. Actual proverbs are sententias, but sententious language can be used to state almost any idea *as if* it were proverbial or deserved to be. King's "We are caught in an inescapable network of mutuality, tied in a single garment of destiny" is such a sententia ("Letter" paragraph 4). Sententias generally involve ornate expression (diction, tropes, schemes, rhythm) to make the statement memorable or striking. The uses of sententious speech include setting up ideas as noble truths that later arguments can build on, and stating enthymematic caps with an emphatic, impressive flourish, thereby giving them an impact that rings in the mind. However, when sententious language is employed for ideas that the audience regards as trivial or false, then it comes across as empty bombast, as phony hot air, as rhetoric in the bad sense.

- **Enthymeme.** This is the *presentational* or stylistic enthymeme that we discussed in Chapter 3—the gesture of summing up a passage, or a whole discourse, and capping it with a pithy (and preferably memorable) statement of the inference or conclusion that the rhetor wants the audience to draw. King's "We will win our freedom because the sacred heritage of our nation and the eternal will of God are embodied in our echoing demands" ("Letter" paragraph 45) is such an enthymeme. King draws the intended claim (victory is inevitable) from the ideational material sententiously summed up by the "because" clause.

- **Erotema (question).** The familiar *rhetorical question*—making an assertion in the form of a question whose answer is obvious, as in, "Shall we, who have been trained in all the noblest things, remain unmoved at a poet's voice?" (Cicero, *For Archias* 19), in which the assertion is that "we" must not remain unmoved. Erotema might be thought of as a variant of sententia—a dramatic, striking, emphatic way to state an idea or draw a conclusion. Who hasn't used an erotema?

- **Paradox (contrary to belief).** The statement of an idea that appears false or nonsensical on the surface, but when understood another way asserts some deeper truth. The ancient philosopher Heraclitus gives us this memorable example: "We step and do not step into the same rivers; we are and are not" (fragment 49a). In such examples, paradox appears as a type of sententia, and has a riddle-like effect.

- **Praeteritio (passing over; Greek *paralipsis*, leaving aside).** The act of *mentioning something by saying that you won't discuss it* as in, "To talk about my opponent's conviction many years ago for tax evasion would be irrelevant and inappropriate, because this election is about issues: so I won't say anything about it." But praeteritio can also be used for more ethically defensible purposes. Cicero employs praeteritio—and calls it that—to magnify the seriousness of a disastrous military defeat: "Here permit me, Romans, just as the poets do who write of Roman affairs, to pass over (*praeterire*) our disaster, which was so complete that no messenger came from the battlefield to tell the general what had happened" (*On the Command of Cnaeus Pompeius* 25). (See also *aposiopesis* and *praecisio*, later.)

- **Aporia (no way).** *Talking about being unable to adequately talk about something,* as when someone declares, "Words cannot describe the beauty of the scene!" Cicero employs aporia in *Against Verres,* in the climactic progression we have seen already, when he caps it with, "what then shall I call this crucifixion?"—as if it were an act so depraved that no word could name it. Lincoln employs aporia (as well as isocolon and accumulation) in the Gettysburg Address when he declares, "But, in a larger sense, we cannot dedicate—we cannot consecrate—we cannot hallow—this ground," and goes on to talk about how anything that he might say would be unequal to what the fallen soldiers did.

- **Aposiopesis (falling silent).** Generally recognized as the gesture of *breaking off in mid-speech, as if unable to continue;* but the term—*apo* (from) *siopesis* (keeping silent)—also suggests the gesture of pointedly not saying something. "I understand that you might have moral objections, but if you won't do what I want, then — well, you understand."

- **Praecisio.** The Latin name for aposiopesis. Sometimes regarded as a more acute form of it—eloquent silence, or extreme brevity. It's hard to illustrate. One might reply to a question by pointedly not answering at all, or with a mute gesture. Another example: Lincoln's Gettysburg Address was expected to last for about fifteen minutes, but he spoke for no more than three. In the Address, as we have noted, he talks about the inadequacy of anything that he might say to the soldiers' self-sacrifice (aporia). Then he stops—in effect concluding the speech with twelve minutes of silence. One might call that either aposiopesis—falling silent—or praecisio—eloquent silence. We leave it to you; we cannot say.

RHYTHMIC COMPOSITION

Rhythm, and the more general concept of *prosody*—the songlike combination of rhythm and melody in speech—get relatively little attention in modern rhetoric, and we will hardly do more than mention them here. Yet the classical tradition gives prosody great importance. The prosody of actual song, after all, is what can give it a nearly hypnotic charm and can affect an audience's mood, as the ancient sophist Gorgias observed. The prosody of *prose*, likewise, can have a comparable effect, especially when it is heard.

The classical tradition approaches prosody mainly under the heading of *synthesis*, or composition—the joining together of words in rhythmically structured phrases, sentences, and larger units. At the most fine-grained level, this involves something like the classical analysis of poetic meter into feet (or measures) composed of stressed and unstressed syllables, and lines composed of a certain number of feet. For example, an iambic foot (an iamb) consists of a weak and a strong stress (- x, ta-DA), a trochee of a strong and a weak (x -), and a dactyl of a strong and two weak (x - -). Shakespeare's favorite line was the iambic pentameter (five measure), composed of five iambs:

    -    x | - x | -   x | - x | - x

That time | of year | thou mayst | in me | behold . . . (Sonnet 73)

In prose rhythm, which is looser, the basic unit is not the poetic foot or the line of verse (such as iambic pentameter), though prose can indeed be analyzed into complex combinations of poetic feet. In prose, the basic rhythmic unit is the individual word, as in telegraph (x - -), telegraphic (- - x -), individual (- - x - -), baseball (x -), and so on. Complex rhythmic patterns thus arise when words are joined in phrases, as in the opening phrases of the Gettysburg Address:

    x x | - x - | x   - x

Four score | and seven | years ago

    -    x x - | x   x | - - x - -

our forefathers | brought forth | on this continent,

    -   x   x -

a new nation, . . .

(We are following Lincoln's punctuation, and devoting each line to what would be a spoken phrase followed by a slight pause; note that *hiatus*—the clashing of similar sounds—enforces a pause between "ago" and "our," if the words are pronounced clearly.) By analyzing the patterns of strong and weak stress carried by the words and dividing them into something like poetic feet, as we have done here, one can get a clearer sense of the rhythmic flow of Lincoln's style. Note the chiasmatic alternations of stress patterns, as well as the repetitions of | x x | and | - x x - |. Note too the relatively low number of unstressed syllables between stresses (or beats), as compared with:

   - - x - - | x -   - - x - | - - x - - x

We are following | Lincoln's punctuation, | and devoting each line . . .

Consider what differences these different rhythmic patterns make to the overall sound and feel of what is being said. Lincoln's sentence seems (to us) more measured and dignified, moving at a slower pace. Ours seems more rapid and talky—more weak syllables between beats (hence more syllables per unit of time), and less highly organized rhythm.

In addition to the pattern of stressed and unstressed syllables, there is also the specific texture of vowel and consonant sounds. For example, Lincoln's "four score and seven" contains such broad vowels as the "oh" sounds of the first two words, and the repeating (and rhyming) liquid "r" sounds, which further lengthen the vowels they follow. This sound texture enhances the stately, slow cadence of the phrase, which is suitable to the mood of solemnity that Lincoln wants to communicate. Further, *assonance* (the repetition or echoing of vowel and consonant sounds) can be used to create complex and distinctive sound textures. Compare "I yearn for your soon return" with "I hope you come back soon."

At less fine-grained levels of analysis, one can look at the *cadences* created by variations and balances in the relative lengths of phrases and sentences. Cadence refers to the larger rhythm created by such units, from pause to pause (hence the Greek term for cadence, *anapausis*, meaning stopping up, pausing). We see this in the phrasing of the opening sentence of the Gettysburg Address:

> Four score and seven years ago
>
> our fathers brought forth on this continent,
>
> a new nation,
>
> conceived in Liberty,
>
> and dedicated to the proposition
>
> that all men are created equal.

Here we focus on the cadence of phrases. Lincoln's sentence has six main phrases. The first two and the last two form couplets of similar length, while the third and fourth are much shorter and seem to stand out and receive some emphasis. Note also the long syllables and assonance of "a *new na*tion." One could continue this sort of analysis to the whole Gettysburg Address, considering the rhythm and cadence not only of the phrases composing sentences, but also of the sentences composing paragraphs, and finally the whole speech.

The point of doing the kind of analysis we outline here is not simply to label rhythmic patterns or figures, but to form a clearer understanding of the sound and feel of any given discourse. What kind of song or music does the rhythm and sound texture of the language produce? This is often an impressionistic matter, but not a matter of arbitrary subjectivity either, if one attends closely to rhythms, cadences, and so forth, and develops an ear for prosody. (One way to do this is by practicing oral interpretation—reading aloud with appropriate rhythm, tone, emphasis.) Despite their having been written in prose, some discourses come close to the sound of music or poetry, while others may sound like random street noise, or like muttering. Either way, the rhythm and sound texture of a discourse contributes to its *tonality* or *mood*, in addition to what is communicated by its diction and figures. Does the discourse *sound* solemn and dignified, nervously chatty, relaxed and cheerful, stressed and angry, heavy with gloom, patiently reasonable? Moreover, is it trying to say, for example, something solemn and dignified with a suitable prosody—or with a prosody that sounds nervously chatty?

WRITE AN ANALYSIS

Following the patterns of classical rhetorical theory, we have focused our discussion of rhythm on oral argumentation. We have focused on the elements in spoken language that establish rhythm: stress patterns, combinations of vowels and consonants, length of major syntactic units. But we would like to stress that rhythm is an important principle in any discourse. Music videos have both aural rhythm (in the pace set by the music) and visual rhythm (in the pace set by the images). Write an analysis of a piece of a music video. Explain the quality of its rhythm. Is it fast, slow, choppy? Then, locate the elements that establish this rhythm. If not vowel and consonant combination, what makes this film, this television ad, or this web animation slow, fast, choppy, accelerate, decelerate, or pause? In your analysis, explain what establishes the rhythm and what rhetorical effect the rhythm has on the discourse. For example, what *tone* or *mood* does the rhythm create?

DELIVERY

Delivery is the actual performance of a discourse, including not only oral interpretation of the words, but also such things as projecting one's voice, control of breath, gesture, posture, appearance (haircuts, clothes, etc.), lighting, props, and stage effects—everything that may be involved in the physical presentation of a discourse to an audience. The classical Greek term for delivery, *hypokrisis*, also means acting. An actor on stage was called a *hypokrites* (from which we get the English word *hypocrite* by an unfortunate derivation). Another term was *cheironomia*, meaning gesture. The most common Latin term is *elocutio*, or speaking out.

As with rhythmic composition, delivery has been somewhat neglected by modern rhetoric, though traditional rhetoric accords it great importance. Demosthenes, generally considered the greatest of all Greek rhetors, is said to have declared that the three most important things in rhetoric are delivery, delivery, and delivery (Quintilian, *Institutio Oratoria* 11.3.6). However, with the rise in importance of audiovisual media—radio, TV, film, audiobooks, CDs, DVDs, the Internet—rhetoric in more recent times has begun to come round again to Demosthenes' view.

METHODS OF ANALYSIS

You can develop a sense of a text's rhythm and style by reading it aloud while trying to repeat the rhetor's intended inflection. Try to deliver the voice, tone, rhythm, etc., embodied in the style *as it is written*. Oral interpretation, though a largely forgotten art today (aside from drama school), is in fact an excellent method of rhetorical analysis, and of stylistic analysis in particular. It is impossible to do a good oral interpretation without a good understanding of a text's situation, argumentation, and style. However, you needn't aim at an Oscar-winning acting performance. The point is to develop an "ear" for the text's voice, tone, rhythm, etc., and to try to deliver what you "hear." It usually takes several rounds of rehearsal and analysis to get close to a satisfactory delivery.

Modern audiences increasingly experience discourse not as a written or printed text but as performance in an audiovisual medium.

Both classical and modern rhetoric have drawn their vocabularies for the analysis of delivery from outside the realm of rhetorical theory proper. Classical rhetoric looked mainly to the art of theater, with some modifications and additions to adapt it to the practice of oratory. Modern rhetoric, likewise, draws vocabulary for delivery from drama, film, music criticism, and media theory, to which we direct you, along with the basic studies in logic, grammar, and graphic design that we have recommended elsewhere in this book.

TYPES OF STYLE

The *virtues* of style and the *types* of style provide convenient conceptual bookends for the details of diction, figures, rhythm, and delivery. While the virtues provide touchstones for the evaluation of style, the types—in which all the details come together—provide two vocabularies to describe style. First, we can divide styles into *plain, middle,* and *grand*. Second, we can list a wide array of *qualitative* types. We will start with the first vocabulary since it is more common and less complex.

The Plain Style

As the name implies, the plain style employs little or no noticeable figuration and avoids excessively elaborate sentence structures. It is what people ask for when they say, "Put it in plain English." Its diction should be familiar, yet precise; its rhythms should resemble natural speech, yet its sentences should be correct. Its chief virtues are those of *clarity*: directness, economy, vividness, and energy. The plain style is used when clarity is most required, especially in the narration of facts and logical explanation. It is the style most suited to logos appeals.

A style that is *too* plain, however, can be monotonous. The plain style can be relieved by the sparing use of figures, short passages of middle style, or (if the kairos is right) grand style. But the plain style has its own sources of charm, if handled well. Through diction, it can create tone, and by varying its rhythms and its phrase and sentence lengths (and sentence structures) it can sustain a sense of liveliness, communicate a straight-talking ethos, and hold the audience's interest and attention.

The narrative section of King's "Letter from Birmingham Jail" is predominantly, though not exclusively, plain style (see, for example, paragraphs 2 and 6–9). So is nearly the whole discussion of just and unjust laws (paragraphs 15–22).

The Middle Style

The middle style presents moderate figuration. Its diction can be more poetic, as can its rhythm; its sentences can be elaborate and ornate, while retaining a sense of poise and balance. The chief virtue of the middle style is *pleasure*. It is the style especially of encomiastic praise, the reflective essay, and the informal public lecture. It *conciliates the audience*—making them more receptive, more willing to listen or read—by enhancing the aesthetic appeal of what the rhetor says.

The dangers of the middle style, when overdone, are self-indulgence, overcuteness, and obscurity. An overdone or unpersuasive middle style appears to be encrusted with artificial, unnecessary, cosmetic ornament—what people call "empty eloquence." The middle style needs to be balanced with, and to retain, the plain-style virtues too.

King, in the "Letter," is not a big user of the middle style—the decorum of his situation works against it. It serves him chiefly as a sort of transition between plain and grand, but here is one example: "The nations of Africa and Asia are moving at jetlike speed toward gaining political independence, but we still creep at horse and buggy pace toward gaining a cup of coffee at a lunch counter" (paragraph 14). Overall this is an antithesis, reinforced by simile and metaphor, which are the most striking figures here. The "cup of coffee at a lunch counter" may be a synecdoche (part-for-whole, attribute-for-essence) for the larger aims of the civil-rights movement. While the point is serious, the witty metaphors seem humorous, highlighting the absurdity of the situation.

The Grand Style

In contrast to the plain and middle styles, with their minimal and moderate figuration, the grand style is often defined in terms of heavy figuration. But *strong emotion* really makes the grand style grand. As Cicero and other authorities in the rhetorical tradition have said, the "duties" of the rhetor are to "teach, persuade, and move." The plain style teaches, explains, or convinces (logos); the middle style persuades or sways the audience with the pleasures of sweet reason urbanely spoken (ethos); and the grand style moves the audience's feelings, especially when the rhetor seeks to motivate them to act (pathos). The grand style, in short, states resonant, emotively significant ideas in a resonant, emotive way.

Therefore, the first requirement of the grand style is that the rhetor must be saying something that feels (to the audience) like an important or transcendent truth or that carries a powerful emotive charge. This is backed by heavy figuration, especially with figures that reflect a suitable emotion. (It would be strange to say things that call for tears or rapture in a completely neutral, emotionless voice.) The figures required for suitably grand expression will depend, of course, on the particular emotion called for and the subject matter, but perhaps the leading characteristic of the grand style is the use of *schemes*, particularly schemes of repetition—parallelism and accumulation.

The grand style has two main dangers. First, if it is used for subject matter that does not warrant high emotion (in the audience's opinion), it will be perceived as empty bombast—hot air—and will be not only unpersuasive but actively off-putting. Second, it generally cannot be sustained for long. It is the nature of an emotional outburst to spend itself quickly. If it continues for too long it seems insincere. For this reason a discourse generally cannot be all grand all the time; the grand style typically alternates with other styles and interrupts them with short, intense bursts of impassioned eloquence.

We have referred to it more than once in this book, but King's "when you have seen" passage ("Letter" paragraph 14) is a good example of the grand style sustained for a longer period. King begins the paragraph with a mostly plain-style sentence: "We have waited for more than 340 years for our constitutional and God-given rights." ("We have waited for 340 years" may be synecdoche, and the closing phrase may be zeugma; but neither feels like much of a departure from plain or proper usage.) This is followed by the middle-style sentence we discussed earlier (about horse-and-buggy speed, etc.) and a third sentence that is mostly plain but incorporates a metaphor: "Perhaps it is easy for those who have never felt the *stinging darts of segregation* to say, 'Wait.'" These three sentences, hovering between plain and middle style, and especially the second one, seem to prepare the audience for what will follow by cultivating their emotional accessibility. It is all sweet reason, so far, calling on the reader's sympathy and sense of fairness.

This plain/middle-style mood of reasonability then suddenly gives way to the grand-style "when you have seen" sequence—an accumulation of nine clauses, each beginning with "when you," enumerating the "stinging darts of segregation" that African-Americans endure, followed by a tenth clause that caps the sequence: "*then* you will understand . . .". The things that are described should move a reasonable, sympathetic person to tears or outrage. Moreover, it is all framed in the second person ("when you . . ."), thus giving the things described more presence by inviting the sympathetic audience to put themselves in "the Negro's" place. Further, the repetitions of "when you" (anaphora) reinforce the enumeration's feeling of compulsive urgency, as if King can barely contain himself. This feeling of a barely controlled emotional outburst is reinforced by the *avoidance* of beautiful or stately schemes such as isocolon or other well-balanced, elegant forms of parallelism. Instead, the clauses are of uneven and varied lengths and structures, building to a climactic crescendo in the fourth and longest clause, but then continuing through five more clauses, again of varied lengths and structures, as if overflowing the original form.

If one thinks of the *delivery* of this passage, it appears that each "when" clause is meant to be delivered as a single breath, as each idea comes and unfolds itself (this is a figure too, called *pneuma,* or breath). As the clauses become longer and more complex, they increasingly strain the speaker's breath. Consider, for example, the third and fourth clauses:

> . . . when you see the vast majority of your twenty million Negro brothers smothering in an airtight cage of poverty in the midst of an affluent society;
>
> when you suddenly find your tongue twisted and your speech stammering as you seek to explain to your six-year-old daughter why she can't go to the public amusement park that has just been advertised on television, and see tears welling up in her eyes when she is told that Funtown is closed to colored children, and see ominous clouds of inferiority beginning to form in her little mental sky, and see her beginning to distort her personality by developing an unconscious bitterness toward white people;
>
> when you . . .

Our point is that delivery of such long clauses would strain the breath. (And that is a figure, too—the stretched or extended pneuma.) This appearance of straining creates a sense of *stress,* as if, again, King is speaking under the pressure of emotion, barely controlling himself. This *stylistic performance* of emotion helps to give the "when you have seen" sequence a feeling of emotional authenticity that almost all readers of the "Letter" feel, and that enhances its persuasiveness and pathetic force.

The "when you have seen" passage also contains a number of tropes: hate-filled policemen; airtight cage of poverty; tongue twisted; clouds of inferiority; mental sky; living at tiptoe stance; plagued with fears; and a degenerating sense of nobodiness. But what mostly contributes to the grandness of this grand-style passage are its schemes of repetition and accumulation, its anaphoras, its avoidance of balanced parallelisms, and its use of stressed pneumata of uneven lengths and forms.

Qualitative Types of Style

As we have noted, besides the plain-middle-grand classification of types of style, there is another tradition of describing styles according to what might be called their *quality* or mood. The Greek rhetorician

---

WRITE AN ANALYSIS

In this section, we focus on the qualities that make a written or spoken argument stylistically plain or grand (or somewhere in the middle). Following classical rhetorical theory, we focus principally on figuration, but we maintain that any form of communication can be described in these terms. Consider the common and popular genre of situation comedy on television today. A show like the American (and the British) *Office* can be described as having a plain style. There is no laugh track. The camera is often shaky or poorly positioned. The lighting is unflattering, the audio simple. *The Office*, of course, borrows many of these cinematic plain-style features from documentary film making. The show lacks any of the stylistic flourishes common to more "urbane" situation comedies—no laugh track to follow particular punch lines, no music to designate the beginning and ending of scenes, no overtly physical gags, no unbelievably flamboyant characters. Thus, *The Office* achieves a kind of trustworthy earnestness that contrasts with the style of other shows in this genre. Select a nonprint or nonoral argument, and write an analysis that characterizes its style as plain, middle, or grand. What makes this rhetorical style? What elements can be described as plain? Explain what rhetorical effect the style has on the entire discourse.

Hermogenes, for example, in his treatise *On Types of Style* identified twenty types, including the styles of clarity, sweetness, sincerity, asperity, vigor, solemnity, grandeur, and florescence, culminating in what he called *deinotes*—literally *awesomeness* (usually translated as forcefulness)—which arose from the perfect combination of the other types according to kairos. (Hermogenes, who refers to these types as "ideas" or "forms" [*ideai*], had great influence on stylistic theory and practice in the Renaissance; see Annabel Patterson, *Hermogenes and the Renaissance: Seven Ideas of Style* [Princeton, 1970].) It is perhaps not necessary here to review Hermogenes' types, but the general principle of description is useful for rhetorical analysis.

As Hermogenes suggests, the quality or mood of any type of style can be described in terms of the subject matter or thought being expressed, the method or figure of thought appropriate to its expression (such as indignation or ratiocination), and the diction, figures, and rhythms that appropriately embody the mood. That is roughly what we did earlier, in our analysis of King's "when you have seen" passage as an example of the grand style. But a more thoroughgoing qualitative approach might enable us to describe the mood and style of that passage with more precision. Similarly, one might describe the dominant style of Lincoln's Gettysburg Address as *solemnity*: a quality—a mood and tone—that arises from his subject matter, his figures of thought, his stately cadences, his figures of speech, and his diction.

STYLE AND DELIVERY IN VISUAL TEXTS: A NOTE

We have referred to delivery in modern audiovisual media already, but here we need to say a little more. As the foregoing discussions make apparent, the traditional vocabulary for the analysis of style and delivery is focused almost entirely on the spoken word. We can speak of diction and figures of speech and rhythm and types of style in written texts, and we can speak, too, of their delivery as an oral performance of the text (like an actor performing a script). But there is also a purely visual aspect to the style/delivery of written or printed text. This has to do with its physical appearance, such as the choice and size of fonts, spacing, the layout of the text on the page, the use of such things as paragraph breaks and headings, and even the paper on which the text appears (or other media, such as a computer screen or a pillar of marble). The function of such elements of delivery, like the voice projection and clear enunciation of a skillful orator in an outdoor assembly, is to make sure the message comes through with maximum clarity and effect. It is easy to take such textual features for granted and fail to appreciate their rhetorical function. But consider, for contrast, what reading a written text was like in Plato's day. There were no small letters, no spaces between words, no paragraph breaks, no punctuation— none of those things had been invented yet—and, of course, the lettering was all done by hand on scrolls of papyrus. Ancient texts did use headings, and usually were laid out in relatively narrow columns to make it easier for the eye to scan the letters. But it is evident how much the visual delivery of modern texts can help the reader as well as help the rhetor's message come through clearly and effectively. The physical shape of the presentation matters. Imagine that this book were printed in a font that looked like this.

Modern texts also can include such visual elements as graphics (charts, graphs, tables of data) and pictures. These perform rhetorical functions analogous to those of figures of speech. One might say, for example, that a bar graph representing a company's sales for each of the last ten years is a sort of metaphor. Each bar is a concrete, visual analogy for an otherwise abstract dollar amount. Moreover, such figures can be manipulated to make the represented idea—such as an upward or downward trend in sales—seem better or worse. (Depending on how the graph is calibrated, the bars can be shortened or elongated, thus making the rise or fall seem smaller or larger.)

A photograph can function as an illustration of an idea, or as a trope. Consider, for example, a public-service ad promoting mentoring that ran in mass-circulation magazines (such as *Newsweek*) a few years ago. The top three-fourths of the full-page ad was occupied by a photograph of two swans, an adult and a baby (a cygnet), spreading their wings. The cygnet was behind the adult, and appeared to be spreading its wings in imitation. The image itself was aesthetically pleasing: the two swans were pure white, standing out against a background of green, lush grass. Underneath ran a heading in large capital letters—SHARE WHAT YOU KNOW. BECOME A MENTOR.—followed by a brief text (in smaller type) encouraging the reader to volunteer. The photograph of the swans clearly was a *metaphor* for mentoring, framing it within the network of ideas associated with swans, the spotless purity of the white swans in the picture, the apparent parent/child relationship between them, and the idea of spreading your wings and taking flight, as well as the physical beauty of the image itself. It all suggests that mentoring is a pleasant, pure, and even beautiful experience analogous to parents interacting with their own young children. Imagine that the swans were placed, instead, in a concrete-floored zoo cage, or that the swans were replaced with a tough-looking young man talking with a grizzled elder in a blighted urban neighborhood. Obviously the effect would be very different.

Note that the overall layout of that ad (picture, text, and all) falls under the heading of structure, as discussed in Chapter 4. Style pertains to the metaphorical function of the swan image (and other aspects of the semiotics of imagery), and to the stylistic features of the heading and the text below it. Delivery pertains to the physical presentation—the whiteness of the white and the greenness of the green, the soft focus of the photograph, the choice and size of fonts, and, in a magazine, such things as the glossiness of the page. If the same ad were published on the Internet, or printed in black and white on antique, recycled, or craftsman (hand-made) paper, or on newspaper pulp, the characteristics of its delivery would be different.

SAMPLE ANALYSIS: ON THE STYLES OF CHRYSLER AND VW

We already have discussed King's use of the plain, middle, and grand styles in "Letter from Birmingham Jail." Here, then, we limit ourselves to a brief analysis of style in the Chrysler and Volkswagen ads in this book's appendices. While we will have a few things to say about visual style, our main focus will be the *prose style* of the texts included in the ads, and the voice—ethos embodied as a voice—that it gives to each carmaker. We'll start with Chrysler.

Our first impression is that the Chrysler ad has a busy presentation, a structure that seems to lack clear focus and direction. In consequence, the main text seems to be left stranded roughly in the middle. Nothing seems to move the reader toward it, or to give the reader a reason to read it. It is almost as if the main text does not expect to be read—in which case it may be no more than an obligatory filler, or may appear as such. Perhaps it is there simply because a car ad is expected to have a chunk of text like that.

Consider, first, the more dramatically presented material that surrounds the main text, which the reader is likely to read first before turning to the text (if ever). The two car pictures that occupy the left side of the two-page spread can be read as synecdoches (part-for-whole) for a larger story, as fragments of a familiar narrative. In each picture the reader sees a parked station wagon, young children, and a youngish parent. In one picture, a thirtyish father seems to lounge behind the wheel, surveying what appear to be his three young boys (the oldest perhaps nine, the youngest maybe four), who are looking at something out of the frame. In the other picture, a late-twentyish mother, thin and dressed in a fashionably sporty all-white outfit, playfully gestures toward her young daughter with teddy bear in the back of the wagon, while two apparently older boys (about nine and seven), one in a baseball cap, look through the tailgate window at something (again, out of the frame). In both pictures the parents, children, and car seem to be at some event or destination, perhaps on a family vacation. The station wagons are large and roomy, and luxurious in appearance. These appear to be scenes of successful middle-class life—a happy *Leave It To Beaver* world (a hit TV show from 1957 to 1963)—or more particularly, the life of young families who have arrived and can enjoy the benefits of affluence, such as an extended car trip or a long drive.

The largest single piece of text in the ad is in the most natural starting point for left-right, top-down processing. The headline in Figure 5.2 is probably the first piece of text that the reader's eye will visit, and it establishes the basic middle-style tone.

The first line is a bit of mildly humorous hyperbole that young parents with multiple children might appreciate—suggesting that kids are the noisiest thing of all and that Chrysler's wagons can make *even them* seem quieter (while "seem" ironically undercuts the hyperbole; the kids will not really be quieter, just further away). Likewise, portraying the parents as "up against" the noisiness of their children introduces a bit of colloquial informality that also functions as mildly humorous hyperbole, since one usually speaks of being "up against" more serious and threatening challenges. ("Up against" also has a metaphorical function, similar to saying that parents are "plagued" with noisy kids.) A further aspect of this headline's humor is that, because it is presented (delivered) in such large, eye-catching type, it seems to shout about being quiet, as if struggling to be heard above the general noise of family life (not to mention the noisiness of the ad's overall presentation). Finally, the way the headline is broken into phrases, and the shift to smaller, italic type in the second and third lines, suggest the probable delivery: slight pauses at the end of each

Even the kids seem quieter
*in the wagons built by people who know
what parents are up against*

Figure 5.2   Text from the Chrysler ad.

line, and a lower volume and smoother/quicker delivery for the last two lines. Interestingly, the pauses cut across what probably would be the normal phrasing in everyday speech (no pause after "know"), thus creating a sort of figure analogous to the metaplasms (especially cutting). This gives the headline a heightened sense of rhythm and cadence, and places an emphasis on "people who *know*" that otherwise would not be there. It is easy to hear this headline as a sort of TV announcer voice, loud and clear, with distinct rises and dips in intonation.

The headline adds another element to the ad. Alongside the pictures' synecdochic evocation of a happy *Leave It To Beaver* world, it adds a suggestion that the parents, as happy and successful as they may be, also need some relief and distance from their noisy, rambunctious kids, a distance provided by the roomy space in the back of the wagon, far back from the driver's seat. (No one ever thought about seat belts in those days.) Apparently the appeal is not so much to those who want to be successful parents. Rather, it is to those who are parents already but want to preserve some space for grown-up pleasures and the trappings of adult success—big station wagons with amenities like a pushbutton dash, a roll-down tailgate window, automatic door locks, a hidden valuables compartment, and a quiet ride provided by "Unibody Construction" (welding instead of bolting the body to the frame) and "Torsion-Aire suspension." This theme is carried through the rest of the ad's texts, including the captions on the pictures of special features, and the main text in the middle.

Three things stand out in these blocks of text.

First, the generally middle-style tone is mostly carried through. We see it in informal locutions such as, "You'll appreciate this on trips" (which is plain in itself, but in its informality and relaxation it creates a feeling of personal closeness and invites identification with the speaker). Or, again, in the main text's opening line, which echoes the headline we first looked at: "Parents will find this hard to believe: these wagons keep you reminded how happy you are to have a family of kids—even on a long haul." Like the headline, it suggests that parents actually are a little weary of their kids and need to be reminded that they really are happy.

Second, this generally informal middle style is interrupted by language that seems to derive from a different register. For example:

> New pushbutton dash puts all the controls at your fingertips.
>
> Rear window rolls down, can be controlled by driver from front seat.
>
> Hidden luggage compartment lets you lock valuables safely out of sight.
>
> New Unibody Construction makes body and frame a solid, welded unit.
>
> Safety features shown at right help put a parent in the right frame of mind to enjoy a drive.

This language often drops articles (a, the) and other noncontent words that normally would appear in natural spoken English. It derives from what might be called an instruction manual register—the language of engineering manuals or product instructions (such as the directions for setting up a computer or assembling a swingset). Such language is in essence an abbreviated notational language that is not meant to be spoken, or even imagined as spoken, and is normally read silently. This is most noticeable in the "rear window" sentence above: If read aloud, it sounds like robot-talk from a comedy routine.

What should we make of this register shift? Is it deliberate, or just a breakdown in "voice"? It may be deliberate. If the ad is directed to a parents-with-young-kids audience, one that wants the sorts of amenities and gadgets that Chrysler offers, the intention may be to give those amenities and gadgets an attractive high-tech aura through technical-sounding language. However, this register shift also may not be deliberate. We can imagine a skilled announcer finding an effective way to deliver these instruction-manual lines; but inescapably they will sound unnatural and will break the illusion of a personal voice connecting with the reader. It will, instead, be a TV announcer voice reading ad copy that strays from natural speech. Moreover, even in the parts that more or less sustain an informal middle style with varied sentence lengths, our admittedly intuitive impression is that, as it goes along, the text fails to sustain a believably speechlike sense of rhythm and cadence. It seems tonally flat and ends up sounding more like an educational film or newsreel from the 1950s. (This impression is based on the evidence of multiple attempts to read the text aloud.)

In sum, the perceivable artificiality of the text's language tends to undercut its gestures toward informality and personal connection, making them ring false. From this we conclude that the register shift most probably is not deliberate. The style as a whole lacks ear appeal, and the high-tech items could have been mentioned without resorting to instruction-manual language. The text appears to have been written by a person (or a committee) focused on transmitting information about these wagons' attractions for the ad's target demographic, but with an unsteady sense of voice. Indeed we question whether the writer(s) hears the text at all, or means for the reader to.

The third thing that stands out for us is the physical/visual delivery of this ad's text. The text elements in the ad are presented in different type sizes and font styles—serif (**like this**) and sans serif (**like this**), roman (**like this**) and italic (*like this*), and all caps and lowercase (with capitalization). Unlike the opening headline, where the font styles and sizes seem to enhance the sense of voice, elsewhere the differences generally seem meant only to provide eye-catching variety or to enhance legibility. We take this as more evidence that the text writer and/or ad designer is thinking of the text primarily as a visual representation of information and not (or very slightly) as a speaking voice. This is particularly noticeable in the main text, a block consisting of five short paragraphs. It is printed entirely in a serif font, and in very small type, possibly the smallest type in the ad. While the designer probably thought the serif font looked more elegant, the font combined with its small size gives the text a quiet or muted feeling—quieter than the booming headlines and the pictures placed around it—and makes it less legible than the small-type, sans-serif captions to its right. This fact alone suggests that the text writer or ad designer may not expect the text to be read, and is counting more on the surrounding headlines, pictures, and captions to do the ad's persuasive work. Again we are drawn to the idea that the main text is perfunctory.

It is quite possible, of course, that the intended readers of the Chrysler ad *don't care* whether the ad projects a believable-sounding voice, or believably sustains an informal middle style that seeks to make a personal connection with them. Perhaps they don't have an ear for style and approach a text as a visual object containing information. Or maybe they believe that the style and content of a text are different things and try to look past the style to focus on the content. Perhaps it doesn't matter that Chrysler's voice sounds artificial, that its gestures at identification with young parents' needs ring hollow, and that it rather appears to be pandering to their desires (for relief from the kids, for adult enjoyments, for some trappings of success, for amenities and gadgets). Perhaps swooping lines and flashy tail fins, an enormous back area to put the kids in, pushbutton dash, smooth-riding Torsion-Aire suspension, and so on are the only things that matter to this audience. This raises issues regarding the normative judgment of style, and theoretical issues about the need to attend to it critically, that we cannot go into here.

Let's turn to the Volkswagen ad.

The argumentation and structure of the ad both lead the reader from top to bottom—from the image of the three stolid-looking VWs (with their mileage figures), to the large-type question "Why?" and finally to the small-type text, which answers the question. The text is not a dead spot in the ad, a perfunctory filler. It is a functional part, indeed the culminating part, so the reader has natural motivations to actually read it. Therefore, the text begins with a reader who probably is more engaged than the reader of the Chrysler ad (who conceivably could skip the main text altogether).

VW then speaks to the reader in a distinctly colloquial, natural-sounding plain style, and with that style's main virtues—clarity, directness, economy, energy, and logicality. This is evident in the opening lines:

Why?

Depends on how you drive it. And where.

Driven by a pro in an economy run, a stock Volkswagen will average close to 50 miles per gallon.

And so on. The language is simple, informal, and direct, and is punctuated in mostly short phrases that reflect the cadences of natural speech. Likewise it employs speechlike sentence fragments (as well as complete sentences). Further, it adheres to a diction that is both proper (to the subject matter) and informal, as in "Notice we lay it right on the line," or "figure on getting about 32 mpg." There are traces of tropical language, such as "lay it on the line" (metaphor), "an indignant letter" (catachresis), "a heavy foot" (metonymy), "has stood up over the years" (metaphor), or "put [this] in your bank-book" (synecdoche), but all of these are well-worn, familiar tropes that generally are perceived as proper (if colorful) diction. There are some register shifts from car talk, like "stock Volkswagen," "stop-and-go driving," or (maybe) "depreciation," but again these are all well within the range of familiar, everyday vocabulary for most Americans. In short, the text presents a lively and believable plain-style voice that speaks the language of its readers—thus inviting identification—and that talks directly *to* them. The voice is not that of an engineer, or of a TV announcer; it sounds more like a mechanic or technician from a VW service department, someone who might have an oil rag in his hand, responding in a no-nonsense way to a po-tential buyer's question. (The Chrysler ad, in contrast, sometimes addresses or refers to "you," but also talks about "parents" in the third person and thereby seems not really to be talking to its audi-ence. Likewise the artificiality of the TV-announcer voice implies not connection but distance from the reader, though the audience may be attracted to the glamour of TV.)

The visual presentation (or delivery) of the VW text is significant also. First, the text is broken into very short paragraphs, often consist-ing of just one sentence. This punctuation visually signals emphatic pauses in the spoken delivery of the lines, which helps to reinforce the sense of speechlike cadences, and to give each sentence and sentence part its full weight as a distinct unit of utterance. Second, the text is arranged in three relatively narrow columns. Aside from creating a visual balance with the three VWs at the top of the page (a sort of iso-colon), this column arrangement performs the same function that it did in ancient papyri, by making it easier for the reader's eye to scan the letters and words of each short line. (There are about 6–8 words per line, compared with 10–15 in the Chrysler ad's main text.) Imagine that, instead, the text was arranged in a single block, with lines that ran unbroken across the page: how easy would it be to read, and how well would the style (and its cadences) come through? Third and finally, the sans-serif font of the text not only is easily legible, but reinforces the plain-style voice, no-nonsense ethos, and minimalist aesthetic of the ad as a whole.

Undoubtedly, the Chrysler Corporation didn't skimp on advertising. Their ad exemplifies state-of-the-art automobile advertising in 1960. It is lavish, compared with VW's. But the Volkswagen ad has a superior sense of style—as well as argument, structure, adaptation to situation and kairos, and rhetoric generally. Perhaps one shouldn't decide to buy a car because of the rhetorical superiority, kairotic inventiveness, or style of its advertising. Certainly one cannot judge a car's quality from its ads, though people do tend to make judgments about a corporation's ethos based on the advertising that it fosters (and stands behind, as the implied rhetor). Surely one ought to consult independent information sources (like *Consumer Reports*), assess one's own desires, needs, and budget, and make a rational decision. (If that is possible; human beings are not quite the rational calculating machines that we sometimes imagine.) But all other things being equal, VW's ad makes an adroit and generally persuasive appeal to its intended audience, stylistically and otherwise. The ad projects a credible plain-style voice with which the reader can connect, a voice that is consistent with the straight-talking ethos that we have noted before, and with the general argument of the ad (i.e., that the car is well engineered; is practical, efficient, and reliable; and has no need to sell itself with gadgets, flashy style, or inflated claims). The style embodies the argument effectively.

WRITING A STYLE ANALYSIS

Analyzing rhetorical style, like analyzing structure, requires that you artificially separate what the rhetor says from how the rhetor says it. This separation is somewhat easier when analyzing structure because the concepts—such as repetitive form or the classical template—provide a clear sense of what you can analyze as structure rather than as argument. Style, however, often refers to a grey area, aspects that could be considered content but that could also be considered form. For instance, several stylistic devices discussed previously (such as the stylistic enthymeme and the analogy) have corollaries in the argument chapter, raising certain questions: When do we treat an enthymeme as a stylistic device rather than as an argument? When is analogy more a matter of presentation than argumentation? Other stylistic devices raise similar questions. When, for instance, is metaphor an argument by comparison rather than a symbolic flourish? (Past rhetoricians have not drawn the stark line between style and argumentation that we propose here. During the British High Middle Ages and the Renaissance, stylistic figures were practiced as devices of argumentation. Students learned to invent arguments by imitating tropes, figures, and schemes.) To help you with this difficult distinction between argument and style, we encourage you to ask the following question of every element that you'd like to analyze: Could this form be adapted to present a completely different content but with a similar rhetorical effect? If the answer is yes, then you probably have a solid case for analyzing the element as stylistic. If the answer is no, then you may be looking at an element of content, a piece of the argument that would change dramatically if you were to substitute new content for what is already there.

After deciding what counts as style and what counts as argument, you still face the difficult task of analyzing the style, which is especially challenging if you've chosen a piece of nonverbal or nontextual argumentation. If you're looking at a speech, then you know to look for metonymy, metaphors, diction, rhythm, and so forth. If you're analyzing a music video, then classical rhetorical theory does not provide you with as many tools to discuss the important stylistic devices. In either case—whether you're analyzing a piece of oral/textual rhetoric or a piece of nonoral/nontextual rhetoric—we encourage you to begin with the stylistic virtues (clarity, correctness, appropriateness, and distinction) and with the three types of style (grand, middle, and plain). These are fairly general terms that should allow you to describe any discourse's style. (The first two sets of questions on pp. 178–179 should help you to apply these general descriptive terms.)

Once you're able to characterize the style, you should look for particular elements that make the presentation clear, distinctive, appropriate, or correct. If you're analyzing an oral or a print argument, then this chapter's discussion of tropes, schemes, and figures will be very helpful. (The questions about tropes, schemes, and figures will guide you toward identifying these elements.) But if you're analyzing a nonoral/nonprint text, you might not get as much guidance from classical rhetorical theory. You may have to discuss elements that classical

QUESTIONS FOR ANALYSIS

- **General questions about stylistic virtues:** What stylistic virtues does the argument exhibit—clarity, correctness, appropriateness, distinction? What can the audience learn about the implied rhetor's ethos (character) based on the virtues exhibited by the argument's style?
    - **Specific questions about stylistic virtues in oral and print arguments:** If you're analyzing a print or an oral argument, what elements of diction or tone make the style clear, correct, appropriate, or distinct? What figures and tropes make the style distinct?
- **General questions about types of style:** What type of style does this argument display—plain, middle, or grand? What elements contribute to this stylistic effect? What makes the style plain, middle, or grand? What does this style say about the implied rhetor's ethos? What does this style contribute to the argument's pathetic appeal?
    - **Specific question about types of style in oral and print arguments:** Looking at the level of figuration (the number and the frequency of tropes and figures), how would you characterize this argument's style—plain, middle, or grand?
- **General questions about tropes:** What sort of tropical discourse (tropes) does the argument employ? How, if at all, do these tropes contribute to the argument's logical or pathetic appeal? Can you find instances of the following tropes—synecdoche, metonymy, simile, metaphor, allegory, irony, litotes, hyperbole?
    - **Specific question about tropes in oral and print arguments:** Can you find instances of the following tropes—catachresis, pun, periphrasis, enallage?
- **General questions about schemes of parallelism:** Do you find any stylistically paralleled elements in this argument? Any set or list of items presented in a similar fashion? What do these paralleled elements emphasize in the argument?
    - **Specific question about schemes of parallelism in oral and print arguments:** Can you find instances of the following schemes of parallelism—anaphora, homoioteleuton, isocolon, chiasmus, anadiplosis, zeugma, and polyptoton?
- **General questions about schemes of accumulation:** Do you find any stylistic elements that repeat or augment principal parts of the argument? Any efforts at accumulation? What does this augmentation contribute to the argument's pathetic appeal? What does the accumulation emphasize?

- **Specific question about schemes of accumulation in oral and print arguments:** Can you find instances of the following schemes of accumulation—climax, antithesis, analogy, enumeration, and correctio?
- **General questions about other schemes:** Do you find other stylistic elements that involve distinctive patterns of arrangement? What do they contribute to the mood or tone of what is being said, what emphases? Can you find instances of polysyndeton, asyndeton, ellipsis, parenthesis, metaplasm, and hyperbaton?
- **General questions about figures of thought:** Do you find any stylistic elements that dramatize the implied rhetor's thought process or emotional state? What do these figures of thought contribute to the argument's logical or ethical appeal? Can you find instances of the following figures of thought—apostrophe, prosopopoeia, dialogism, sententia, erotema, paradox, praeteritio, aporia, aposiopesis, and praecisio?
- **General questions about rhythm:** How would you describe the argument's rhythm? Slow, fast, choppy, smooth? What elements contribute to that rhythm? What does that rhythm add to the argument's pathetic or formal appeal?
- **Specific questions about rhythm in oral and print argument:** What syllabic stress patterns (iambs, trochees, etc.) do you notice? What combinations of vowels and consonants? What patterns in sentence and phrase length?
- **Specific questions about delivery of oral arguments:** How would or can you deliver this argument as a speech? What do you notice when reading the text aloud?

---

rhetors never considered (such as camera angle, visual layout, web or game design). Whatever specifics you discuss, you should explain how the particular stylistic features contribute to the general quality. How do these schemes—or these camera tricks—make the style distinctive?

Finally, after characterizing the style in general terms and finding elements that contribute to the qualities that you want to emphasize, you should try to explain what this style contributes to the discourse. How would a distinct style of cinematography help a rhetor make the audience feel emotionally overwhelmed at key moments in a movie? How would a plain style of writing make a rhetor appear credible? You'll notice that we couch the previous two questions in terms of Aristotle's three appeals. We think that's a good place to start: Does this style (comprised of these elements) contribute to a key logical, pathetic, or ethical appeal? But, as our analysis of the Chrysler and the VW ads demonstrates, style can be discussed in a variety of ways, as an important contribution to a variety of argumentative or structural components. No matter what you choose to argue, we think these three questions should guide your initial efforts at rhetorical analysis of style:

1. How would you characterize this style (clear, correct, appropriate, distinct, grand, middle, plain)?
2. What elements contribute to the different qualities attributed to this argument's style? What makes it distinct, plain, grand, etc.?
3. What do these stylistic qualities (and elements) contribute to the overall discourse?

Following is a student-authored analysis of style in a 2009 video Public Service Announcement (PSA) produced and originally aired in England. Notice that the author, Tara Hall, characterizes the discourse's style using general terms provided by this chapter. She then explains which elements contribute to these general qualities. According to Tara, the PSA uses particular camera angles, viewpoints, and slow-motion video to achieve stylistic clarity. In each case, the analysis offers a general description that is then explained by focusing on specific stylistic elements. Also notice Tara's effort to relate the style to the argument. She maintains that the PSA's clear style contributes to two important pathetic appeals. Thus Tara *analyzes* the style that she's *labeled* as clear.

STUDENT ANALYSIS OF STYLE IN A TELEVISED
PUBLIC SERVICE ANNOUNCEMENT

Hall 1

Tara Hall
Professor Jacqueline Boulos
ENG 221 Textual Analysis
May 30, 2010

Clarity and Rhythm in a British PSA

In an effort to bring attention to the rising trend of
texting while driving and its inherent dangers, England's
Gwent Police Department hired filmmaker Peter Watkins-
Hughes to create a gripping public service announcement.
(You can view the entire video at YouTube.com by searching
for "PSA Peter Watkins-Hughes.") What Watkins-Hughes
produced is a stylistically clear and concise four-minute
segment that leaves little to the viewer's imagination.

Watkins-Hughes—the actual rhetor—uses a few precise
techniques to develop a clear style. First, he maintains
throughout the majority of the piece a camera angle that
presents the action from a first-person perspective, as if the
viewer is in the car experiencing whiplash or on the side of
the road watching emergency workers use the jaws of life to
rip into a demolished vehicle. In certain areas, the rhetor
employs slow-motion cinematography to visually march the
viewer through each and every step of the situation. Finally,
he carefully alters the pace of the video, keeping the message
clear by subtly dividing it into digestible segments so as not
to overwhelm the audience.

Throughout the announcement, which plays out more
like a movie than a traditional PSA, Hughes shifts the position
and angle of the camera. For much of the video, the scenes
are shown from the perspective of specific viewers—Hughes'

Annotation (left margin): Tara says the PSA exhibits a stylistic virtue—clarity—thus offering a general description without having to get into the specific elements that contribute to this video's style.

Annotation (right margin): Tara explains what particular elements make this video's style clear—camera angle, slow motion, and rhythm. Since the tropes, figures, and schemes discussed in this chapter may not apply to this video, Tara must invent her own terms to discuss the stylistic elements of a clear video.

Notice that here, and elsewhere, Tara describes segments of the video to show the audience that the style really is clear in the ways she claims. Tara must present descriptions of the video to give the reader examples of the elements that Tara wants us to notice in this text.

implied rhetors. In the opening scene (0:03), a young female driver types out a text and, because the camera is positioned from the driver's assumed sightline, the audience feels like the driver. A few seconds later, the perspective shifts outside the car, for a second or two, as if the viewer were standing on the side of the road witnessing the slow drift of the texter's vehicle into oncoming traffic. With the frequent shift from the first-person perspective to the third-person perspective, the rhetor makes his argument clear without words, but through visual presentation.

This filming technique gives the audience the sense that they are also experiencing the event, one that most of them probably haven't faced before. This in turn creates a substantial pathetic appeal. Watkins-Hughes matches the position and angle of the camera with his desired audience reaction, making his argument clear from many perspectives: from the eyes of the texter, innocent victims, and bystanders/media alike.

In the crash sequence (0:13–0:34), the rhetor employs a different sort of cinematography from the rest of the video in an effort to clearly exhibit the injuries inflicted in a high-speed car accident. By doing this, Watkins-Hughes chooses not to gloss over the "gross" parts of an accident like traditional PSAs might. Instead, he uses a slow-motion style to capture exactly how the body reacts in the accident. The slower exhibition of frame-by-frame images, coupled with the sounds of glass shattering, bones breaking, etc, is one of the clearest ways to reinforce the argument that texting is dangerous.

The graphic style of the cinematic technique exemplified in this segment not only contributes to the

Notice that Tara explains how the element she's describing (the camera's perspective) contributes to the video's stylistic clarity.

After explaining how the camera's perspective contributes to the video's clarity, Tara explains how this stylistic clarity contributes to the video's argument (its pathetic appeal).

Tara introduces the next element that she will discuss, explaining how slow-motion video contributes to stylistic clarity.

Hall 3

pathos by leaving the audience shocked, sad and possibly afraid, but it also gives inexperienced viewers an inside perspective of a serious car accident, which builds a strong ethical appeal. Since many haven't experienced a major crash first hand, they take this factlike presentation for truth because of its clear delivery.

The PSA's subject matter and the manner in which it is delivered are both intense, which might explain the rhetor's decision to occasionally alter the pace of the video. The first 13 seconds is upbeat with lively chatter between driver and passengers while up-tempo music plays in the background. The mood, though not the pace, shifts as the accident occurs, but a short pause is thoughtfully placed between the impact with the first oncoming car and a subsequent one a few seconds later (0:23–0:27). This short four-second break between graphic scenes relieves the weight of the heavy content, giving the audience a sort of visual breather. With the second impact (0:27–0:36), the pace quickens again until the cars come to a rest around the 37-second mark. At this time, another short-lived break ensues.

This quick-slow-quick rhythm uses the audience's attention span to the actual rhetor's advantage in a complex way. Watkins-Hughes heightens the viewers' emotional response—he makes them feel—by quickening the pace of the video during the most important, telling scenes: the causal act of texting and the bodily injuries being sustained. The slower portions serve as a period of subconscious reflection, a time to process the effects of texting while driving. This technique, though in no way subtle, economizes viewer energy, making the argument clear while also heightening the pathetic appeals.

After explaining how slow-motion cinematography contributes to the video's stylistic clarity, Tara analyzes its contribution to the argument (the pathetic and ethical appeals that this style reinforces).

Tara summarizes her argument about how the rhythm contributes to the video's stylistic clarity and to its pathetic appeals.

Hall 4

With the use of a handful of filming tactics, Watkins-Hughes portrays the PSA's message in a clear way. Though the process and storyline seem simple, the camera angles and perspective changes create a well-rounded style. By employing a slower cinematic style during the impact scenes, the rhetor keeps the viewer clearly focused on the exact repercussions, leaving little room for refutation. Finally, controlling the pacing of the video's intensity deftly shapes the audience's retention of the argument's faster-paced take-home message.

6
Ideology (Logos Revisited)

At a number of universities in the United States today, students can take courses with the word *rhetoric* in the title. At some colleges, people can even earn a degree in rhetoric. We often wonder how these students explain their course of study to people who probably associate the term *rhetoric* with lying or spin. Would it be worse if they had to say, "I'm majoring in ideology with a minor in rhetoric"? *Ideology* is the only political term that might nowadays provoke a more negative reaction—the only college major that might sound more questionable—than rhetoric. Take the following headline from a recent issue of *Human Events Online* (2 March 2010): "Obama Continues Selecting Judges by Ideology, Not Skill, Intelligence or Experience." According to this article's title, *ideology* is the opposite of good qualities, such as skill, intelligence, and experience. Those who follow ideology are blindly dedicated to a rigid set of beliefs, regardless of what these beliefs recommend, regardless of whether or not these beliefs match reality, regardless of whether or not they are ethically right or practically helpful. If most people hear *lies* when we say *rhetoric*, then, likewise, most people hear *foolish dogma* when we say *ideology*.

Why analyze something so sinister? If our behaviors, our habits, and our relationships are conditioned by our beliefs—what we called presuppositions in Chapters 2 and 3—then the study of rhetoric is necessary to understand how people communicate. We want to see how presuppositions make arguments believable. We study ideologies for a similar reason. An ideology, as we will use the term in this chapter, is a system of presuppositions. When we look for an ideology, we try to find stable collections of ideas that shape who people are and what they do. Before getting too deep into the subject, allow a brief definition. For the moment, let's define an *ideology* as a set of presuppositions that influences most everything—people's family lives, their political choices, their intimate and professional relationships. These presuppositions must be held by an entire social class, culture, or community. And people must commit to and depend upon these presuppositions for a notable stretch of time. An ideology is bigger than you or us, bigger than the rhetor or the argument. It is probably older than its adherents and will likely outlive recent initiates. For this reason, Kenneth Burke contended that an ideology can persuade without a rhetor. And for this reason, we must wonder if any human community can persist without sharing a broader set of beliefs, without relying on an ideology. Arguments depend on presuppositions. Communities depend on ideologies.

SIDEBAR: A BRIEF HISTORY OF IDEOLOGY

Though the term *ideology* has been around since the late eighteenth century, we can begin to trace its critical origins by briefly mentioning Karl Marx and Frederick Engels's tome, *The German Ideology* (1845). Marx and Engels believed that an ideology was an upside-down mental representation of a "real" or "material" circumstance. They famously compared an ideological constellation to the image offered by a camera obscura, a nineteenth-century device that allowed artists to capture a two-dimensional representation of three-dimensional space by refracting an upside-down image through a lens and into a dark box where it could be traced. The inverted nature of an ideology was important to Marx and Engels because they believed that mental representations lead people to think that ideas precede—or cause—their lived economic circumstances when, in reality, lived economic circumstances really precede and thereby cause mental representations. For example, Marx and Engels might argue that the beliefs about liberty, as we discuss them later, are an inverted representation of a real contradiction between a legal system that preserves people's formal freedom to speak, truck, and barter and an economic system that denies their real freedoms by stripping workers of the capacity to alter, resist, or avoid cruel economic conditions (such as a grueling 16-hour workday in a nineteenth-century British factory). For the classical Marxist, the real contradiction causes and conditions the ideology of liberty. A number of writers follow in this classically Marxian vein. For example, anthropologist Claude Levi-Strauss maintained that myths and other symbolic utterances are an effort to manage material circumstances, such as tribal division, through symbolic structures, such as art or orally preserved stories. In addition, literary critic Frederic

Jameson argued that great works of literature are the inverted representations of class divisions and economic tensions. The inheritors of a classically Marxian approach practice *materialist* analysis insofar as they insist on some *material* circumstance that determines an ideology's existence and shape.

In the late twentieth century, another mode of ideological analysis has challenged the primacy of materialist analysis. *Immanent* analysis focuses strictly on the ideology itself, making no claims about a deeper or determining cause. The rise of immanent analysis is often traced to the French philosopher Louis Althusser, who contended that an ideology shapes the very fabric of our being and understanding (so it is impossible to clearly see any material reality without an ideological lens). In Althusser's terminology, an ideology interpellates (or calls) you, calling you to be as you are, to understand as you do, and to behave as you may. To get outside of ideology would require descent into madness or death. Althusser also argued that ideologies are determined not by one single factor (such as an economic circumstance) but rather by a whole network of causes, including economic pressures, religious inculcation, educational institutions, personal habits, social mores, linguistic norms, and so forth. Thus, Althusser contended that an ideology is not *determined*, but rather *overdetermined* by all of these factors, none more causally primary than the others. Althusser's inheritors include the philosopher Michel Foucault, the literary critic Pierre Macherey, and the sociologist Göran Therborn.

Most often, in contemporary scholarship, ideological analysis refers to immanent analysis, though there are some critics who insist upon the possibility of a materialist rhetorical analysis. Materialist analysts compare the ideology to the real systems of oppression that the ideology perpetuates. For the purposes of this chapter, we will focus on immanent analysis, though we do not preclude the possibility for a materialist rhetorical analysis. We maintain that both the immanent and the materialist critic must begin with the ideology itself, studying the assumptions that shape its contours and the arguments that maintain its presence. Even the materialist analyst must begin immanently, from within the argument(s).

Ancient Greeks believed that rhetoric depends upon commonly accepted opinions—what they called *doxa*—which can be separated from absolute, universal, and uncontestable knowledge, which some called *episteme*. Ideological analysis investigates a community's *doxa*, its shared presuppositions. Therefore, ideological analysis is cultural analysis. However, ideological analysis can also be a way of preparing for argumentation. Just as Cicero insisted that rhetors argue *in utramque partem* (from every side), we contend that students of rhetoric should learn to think from all ideological perspectives to understand how communities come together.

Rhetorical analysis of an ideology requires a study of ideas in argumentation. Thus, ideological analysis requires attention to two things: commonly shared presuppositions and the presuppositions that support an individual argument. Rhetorical analysis of an ideology also requires a broader understanding of *logos*. In Chapter 3, we discussed *logos* with reference to the individual argument. Here, we will talk about *logos* as something that does not stop when the argument reaches its conclusion. Borrowing a term from Michael Calvin McGee, a twentieth-century rhetorical theorist, we suggest that rhetorical analysis of an ideology searches for an *ideograph*, a constellation of presuppositions. Despite its ultimate and sprawling object, this investigation depends upon analyses of specific persuasive efforts. To begin rhetorical analysis of an ideology, you must suspect that an ideograph exists—that a collection of presuppositions persists and that these presuppositions warrant a number of arguments. It is useful to try summarizing the ideograph. What term or symbol captures this set of ideas? McGee recommended inventing a value-heavy and abstract term to capture the ideology. As sample American ideographs, McGee mentions liberty, religion, and property.

Once you've hypothesized that an ideograph exists, you should find and analyze an argument that depends upon its presuppositions. In this chapter, we will describe and model ideological analysis using four methods: (1) searching for a stable set of presuppositions, (2) noticing how one set of presuppositions overlaps and interacts with another in the same argument, (3) locating extensions of those presuppositions into (an)other argument(s), and (4) finding common tensions (what we call *paradoxes*) within an ideology and a single argument. We will explain each of these methods and then briefly demonstrate their application. Throughout this explanation of method, we will refer to one of the core documents building upon presuppositions about liberty—the Declaration of Independence. We conclude this chapter with a sample analysis of two ideologies in King's "Letter."

SEARCHING FOR IDEOLOGICAL PRESUPPOSITIONS

In Chapter 3, we discuss one key method used to locate presuppositions: enthymeme analysis. Here, we will add something to the process. In addition to locating enthymemes and their presuppositions, ideological analysis requires you to look for systems of ideas that get invoked, often without explicit mention, in various arguments. Not all presuppositions are part of an ideology because not all presuppositions are part of a cohesive or historically important set of beliefs. We start our analysis of an ideology by hypothesizing an ideograph—a weighty term or symbol. Let's take *liberty*. Then we work from a specific argument, asking ourselves what this rhetor wants us to assume about X (the ideograph's topic). To apply this question to a particular case, we would ask what the authors of the Declaration of Independence want us to believe about liberty. See Figure 6.1.

We hold these truths to be self-evident, that all men are created equal, that they are endowed by their Creator with certain unalienable Rights, that among these are Life, Liberty and the pursuit of Happiness.—That to secure these rights, Governments are instituted among Men, deriving their just powers from the consent of the governed, — That whenever any Form of Government becomes destructive of these ends, it is the Right of the People to alter or to abolish it, and to institute new Government, laying its foundation on such principles and organizing its powers in such form, as to them shall seem most likely to effect their Safety and Happiness. Prudence, indeed, will dictate that Governments long established should not be changed for light and transient causes; and accordingly all experience hath shewn, that mankind are more disposed to suffer, while evils are sufferable, than to right themselves by abolishing the forms to which they are accustomed. But when a long train of abuses and usurpations, pursuing invariably the same Object evinces a design to reduce them under absolute Despotism, it is their right, it is their duty, to throw off such Government, and to provide new Guards for their future security.—Such has been the patient sufferance of these Colonies; and such is now the necessity which constrains them to alter their former Systems of Government. The history of the present King of Great Britain is a history of repeated injuries and usurpations, all having in direct object the establishment of an absolute Tyranny over these States. To prove this, let Facts be submitted to a candid world.

Figure 6.1 The second paragraph in the Declaration of Independence.

The Declaration of Independence, drafted in 1776, is a classic text in American history because it explicitly states beliefs that have shaped a government and a national identity. To find explicit mention of many presuppositions about liberty, we need look no further than the Declaration's second paragraph. (See Figure 6.1.) The first two sentences, in fact, constitute an enthymeme based upon a set of "self-evident" truths:

Datum:	All men are created equal [. . .] endowed by their Creator with certain unalienable Rights [. . .] among these are Life, Liberty and the pursuit of Happiness.
Claim:	To secure these rights, Governments are instituted among Men, deriving their just powers from the consent of the governed.

The warrant to this enthymeme can be stated as a "since" clause: Since these free individuals existed before their government and would only associate to protect the rights that they enjoyed before joining a community. Thus, we have the first presupposition in our ideology.

WRITE AN ANALYSIS

Though we encourage you to look for as yet undiscovered ideologies, we acknowledge that most rhetorical analysts begin by reading and building upon other people's work. Ideology analysis requires such a large knowledge of culture, context, and history, that few can achieve the task alone. We often allow other people to describe the ideology, and we contribute to that conversation by offering one more analysis or a set of analyses to contest or support a given position. This chapter and the analyses contained therein are both heavily indebted to previous arguments. The two of us did not discover these ideas about liberty. We've read a number of books about liberalism and its central tenets. And we decided to write about this ideology and two of its iterations in part because one of us has expertise in early-American political discourse. So, in this chapter, we are building upon cultural, historical, and rhetorical work that we've inherited. Read another other person's description of an ideology. We recommend a few sources:

- The historian David M. Kennedy contends that Franklin Delano Roosevelt redefined liberty. FDR contended that liberty should include freedom from the insecurity, want, and fear created by the Great Depression and the two world wars. (See Kennedy's book *Freedom from Fear: The American People 1929–1945* [1999].)

- Paulina Borsook claims to have located an ideology of *cyberlibertarianism* in many persuasive efforts that appeared during the dot-com boom of the late 1990s. (See her article "Cyberselfish." *Mother Jones* July/August 1996, <http://www.motherjones.com/news/feature/1996/07/borsook.html>.)

- Thomas Frank claims to have located an ideology of *market populism* in many political arguments made by right-wing pundits and conservative politicians in the late twentieth century. (See his article "The Rise of Market Populism: America's New Secular Religion." *The Nation* 30 Oct 2000, <http://www.thenation.com/doc/20001030/frank>.)

- Walter Newell claims to have located an ideology of *postmodernism* in many arguments made by Western leftist philosophers and radical Islamicists in the early twentieth century. (See his article "Postmodern Jihad: What Osama Bin Laden Learned from the Left." *The Weekly Standard 26* Nov 2001, <http://www.weeklystandard.com/Content/Public/Articles/000/000/000/553f-ragu.asp>.)

Then, write an analysis of a particular argument to show that this discourse does (or does not) depend upon the ideology that one of the previously mentioned writers describes.

- Does Norman Rockwell's *Four Freedoms*, a painting designed to trumpet FDR's expansion of government and the U.S. involvement in World War II, offer new presuppositions about liberty?

- Does "Cyberspace and the American Dream," one of the most commonly read documents in high-tech culture (available at <http://www.pff.org/issues-pubs/futureinsights/fi1.2magnacarta.html>) appeal to a cyberlibertarian ideology as Borsook describes it?

- Does a recent opinion article in the *Wall Street Journal* draw on the presuppositions of market populism, as Frank describes it?

- Does postmodern ideology, as Newell describes it, warrant the arguments in one of the articles that Newell cites?

The second paragraph in the Declaration continues to build upon the claim established by the first two sentences, thereby forming an epicheireme that depends upon another unstated warrant (a presupposition):

Datum: To secure these rights, Governments are instituted among Men, deriving their just powers from the consent of the governed.

Claim: SO Whenever any Form of Government becomes destructive of these ends, it is the Right of the People to alter or to abolish it.

Warrant: SINCE Preservation of these rights (to freedom) is good and desirable for the individuals who possess them.

A series of arguments (enthymemes) follows, but we will skip ahead to one in particular:

Datum: When a long train of abuses and usurpations, pursuing invariably the same object evinces a design to reduce them under absolute Despotism, it is their right, it is their duty, to throw off such Government, and to provide new Guards for their future security.— Such has been the patient sufferance of the Colonies.

Claim: SO such is now the necessity which constrains them to alter their former Systems of Government.

Warrant: SINCE Suffering under tyranny makes it possible to rebel in the name of liberty.

We skip ahead to this particular enthymeme because it relies upon a key presupposition in the ideology we're investigating (and arguably a key presupposition in any ideology). To explain, allow us a brief digression.

As we mentioned in Chapter 3, material topics provide the rhetor with presuppositions on which to build arguments. Aristotle (*Rhetoric* 2.19) pointed to three that we find particularly useful and that have been repeated in sociological writing about ideology. (For application of these topics in contemporary theories of ideology, see Göran Therborn's *The Ideology of Power and the Power of Ideology*, 1980).

- Past and future fact. What has happened? What exists? (This can also be discussed as a material topic of the real.)

- Greater/lesser. What is better or worse? (This can also be discussed as a topic of the preferable or as a topic for arranging hierarchies of value.)

- Possible/impossible. What is probable (likely or unlikely)? What is likely (easy or hard)? (This is another material topic of the real.)

Based on our above analysis, it is evident that the Declaration would have us believe the following: Free individuals exist prior to any government (past fact). Preservation of freedom is good and its opposite, despotism, is bad (greater/lesser). Rebellion in the name of liberty is possible (possible/impossible) in certain circumstances.

FOR FURTHER DISCUSSION

We have explained, at various points in this book, that all arguments (print, oral, visual, etc.) depend upon presuppositions and can be analyzed as enthymemes. Though we focus on two textual arguments in this chapter, we'll note that the constellation of ideas associated with "liberty" gets invoked in a number of visual arguments as well. Take the following political cartoon by Lisa Benson (8 March 2010, retrieved from http://townhall.com/cartoons/cartoonist/LisaBenson). How does this image's argument depend upon the belief that liberty exists, that it's good, or that it is possible to rebel against any institution that curtails liberty?

SEARCHING FOR IDEOLOGICAL OVERLAP

In our discussion so far, we've pointed to one ideology in one discourse. We do this to emphasize how important these presuppositions are to a particular argument. But we don't want to give the false impression that each and every discourse relies on only one ideology. Far from it. Most discourses, like most people, rely upon a range of beliefs. In this next section, we will talk about analyzing multiple ideologies in one argument. We call this an analysis of *ideological overlap*.

We begin with a method not unlike the one just described. We analyze enthymemes, searching for their warrants, and particularly looking for constellations of warrants—presuppositions about what is, what is good, and what is possible. In this case, however, we will look for multiple ideologies. Having identified one constellation of beliefs associated with liberty, we will consider another constellation of beliefs associated with Christianity.

In this case, the search for presuppositions in enthymemes is not entirely necessary because the authors of the Declaration explicitly state a Judaeo-Christian belief: A Creator exists and endows people with certain inviolable characteristics. Genesis 1:27 reports that God created Adam in God's likeness, thus giving people unique characteristics. But the answers to the next two questions (what is good and what is possible) require a bit more searching. Returning to the second enthymeme analyzed, we find that another religious belief provides backing to support the warrant:

Datum:	To secure these rights, Governments are instituted among Men, deriving their just powers from the consent of the governed.
Claim:	SO whenever any Form of Government becomes destructive of these ends, it is the Right of the People to alter or to abolish it.
Warrant (unstated):	SINCE preservation of these rights (to freedom) is good and desirable for the individuals who possess them.
Backing (unstated):	BECAUSE it is good to preserve rights that have been given to people by their Creator.

Similarly, a religiously grounded presupposition backs the warrant of the third enthymeme analyzed:

Datum:	When a long train of abuses and usurpations, pursuing invariably the same object evinces a design to reduce them under absolute Despotism, it is their right, it is their duty, to throw off such Government, and to provide new Guards for their future security.—Such has been the patient sufferance of the Colonies.
Claim:	SO such is now the necessity which constrains them to alter their former Systems of Government.
Warrant (unstated):	SINCE suffering under tyranny makes it possible to rebel in the name of liberty.
Backing (unstated):	BECAUSE the divine grant of freedom makes liberty a just and defensible cause sanctioned by "the laws of nature and of nature's God."

In fact, we might consider the sentences about what "prudence [. . .] will dictate" as a qualification to the previously stated enthymeme. Everything just stated is true *unless* people can suffer having their divine rights violated.

With or without the qualification, we have stumbled upon another constellation of ideas about what is, what is good, and what is possible: A creator is. The rights endowed by that creator are good. It is possible to rebel against a government that violates these rights in an insufferable way. We can also see that the ideology associated with liberty and the ideology associated with Judaeo-Christian religion overlap one another in the Declaration of Independence. Each ideology contributes to a common set of inferences in interesting and related ways. (Of course, this need not be the case. One can build an argument on the presuppositions about liberty without believing in a creator or a set of divinely granted rights.) Noticing ideological overlap allows us to see how complex and interrelated beliefs make an argument persuasive. This analysis also explains how ideologies can change. Allow a brief theoretical digression.

The theory of ideologies, as sketched previously, assumes that there is no entirely nonideological existence, just as there is no entirely nonrhetorical existence. People are social animals. We need symbols to get along with one another and to make sense of our world. And we inherit those symbols from others. We don't each decide for ourselves what is, what is good, and what is possible. Other people teach us what they have learned from other people.

It is safe to say that people believe multiple and often conflicting ideologies, just as they participate in many communities. People may identify with a nationalist ideology and a religious ideology, both at once, claiming that they are both British and Protestant, both Italian and Catholic. People identifying with several ideologies are able to leverage one set of beliefs against another, sometimes reconciling them, sometimes synthesizing them, sometimes discarding them and integrating novel ideas. (Behavioral psychologists often use the term *cognitive dissonance* to reference the conflicts among ideological presuppositions within one person's understanding.) Like the contemporary rhetorical theorist Barbara Biesecker, who borrows heavily from Kenneth Burke, we are suggesting that rhetoric begins with people, not with ideology. Or, paraphrasing Biesecker (who paraphrases Burke)—not language, but *homo dialecticus* (the dialoguing animal) is the zero ground for society. (See Biesecker's *Addressing Postmodernity: Kenneth Burke, Rhetoric, and a Theory of Social Change*, 1997.) Societies—and arguments—begin with people. Individuals encounter languages, learn beliefs, join communities. But these same individuals can find novel ways to use these languages, these beliefs, and these communities. And so the authors of the Declaration can find ways to be both devotees of liberty and Christianity. Moreover, they can invent a new national identity—citizens of the United States—as well as a relatively new set of beliefs that make others feel like they, too, are U.S. citizens.

METHODS OF ANALYSIS

When discussing ideologies in this chapter, we have often invoked the "constellation" metaphor to emphasize an ideology's organic nature. A constellation is a collection of otherwise distinct objects whose relationship only becomes evident when they are placed in proximity and in a certain relation to one another. The items in a constellation aren't arranged vertically; none appears more foundational than another, though some terms are more central and others more distal. You can similarly think of an argument as a constellation of proofs. We are preceded in our "constellation" metaphor by Kenneth Burke, who developed a method of cluster analysis, which we find useful in describing both ideologies and arguments. (See the title essay in Burke's *Philosophy of Literary Form* [1941].) Burke hypothesized that some "clusters" are "public"; such clusters are shared by many people. He also contended that the items in a cluster "identify" the other items; the meaning of each is determined by its relationship to the other terms. We have said similar things about ideologies—ideologies are shared by many people, they are appealed to in public circumstances, and an ideology is made of both its presuppositions and their relation to one another. Burke provides a method of cluster analysis that we can easily apply to ideologies. Following Burke, we can draw a cluster of the terms and ideas associated with liberty, placing the central presuppositions at the center and the distal presuppositions toward the outer edges. Thus, we invent a new map of this ideology. Taking our cluster analysis below as a model, try to draw your own cluster of ideas and terms associated with the ideology you want to analyze.

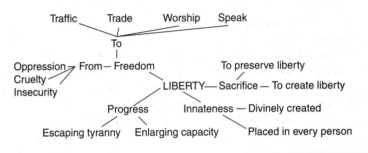

SEARCHING FOR IDEOLOGICAL EXTENSION

The Declaration of Independence may be one of the first, but certainly not the last, arguments about liberty in American history. It is, nonetheless, one of the most persuasive. In the eighteenth century, the Declaration was printed in newspapers across the colonies, inciting agreement among those who loved liberty and those who opposed the British. The Revolutionary War is a testimony to this document's persuasive impact. For more than two hundred years, American citizens have been introduced to the Declaration and invited to accept its presuppositions. For more than two hundred years, Americans have sided with liberty and against oppression, with divine law and against human law, with democracy and against tyranny. Liberty, therefore, persists and is given new life every time a seventh-grade civics class is inspired by the words, "We hold these truths to be self-evident." This ideology, like all others, lives in specific arguments. And ideology in general, as Burke once explained, "derives from [human] nature as a 'symbol-using animal'" (*Rhetoric of Motives* [Berkeley: University of California Press, 1969], p. 146).

As we've already explained, analysis of ideology often begins with a belief that people exist before language. Though our beliefs and our identities may depend upon language, we precede these beliefs and identities. We can therefore change them. We can do things to ideologies—like bringing them together in an argument. In this section, and in the following method of analysis, we will explain another theory of language and of social change. Doing so will require another theoretical digression on performance.

A number of contemporary rhetorical theorists question the separation of individual people from ideologies. They wonder if the human agent really is the zero-ground for societies. Perhaps societies (and people's identities) begin with language. Perhaps *we* don't exist before or without our beliefs about who *we* are. Contemporary rhetorician Judith Butler, for instance, asks us to question whether or not a person's "substantive being" precedes language. She invites us to consider Burke's *homo dialecticus* as a creation of language: "a relative point of convergence among culturally and historically specific sets of relations" (*Gender Trouble: Feminism and the Subversion of Identity* [New York: Routledge, 1990], p. 10). If Butler is right, if our identities don't come before our beliefs, then we cannot suppose that individual people adopt and alter beliefs to suit their purposes. In the words of Friedrich Nietzsche, the nineteenth-century German philosopher whose work influenced Butler and many of her contemporaries: "there is no 'being' behind 'doing' [. . .]; the 'doer' has simply been added to the deed by the imagination" (*Geneology of Morals*, 1887, XIII). We don't speak language. Language speaks us. So we can't look to the individual agent (the person doing the talking) to find out how ideologies and arguments change because that individual person doesn't exist without those ideologies and those arguments.

We're left with a troubling question: If ideologies and individuals are all part of the same rhetorical mix, then how do ideas and communities change? Butler offers an answer with her theory of performativity. Butler contends that ideologies do not exist independently of arguments. In fact, when we speak of an ideology as if it were a stable object outside of its manifestations, we may misrepresent the situation. An ideology may not exist independent of the symbols constituting it, any more than a dance exists independent of its performances. A skilled dance instructor can sketch the foot traffic of a tango or a waltz, just as a skilled rhetorical critic can sketch the points in an ideological constellation, but these sketches do not represent anything real. The dance happens in the performance. The ideology emerges in the argument. Since ideologies don't exist independent of their performances, there is always the chance that a rhetorical performance, by differing slightly from its predecessors, can change an ideology altogether. In fact, we might go so far as to say that every appropriation of an ideology is unique, just as every dance is slightly different from previous performances. The performative nature of ideologies leads us to conclude that they are not static objects. Furthermore, the performative nature of ideologies accounts for change without supposing that ideological change requires a person. Ideologies (and communities) change because they keep getting performed in arguments, and every argument is a little different from those that it resembles.

To analyze an ideology's performance, you must concentrate on change without worrying about the agent. Later in this chapter, we will look at King's extension of liberty in his "Letter." For the time being, however, we will discuss one more method of ideological analysis: searching for paradoxes.

SEARCHING FOR IDEOLOGICAL PARADOXES

Before we explore this last approach to ideology analysis, we'll ask for your patience as we present our last theoretical digression, an explanation of the difference between willed and organic ideologies. According to the early twentieth-century political theorist Antonio Gramsci, willed ideologies are explicitly stated and developed by particular people or groups of people. Since willed ideologies are invented all at once and are explicitly stated, they tend to be internally consistent. One will find few evident contradictions in such a system of belief. Think of a platform statement for a political party, for instance. A committee sits down to hash out these ideas and is thus likely to notice two presuppositions that openly contradict one another. Organic ideologies, on the other hand, develop over time, as arguments get made and communities get formed. Organic ideologies can take years, decades, centuries, even millennia to develop. Therefore, organic ideologies tend to remain both unstated and commonsensical. And they tend to tolerate more inconsistency, more contradictions. Organic ideologies tend to be *paradoxical*. They often include apparently nonsensical combinations of ideas.

The word *paradox* derives from two Greek roots: *para*, meaning "alongside of" or "standing apart from and contrary to" (as in parallel lines); and *doxa*, meaning "commonly held belief." This brief reference to the word's Greek roots suggests a definition that we find analytically useful. A paradox can be defined as two commonly held opinions standing side by side but not meeting (perhaps seeming to contradict) one another. For the rhetorical analyst of an ideology, a paradox consists of two conflicting ideas contained in a common doxa. These paradoxes sometimes reflect and sometimes promote the conflicts within a given society.

The notion of a paradox helps us to understand how an ideology makes a logos appeal possible without also requiring the consistency normally associated with logic. We emphasize the paradoxical nature of ideologies to offer one final technique for rhetorical analysis but also to explain something about *logos*. *Logos* includes any proof that depends upon ideas and their use in argumentation. The ideas themselves may contradict one another. Arguments are collections of proofs to form an argument. Ideologies are collections of ideas to form a community. Looking for paradoxes within an ideology helps us to see the tensions that have developed over time and over numerous arguments in specific rhetorical situations. Once you've established that an ideology exists (by searching for presuppositions in one document), that multiple ideologies overlap one another (by looking for competing or complementary ideographs in one argument), and that an ideology has been variously performed in different circumstances (by investigating the multiple and differing extensions of this ideology), you can argue that the ideology has certain productive tensions resulting from its organic nature. Locating these tensions (what we call *paradoxes*) is one useful manner of rhetorically analyzing an ideology because convincing arguments are often able to synthesize potentially conflicting ideas in an ideology by applying them to a particular kairos.

Next, we explore King's "Letter," demonstrating that he invokes many of the core presuppositions associated with liberty, that he extends them in interesting ways, that Judaeo-Christian beliefs underpin his assertions about liberty, and that his "Letter" is so persuasive in part because it is able to resolve a paradox found among this ideology's presuppositions.

SAMPLE ANALYSIS: PARADOXICAL LIBERTY IN KING'S "LETTER"

American ideas about liberty include a paradox: Those who wish to enjoy liberty must sacrifice their own freedoms. Of course, anyone who identifies with this ideology will quickly assert that this statement is only contradictory at an initial glance. Citizens are asked to sacrifice their ability to do whatever they choose by agreeing to a rule of law. This rule of law, when equally enforced, will allow everyone greater freedom. For example, early Americans agreed to a stronger national government and a tighter rule of federal law so that the entire nation could enjoy greater liberty. In fact, during the eighteenth century, many worried that a standing national army would take away people's freedom. Those championing such an army, however, pointed to Shays' Rebellion (1786), saying that the minor sacrifice of liberty to a federal army would protect freedoms threatened whenever individual citizens took up arms and broke laws. This claim's persuasive appeal depends, in part, on the rhetor's ability to resolve the paradox. Thus, we can explain an argument's persuasive ability by noting its ability to synthesize conflicting beliefs in a single ideology. Martin Luther King, Jr.'s "Letter from Birmingham Jail" is persuasive, as we will argue later, in part because the argument makes sense of a paradox in the ideology of liberty.

To explore this ideological paradox, we should first notice that liberty is central to many of King's arguments. His beliefs about liberty overlap with his Judaeo-Christian beliefs. King invokes liberty in many of his most persuasive enthymemes. As early as the third paragraph, he presupposes the existence and the value of human liberty in a key logos appeal:

Datum: Just as the prophets of the eighth century B.C. left their villages and carried their "thus saith the Lord" far beyond the boundaries of their home towns, and just as the Apostle Paul left his village of Tarsus and carried the gospel of Jesus Christ to the far corners of the Greco-Roman world . . .

Claim: SO am I compelled to carry the gospel of freedom beyond my own home town.

Needless to say, the above argument relies upon many presuppositions. To accept this argument, for instance, we must accept that those who seek to protect human rights must often travel to foreign places. Also among the presuppositions required to believe this enthymeme, however, are the following ideas—each associated with liberty and Judaeo-Christian religions: Freedom exists in every person; freedom is guaranteed by God and presented in a Gospel that God's followers must preach. At numerous other points in the argument, King invokes "freedom" and Judaeo-Christian tradition together in arguments about his purpose and his methods in Birmingham.

Furthermore, King extends these ideologies into a defense of direct action. While Federalists in the late eighteenth century contended that a more robust state with a stronger army would increase human liberty, King insists that direct action may violate the law, but it will promote freedom for all humankind. In paragraph 24, he contends that direct action can reveal the tensions already present in society, the injustices that interrupt human liberty. Direct action can force people to see and to correct injustice—to increase freedom. King's ability to persuade surely depends upon his extension of liberty into a defense of direct action. Likewise, his "Letter" is moving in part because it draws upon two long-standing and oft-allied ideographs—liberty and Christianity. But the "Letter," perhaps, is most persuasive because King resolves a paradox often found in the cluster of beliefs about human liberty.

In paragraphs 15–22, King himself wrestles with the paradox of liberty and its most commonly accepted resolution as he defends his decision to break laws through a campaign of nonviolence. King found himself in the same position as the Massachusetts rebels who followed Daniel Shays into an illegal course of resistance against a local government. Those identifying with American liberty, those familiar with and accepting of the presuppositions that make up the paradox of liberty, may be inclined to label King a threat to liberty. They have heard a number of arguments contending that we must sacrifice some liberties (such as our ability to parade in any city at any time) to ensure greater liberty for everyone. This commonly argued resolution stands as part of the community's *doxa* and must be addressed if King is to clear the way for his own resolution to the paradox of liberty. King must convince his audience that his actions don't violate liberty. If he fails to do so, his readers may conclude that he does not hold dear their beliefs. He does not accept their ideology, and is therefore not part of their community. From this perspective, what appears most interesting is King's ability to assert certain ideological mainstays, while rhetorically reaching toward a new synthesis, a resolution that does not divide him from those who champion American freedom.

At the beginning of paragraph 15, King concedes that his course of action appears to threaten liberty by encouraging protesters to break some laws even as he insists that everyone obey other laws to guarantee the freedoms so long denied to African-Americans. Some in King's audience may be inclined to believe that selective obedience to the law threatens freedom. An audience who identifies with this ideology may therefore separate themselves from King and the civil-rights movement. To prevent this, King proclaims his dedication to liberty in this crucial paragraph, saying that those worried about his decision to break laws have voiced "a legitimate concern." He also offers his own resolution to the paradox of liberty by distinguishing between "just and unjust laws." (King's argument about just and unjust laws invokes the formal topics of "genus and species" and "difference," which we discuss in Chapter 3.) King argues that enemies of liberty break just laws, while liberty's proponents often violate unjust laws to preserve just laws. He identifies with the champions of liberty. He divides the civil-rights movement from those who support unjust laws. The intended audience, those already believing in liberty, will imagine that they belong to King's community because they share his commitment to just laws. And they will separate themselves from any community defending Birmingham's unjust laws.

We can extend this analysis by noticing King's simultaneous appeal to liberty and to Judaeo-Christian beliefs. Since the Declaration of Independence, Americans have argued that liberty is a God-given right, forming a community that loves freedom and follows a divine order. King echoes these presuppositions when he quotes St. Thomas Aquinas, saying, "An unjust law is a human law that is not rooted in eternal law and natural law." Since "segregation distort[s] the soul and damages the personality," any laws supporting its continuance must be unjust, so supporting such laws opposes liberty. King even broadens his appeal by quoting Martin Buber, a Jewish philosopher. Just laws are not only for Christians who follow Aquinas. They are also for Jews who agree with Buber. All people identifying with these figures should obey the 1954 Supreme Court ordinance and should disobey segregation statutes.

In the space of two paragraphs, King has adopted a stance that includes justice, the Judaeo-Christian tradition, and obedience to divine laws that further liberty. He has also divided himself from those who obey human laws that rob African-Americans of their liberty. Finally, he has offered a new solution to the paradox of liberty: Those who wish to enjoy liberty must sacrifice their own freedoms by obeying divine just laws and by disobeying human unjust laws.

In paragraphs 17–19, King continues his exposition on just and unjust laws, further asking the audience to accept his understanding of liberty. We are told that unjust laws compel a minority to follow a rule that is not imposed on the empowered majority, that Alabama voting statutes are unjust, and that a law can be "just on its face and unjust in its application" as when King was arrested for violation of a law against parading without a permit. In paragraph 20, King begins to reassure his audience that he adheres to the ideology of liberty by refusing to join a community that advocates anarchy. King says, "In no sense do I advocate evading or defying the law, as would the rabid segregationist. That would lead to anarchy." Only a "rabid segregationist" who favors a particularly heinous ideograph—"anarchy"—would refuse to suffer the penalties for his actions. King, a proponent of liberty, accepts his penalty, as he sits in a Birmingham city jail scrawling his missive on scraps of paper.

In paragraph 21, King compares himself to past advocates of liberty: early disobedient Christians who fought unjust Roman laws and bravely faced "hungry lions," Socrates who willingly suffered death rather than recant his beliefs, and early-American revolutionaries who threw British tea into the Boston harbor to protest unjust British taxes. The readers are invited to join a community of admirable figures, presumably all adhering to the ideology of liberty and its newly resolved paradox. Readers are also invited to leave a community of segregationists: Alabama's legislative representatives and the state's citizens who oppose the civil-rights movement. Paragraph 22 continues in this vein, reminding the readers that Adolph Hitler and communist governments have created and obeyed unjust laws, while those who disobey such laws champion liberty by aiding and comforting Jews or by continuing to practice their freedom of worship despite the consequences. King places himself in good company, making it difficult for readers to divide themselves from such an admirable, and admirably just, community.

These paragraphs from King's "Letter" are not the only novel invocation of liberty. In fact, this ideology persists in American public discourse in part because arguments continually repeat these principal ideas in peculiar rhetorical situations. We are continually rethinking the paradox of sacrificing our liberties to preserve them. Our ideas about liberty persist because of these reiterations, these reinterpretations in new circumstances. King, therefore, fits in a long tradition of Americans, including Thomas Jefferson and Alexander Hamilton—people who seek to continue a valuable ideological constellation by rhetorically reiterating its core paradox in kairotic ways. This analysis not only explores a particular argument, it also explores an element common to many arguments about liberty. In American public discourse, to speak of liberty is to wrestle with its central contradiction—to rhetorically seek out a resolution to this contradiction in specific rhetorical situations. Persuasive efforts that fail to resolve this paradox will appear less substantial, less convincing. Perhaps so many people identify with King and the civil-rights movement today because of his rhetorical solution to an enduring contradiction in a distinctly American ideology.

QUESTIONS FOR ANALYSIS

Rhetorical analysis of an ideology requires summary and description of two things: (1) a persuasive effort; and (2) the ideology that you claim has shaped and been shaped by this persuasive effort. Therefore, this mode of rhetorical analysis poses unique challenges that we have not yet explored. Since the critical scope is no longer limited to one argument, performance, parade, or picture, the analyst must continually shift between the narrowly focused description of an argument and the broadly focused description of an ideograph. At the outset, you might consider summarizing and describing these two things separately from one another. Consider the following questions as probes into a particular argument and the ideology that this argument depends upon:

Questions About the Argument

- What does the rhetor want you to believe when you get to the end of this argument? What's the principal claim?
- What must you do, care about, or accept if you are persuaded by this argument?
- What appeals does the rhetor present in support of his argument?
- What presuppositions (warrants) do these appeals invoke?

Questions About the Ideology

- What stance would you adopt if you accepted this ideology? What kind of person would you be? What kind of person would you separate yourself from?
- What single word, image, icon, or phrase—what ideograph—encapsulates this ideology?
- What must you believe exists, is good/bad, and is possible in order to identify with this ideology?
- What paradoxes or contradictions appear among this ideology's core presuppositions?

CODA: IDEOLOGICAL ANALYSIS AS CULTURAL ANALYSIS, OR THE FIFTH RHETORICAL CANON OF MEMORY

In the first four substantive chapters of this book, we introduced you to three of the five canons of rhetoric: invention, arrangement, and style. We also briefly touched on delivery in Chapter 5. A brief introduction of the remaining canon is in order. The canon of memory in ancient times helped students to remember their arguments so that they could speak without a script. Even today, memory is often treated as the art of remembering an argument in its entirety—a task rarely necessary in an age of teleprompters. And so, the canon of memory does not seem particularly relevant to contemporary rhetorical analysis. But there is another facet of memory that deserves our attention—public memory. Whole societies remember things that are important to them. Monuments, celebrations, important works, and references to common histories invoke public memory in the interest of creating communities of common belief.

Public memory has an ideological component. Ceremonies commemorating U.S. history invoke liberty. The good rhetor and the accomplished rhetorician, therefore, must have a vast memory of common beliefs, commonly invoked sentiments, commonly read texts. For this reason, many teachers of rhetoric from ancient times to the present have advised their students to study widely in the liberal arts and sciences. Rhetorical analysis requires a great deal of remembered information to piece together the ideologically charged components of a community's shared culture.

Rhetorical analysis of an ideology can illustrate how a society remembers the beliefs and values that its denizens hold most dear. Americans, for instance, remember liberty by constantly considering new arguments about what it means to be free. A rhetorical analysis of liberty's appearance throughout U.S. history can provide insight into cultural memory and can develop the analyst's memory as well.

7

Affect (Pathos Revisited)

While writing this chapter, one of us is also raising a four-year-old child. Often, when asked about her reasons for doing something, she simply says, "Because I felt like it." Why did you take off your shoes? Because I felt like it. Why did you stop playing hide-and-seek with us? Because I felt like it. Why did you hit your sister? Because I felt like it. Her reasoning can frustrate. It's hard to accept that feelings can sufficiently explain anything. After all, we're supposed to reason our way toward a conclusion. We're supposed to be guided by rational deliberation. We're supposed to think—not feel—before we act. Never you mind what adults suppose—the four-year-old understands something that we regularly forget. Our emotions are a big part of who we are, what we believe, and how we behave.

During the nineteenth century, William James's empirical psychology and Charles Darwin's evolutionary biology both suggested that intelligent adults reconsider the four-year-old's rationale. They told us to take emotions seriously. Darwin and James were a little late to the conversation. Four-year-old children have had good company for more than 2,000 years. Rhetoricians have been theorizing emotion and human motivation since the ancient Greeks. In fact, Aristotle offered one of the first recorded Western efforts at a psychology of emotion. Aristotle's extensive treatment of the emotions in Book II of his *Rhetoric* was probably a response to Plato's recommendation that rhetors study the psyche (see Plato's *Phaedrus* 271A-E). During the last 30 years or so, developments in social psychology, neuroscience, anthropology, and philosophy have asked many people outside of rhetorical theory to consider emotion. Some have become especially interested in the social function of bodily conditions (what we will call *affects*). In this chapter, we offer an extended look at emotion's place in rhetorical inquiry, beginning with the groundwork that Aristotle laid for us and building on his theories by importing our knowledge of contemporary developments in a variety of disciplines. Our goal is to update the classical notion of pathos.

INTERPRETATION AND AFFECT

Let's begin with Aristotle's complex picture of human emotion. Aristotle presents states such as anger and shame as psychological conditions with several roles. He specifically attributes three functions to any emotion: a bodily condition, a cognitive interpretation, and a behavioral disposition. Let's begin by exploring the first two: the bodily disposition and the cognitive interpretation. We will call these *affects* and *interpretations*, respectively. Though we separate affects and interpretations, like Aristotle, we want to emphasize that this separation does not necessarily indicate a real division. When people feel anger, it is difficult to say that they think one thing in one part of themselves and feel something else in another part of themselves. Rather, it is more elegant to propose that anger is a condition incorporating both interpretive and affective functions. Rhetorical analysis explains how these two come together, how they influence the audience, and how they are invoked by a discourse.

Later, we will offer specific methods to help you explore the affective dimension of a persuasive effort. For the moment, however, we will further explore our key terms: *affect, interpretation,* and *behavior.* We can do so by analyzing two common experiences.

Affect and Interpretation in a Typical Horror Movie

Remember the last time you watched a horror film—not an especially well-made piece of cinema, but an entertaining one. Remember the first really tense scene, the initial moment, probably twenty minutes or so into the movie, when you knew that someone was about to arrive at a grisly end. Maybe the foreboding music tipped you off. Maybe you knew something this unfortunate character didn't. (There's a killer with a chainsaw stalking the woods where you've decided to schedule your midnight romance!) Or, maybe you just had a bad feeling about one character's decision to investigate that strange noise in the darkness.

For whatever reason, you felt suspense, and you probably also felt a series of other things as the scene unfolded: terror, disgust, and then relaxation, as the tension in your body quickly dissolved. Each of these emotions can be parsed into a bodily disposition (an affect) and an interpretation. Suspense can be separated into a feeling of excitement (accelerated heart rate, dilated pupils, sweaty palms, etc.) connected to an interpretation of the situation: Something is about to happen. Terror can be separated into a similar feeling of excitement along with a different interpretation: Unspeakable danger is nearby. (Who wouldn't be terrified of a vengeful, chainsaw-wielding arborist?) Disgust can be separated into physical nausea and an interpretation of its object: You don't want to ingest or come anywhere near someone's guts, especially when dangling from a rusty gardening implement. Even the sense of relaxation can be parsed into a fading excitement and an interpretation of the situation: Finally, this horrible event is over.

Affect and Interpretation in the Fear of Looming Predators

Another common experience explains the connections among affects, interpretations, and behaviors. The "looming" phenomenon triggers a common affect (excitement) and a common behavior (duck and run for cover). This is true for many animals, humans included. Even if we perceive nothing more than a dramatic change in light, as if a bird of prey were flying over us, we feel and do these things. It is difficult to say that, while feeling excitement and fleeing the scene, we consciously interpret the situation. Our behavior is too quick to allow such a conscious appraisal. Furthermore, there is neurological evidence suggesting that our visual registration of looming may bypass the brain systems (the executive centers) that conscious deliberation depends upon.

But this does not mean that interpretation doesn't occur. It just means that we can't restrict our definition of *interpretation* to consciously experienced, higher-order cognition. For the purposes of rhetorical analysis, we advance Aristotle's solution, which gains support from contemporary empirical psychology and neuroscience without offering a final understanding of how things really work in the mind. Rhetoricians can accept that emotions involve interpretations (broadly defined), affects, and behaviors without making the effort to figure out where things happen, what comes first, or what is most important.

HOW CAN WE OBSERVE/ANALYZE AFFECT?

For the rhetorical analyst, affect presents a curious challenge—how to discuss or identify an affect when it is wound up with other psychological elements. So far, we've hinted at one approach. You can observe the bodily dispositions that participate in an experience. Therefore, the rhetorical analyst interested in closely dissecting a pathetic appeal must further separate the audience's response into affective, interpretive, and behavioral dimensions. Take one emotion in particular—disgust. Our earlier treatment of pathos helps us to analyze a horror film's ability to make the audience feel disgust, and this vocabulary may explain what this pathetic appeal does for the film's larger argument. But if you're interested in further picking apart how this appeal works, then you will need a more fine-tuned vocabulary. Let's see where *affect, interpretation,* and *behavior* get us.

Disgust is usually accompanied by several bodily dispositions (affects), such as nausea. You may even turn away (a behavior) to shield your senses. These affects and behaviors are often triggered by exposure to something that you don't want to eat or even touch. So far, we've been noticing the emotion's affective and behavioral dimensions. But when declaring something disgusting, we often comment on a physical reaction combined with something else. Our bodily disposition simply says, don't eat that, and get it away from me. But our interpretation adds to these responses. We may decide that the cinematic gore is revolting. We may cover our eyes or mouths. And we may also incorporate these bodily responses into a larger interpretation of the scene and its characters: This act and the person committing it are so vile that we cannot consider them human; this must be the work of an unsympathetic animal. Disgust can be parsed into an affect (nausea), a behavior (revulsion), and an interpretation (a belief that the killer is inhuman).

This method of analysis can help us to explain and to invent pathetic appeals. For example, the connection between revulsion/nausea and the judgment that someone is not human plays a key role in some horror films. We aren't upset when we see the maniacal gardener fall into his own wood chipper just as we are not distraught when we see a rabid dog get shot. We have been persuaded that neither deserves a dignified end because neither is human. Similar emotions have played an important role in the past century. During the Nazi pogrom, Jews were often made to do disgusting things—scrub toilets, relieve themselves publicly—to make them seem less human and more deserving of cruel treatment, even mass extermination. In our own times, prisoners are often refused access to restrooms or sanitary facilities. As the prisoners become increasingly soiled, their captors begin to feel nauseous at their presence, and more willing to see the imprisoned as less than human. This affect and its allied interpretation can be quickly tied to a set of behaviors that include indifference, cruel treatment, and perhaps torture.

Separating the affective, the behavioral, and the interpretive components of an emotion also helps us to see that we can disagree about our feelings. We believe that this ability to understand disagreement over pathos is the most significant contribution that rhetorical analysis can make to the emerging study of emotions. Too often, we imagine emotion as something that cannot be debated or changed. People declare, "That's just how I feel," as if their feelings were incontestable. But rhetorical analysis helps us to see how we can argue for different feelings about and different behaviors toward the same object.

Returning to our previous example of how one might feel when confronted with a soiled and unsanitary prisoner: You may have no control over the nausea washing over you, you may be unable to keep from recoiling, but you can incorporate these bodily responses into various interpretations, making for very different emotions. Rather than deciding that soiled prisoners are less than human, you may believe that their captors are cruel for allowing such indignity. When searching for new persuasive techniques, rhetorical analysis moves beyond an exclusive attention to reflexive behaviors and immediate affective responses. If we are always moved before we can think, then we will have no capacity to disagree or reinterpret. There will be no room for persuasion, only subliminal coercion. One famous neuroscientist, Joseph Ledoux, agrees: "The hallmark of cognitive processing is flexibility of responses on the basis of processing. Cognition gives us choices" (*The Emotional Brain: The Mysterious Underpinnings of Emotional Life* [New York: Simon and Schuster, 1996], p. 69). Noticing such choices, as they are made available by the interpretive dimension of an emotion, is an important step toward advocacy. The astute rhetorical analyst can locate an affect, can notice a behavior, can find their allied interpretation, and can theorize a new emotional appeal, incorporating the same affect into a new interpretation, a new behavioral response, and thus a wholly different argument.

Before we move on to a more extensive explanation of how to analyze pathetic appeals, we would like you to entertain a brief digression about another contemporary theory about pathos. Like Aristotle, we emphasize the interpretive part of pathos, asking you to conceptualize emotion as a cognitive as well as bodily condition. Contemporary philosophers (such as Ronald de Sousa) and contemporary psychologists (such as Richard Lazarus) have termed this a *cognitivist* approach to emotion. In contrast, you might consider a newly prominent line of rhetorical theory, which contends that affective states overtake us in a *precognitive* fashion. If the *precognitivist* theorists are right, then the element that we stress in this chapter—the interpretation—may be unnecessary or even unimportant. (See the works of psychologist Robert Zajonc, philosopher Brian Massumi, and rhetorician Diane Davis.) This theory captures something important about affect. Sometimes it is impossible to control our bodily reactions. Also, affects move from one body to another, often without an apparently interrupting interpretation. Since this is an introductory textbook, we won't venture past a quick aside about the precognitivist approach to pathos. We mention it here to explain that this chapter is not the only and certainly not the last word on rhetoric and emotion.

PATHEMATA, OR WHAT TO LOOK FOR WHEN ANALYZING AFFECT

So far, we've offered a vocabulary that is useful to rhetorical analysis of emotional appeal. Surely, *affect, interpretation,* and *behavior* will help you to explain certain appeals and to imagine other means of persuasion. But this vocabulary is not very helpful when staring at an opinion article or a commercial advertisement. Though a useful explanatory vocabulary, these terms won't help you to locate or to label the parts of an

FOR FURTHER DISCUSSION

In the documentary *Supersize Me* (2004), Morgan Spurlock eats fast food every day for three meals a day to document what this diet can do to a person. Several scenes in the movie are, quite frankly, disgusting. One in particular (23 minutes into the film) features Spurlock eating an enormous meal and then vomiting. Needless to say, the video segment (just a few minutes long) is quite difficult to watch. (You can find the entire film on YouTube.com by searching for "Supersize Me." You can find this scene in particular by searching for "Supersize Me—Morgan Spews.") Let's assume that we're right about the bodily condition that you experience while watching this. You feel nauseous, and you don't want to ingest anything that you've witnessed. What is the interpretive component in this emotional appeal? Is there room for disagreement here? For instance, can we fairly say that different audiences might interpret the scene in different ways?

1. AFFECT: Nausea

    INTERPRETATION: This person is really gross.

    EMOTION: Disgust with Spurlock.

2. AFFECT: Nausea

    INTERPRETATION: This food is really gross.

    EMOTION: Disgust with McDonald's.

Do you see other possible interpretations and therefore other possible ways to read the argument? What elements in the film might lead an audience toward one interpretation or the other?

---

argument. So far we have explained *how* a symbolic action is moving, but we have not explained *what part* of the symbolic act moves the audience. In the interest of finding these emotive elements, we resuscitate a term that was introduced briefly in Chapter 3: *pathemata*. *Pathemata* are things that provoke *pathos*. We can further subdivide them into vivid presentation and symbols with strong emotional resonance. The first step toward a complex rhetorical analysis of pathos will involve locating and labeling *pathemata* and further explaining their affective, behavioral, and interpretive dimensions.

Vivid Presentation

Why do we have such strong reactions to images rather than words? While browsing a news site, you may read that thousands of people have been injured, killed, or dislocated by a national disaster, and you may feel sympathy but no strong reaction. However, if the site presents a photogallery—or even a lone image of one victim, bloody amidst the wreckage—you are likely to feel something much stronger. Images affect us emotionally because they are vivid—they present life as it is. Video is even more vivid. While images are static, videos move and speak before us. Why read about something when you can watch it? Why stare at a still picture when you can witness the event unfold? During the early twentieth century, movies quickly supplanted radio as the dominant entertainment medium. During the early 1990s, the Internet was mostly taken up with textual information: bulletin boards and email, for instance. In the last few years, video has flooded the worldwide web. Though video's dominance in our culture is not even a century old and its dominance on the Internet is not even a decade old, rhetoricians long ago would have predicted video's ascent. Rhetoricians have long known about vivid presentation's emotional impact.

The ancient Greek term for vivid language is *enargeia*—making things move as if they were alive. This term refers to vivid description that uses words to recreate the visual (and aural and even bodily) experience of witnessing something.

SIDEBAR: A BRIEF HISTORY OF VIVID PRESENTATION

Aristotle talked about a rhetor's vivid description designed to make the audience feel a certain way about a situation, a person, or an event. Such description, said Aristotle, lays the object before the audience's eyes, making everything move and live. Several centuries later, Longinus (in his treatise on the sublime) discussed the rhetor's ability to emphasize portions of an argument by employing certain stylistic contrivances. In the twentieth century, Chaim Perelman and Lucy Olbrechts-Tyteca argued that a rhetor can give "presence" to particular beliefs and values by describing them vibrantly, by making them seem near to the audience, and by using striking rhetorical figures.

The theorist most preoccupied with vivid description and emotional appeal, however, is George Campbell, an eighteenth-century rhetorician who developed an elaborate psychological theory of how stylistic animation contributes to people's emotional responses. (Campbell relied heavily on David Hume's belief that knowledge begins with either immediate experience—sensation—or remembered experience—reflection. Since sensation is more vivid than reflection, it will be more moving.) Campbell argued that vivid representation can engage the audience, making them feel like they are actually experiencing whatever the rhetor describes. A lively representation, therefore, is not only more memorable, but it is also more inclined to elicit the affective response that we would have in a real encounter.

Campbell's theory, now more than 200 years old, presaged what contemporary neuroscientists are discovering about human perception. When we imagine an experience, our brains behave as if we were confronted with the object itself. Of course, the imagined experience will not be as intense as the immediate experience, even though the neurological activity behind each is very similar. This is all to say that, for your brain, the affective result of an imagined experience is very similar to the affective result of a sensed experience. Neuroscientist Antonio Damasio calls this phenomenon an "as if" response. Triggered by an imaginative invocation begun in one portion of the brain, another portion behaves "as if" it were responding to an external stimulus. See Damasio's *Descartes's Error: Emotion, Reason, and the Human Brain* (1994).

If rhetors can learn to present their ideas more vividly, they can increase our emotional response to portions of their arguments. We might say that the rhetor will try to get the audience affectively invested in a key part of the argument in order to move people toward a strongly felt interpretation and a related set of behaviors. To put this in George Campbell's vocabulary, "lively ideas have a stronger influence than faint ideas to induce belief" (*The Philosophy of Rhetoric*, ed. and intro. Lloyd F. Bitzer [Carbondale: Southern Illinois University Press, 1963], p. 73).

Not only visual but also textual argumentation can be analyzed through the vocabulary of vivid presentation—*affect* and *interpretation*. Consider a famous paragraph in King's "Letter." Paragraph 14 is probably the most commonly remembered passage in this document, in part because King's lively images encourage us to imagine and to understand the indignity of African-Americans' experience in the segregated

South. King describes the particular indignities that African-Americans must endure each day.

His most visually descriptive passages show the audience what segregation has inflicted upon African-Americans. King mentions "the hate-filled policemen [who] curse, kick and even kill" African-Americans. This particular image would become especially poignant shortly after the "Letter" was published in April 1963. Just one month later, the Commissioner of Public Safety, Eugene "Bull" Connor, turned attack dogs and fire hoses on nonviolent marchers, women and children included. Images of this brutality were broadcast all over American television sets. King's description surely brought to mind the cruelty that Americans saw on the evening news. But there are other vivid images that the audience can relive—having to tell your child that she must endure blatant injustice, having to sleep in a car because a motel is designated "whites only," having to witness lynch mobs that abuse your neighbors and friends without risking criminal charges, and so on.

By the end of paragraph 14, the readers who imagine these events will surely feel a series of indignities and outrages. They will experience the shame of having to tell their children of cruelties that they cannot set aright. They will feel the discomfort of having to sleep in the cold and cramped cab of an automobile when more suitable lodging should be available. If they dwell on these images long enough, their bodies may even mimic the behaviors that would accompany a real experience. They may feel a chill as they imagine a cold night spent in the car with no heat. They may feel angry tears well up as they imagine seeing their children's disappointment. Their behaviors, when conjoined with the interpretation that King advances (such occurrences are unjust), will constitute a judgment on segregation and on those who wait for reform. It will become difficult to feel all of these things and then to believe that civil-rights marchers should wait for slow-paced reform. Of course, the conclusion to this paragraph implies a behavior: Don't wait for change; fight for it now. Paragraph 14, therefore, asks us to feel a certain way, to interpret the situation in a particular light, and to follow a prescribed course of action. It is a pathetic appeal inclusive of an affect, an interpretation, and a behavior. And the pathetic appeal happens through vivid description.

FOR FURTHER DISCUSSION

Public Service Announcements (PSAs) have recently adopted many of the cine-matographic effects developed in film making to enhance their emotional impact by making the video more vivid—more like real life. We'll suggest a couple for analysis but with a word of caution. These are graphic and very disturbing videos.

- A Helen Bamber Foundation video encourages people to fight human trafficking by asking the viewer to feel like a sex slave. (This video can be found at Dailymotion.com. Search for "I am Elena" by relevance.)
- A British PSA against texting and driving makes the viewer feel like she's in the car while several teens get into a violent crash. (You can find this video on YouTube.com by searching for "PSA Peter Watkins-Hughes.") You might also consult Tara Hall's analysis of this PSA's style and its emotional appeals at the end of Chapter 5.

Each of these videos—or any other especially vivid and emotionally moving piece of video—asks two questions that deserve further discussion. First, how did the video create such a vivid experience? To ask this question another way, what particular elements make you feel like you're in the car with a bunch of injured teens or living the life of an enslaved prostitute? Second, when is an emotional appeal too vivid? In other words, at what point will the audience say we've gone too far, made the experience too real, produced an argument that's too much like real life? These questions are particularly relevant to the British PSA because this video was widely criticized for being too graphic, too realistic, too emotionally intense.

Even video—arguably the most vivid medium today—tries to recre-ate experiences to elicit strong emotional responses. Consider two elements in film making—direct cinema and the shaky camera. Direct cinema tries to recreate a "fly on the wall" perspective by videoing people who seem unaware of the camera's presence. In direct cinema, the audio quality is typically poor (as if recorded on site with no sophisticated equipment). The camera position is rarely opportune. And the people play to one another, not to the camera. The resulting experience, for the viewer, is strikingly realistic. Documentaries often reproduce techniques from direct cinema to make the argument seem more trustworthy, vivid, and real. The shaky camera (or free camera) is a cinematographic effect achieved by filming with a hand-held camera. The viewpoint is not stable—as if the viewer were watching through his or her own eyes, not through a camera on a tripod. Both the free camera and direct cinema try to make the video experience more vivid, just as King used descriptive language to make his audience live the experiences that he described.

Emotionally Resonant Symbols

We've looked for pathetic appeal in vivid presentation of text and video, but there are other kinds of *pathemata* that deserve analysis. Specific terms or symbols, if woven into emotionally powerful associative networks, can likewise lay before the audience something moving. We will discuss two such networked *pathemata*: those dependent upon an associative network established by the rhetor and those dependent upon an associative network provided by the audience.

We'll begin with *pathemata* that depend on emotional associative networks that the rhetor presents. Rhetorician I.A. Richards once posited that words are all connected into associative networks that include memories, convictions, relationships, and other words (see *The Philosophy of Rhetoric* [New York: Oxford University Press, 1971]). If his contention has any merit, then it would be difficult to believe that any single word lacks emotional resonance. Each word must be tied to some feeling. Take the word *hope,* for instance. Already, among contemporary U.S. citizens, this word has an emotional resonance, but a skilled rhetor can tie it to concepts and beliefs that are themselves emotionally resonant, giving the term even stronger pathetic appeal. To demonstrate, we turn to an Illinois state senator's attempt to tie the word *hope* to a series of emotionally resonant concepts and experiences, thus crafting a word with strong emotional impact. Listen to what Barack Obama told the Democratic Party at its 2004 convention:

> I'm not talking about blind optimism here—the almost willful ignorance that thinks unemployment will go away if we just don't think about it, or the health care crisis will solve itself if we just ignore it. That's not what I'm talking about. I'm talking about something more substantial. It's the **hope** of slaves sitting around a fire singing freedom songs; the **hope** of immigrants setting out for distant shores; the **hope** of a young

naval lieutenant bravely patrolling the Mekong Delta; the **hope** of a mill-worker's son who dares to defy the odds; the **hope** of a skinny kid with a funny name who believes that America has a place for him, too.

Obama, in this one paragraph, takes a single term and situates it in a network that includes moving episodes from America's history (slaves fighting for freedom; immigrants coming to a new world) and from the lives of the Democratic nominees for President and Vice President (John Kerry was a soldier in Vietnam; John Edwards was the son of a North Carolina millworker).

Visual arguments often similarly create networks of association in order to make emotional appeals. A recent commercial, for example, associates several emotionally compelling elements with the Blackberry corporation, thus attempting to make the audience feel something about a brand that, at the time of this commercial's production, had little emotional resonance. In 2009, smartphone users were more likely to respond enthusiastically to the Apple brand because of the very popular iPhone. This Blackberry commercial tried to generate similar enthusiasm by connecting the brand to a network of moving elements: a new band that struggles to succeed while doing something they enjoy, a popular song (the Beatles' "All You Need Is Love"), a high-energy rock concert. At the end of the commercial, as shown in Figure 7.1, all of these elements come together in a single frame that layers the words "Do what you love" (an emotionally resonant message) over the Blackberry logo (a series of ovals with one flat side), against the backdrop of a live music show. The Blackberry logo (itself not a very inspiring symbol) becomes associated with an emotionally powerful network of music, images, and narrative. The symbol itself, thus, becomes a *pathema* because of the associative network established in this commercial.

Obama and the Blackberry corporation have to go to great lengths to make their symbols (the word *hope* and the corporate logo) into pathetic appeals. But some words and symbols maintain their resonance even outside of a given argument. They become central to our ability to deal with and to understand the world. By themselves, they invoke powerful associations.

We are into the territory of associative networks that an audience already knows. One such association is invoked whenever the Apple

Figure 7.1 Closing screenshot from the Blackberry "Love What You Do" commercial (2010).

logo is presented to people who know about and like any of Apple's products. Merely showing the logo invokes a host of experiences and emotional investments. Something similar happens in political arguments. Contemporary pollsters and politicos in the United States have realized that words—like brands—resonate with people's beliefs, their experiences, and their emotions. Speechwriters, public-relations consultants, and even party leaders have become especially attentive to the emotive appeal in our day-to-day diction. They have become particularly concerned with *framing*. A speaker frames an object (a term, an idea, an institution) by carefully connecting it to emotionally moving words. For example, take the words *government* and *Washington,* two terms that have become very important to Frank Luntz, a linguist and political strategist.

In 1994, the Republican Party orchestrated their Contract with America, a series of policy statements that would help Republicans take back the House of Representatives after an extended period of Democratic dominance. Since the Contract with America stipulated that many federal programs should be reduced or eliminated, Luntz realized that he should frame these programs in a language that would bring to mind bad experiences and negative emotions. In a memo to others in his party, Luntz encouraged people to frame federal efforts

---

FOR FURTHER DISCUSSION

We've discussed a corporation's effort to create an emotionally resonant network that involved a corporate logo. Such an argument would be necessary if the logo itself didn't already evoke emotions. But many corporate logos have been around for so long that they function as values. We feel strong emotions at the mere presentation of the logo, without a network of emotionally resonant images. Take the Coca-Cola brand, for instance, or the Nike Swoosh. These logos have been around for so long and have been involved in people's daily lives so much that they evoke emotions by themselves. The companies dare not change the logos' appearance for fear that they would lose emotional appeal. Analyze an ad that includes an emotionally powerful logo. What emotions will people likely feel when they see this brand? Does the Coke logo make people feel nostalgia? Does the Nike swoosh make people feel empowered? How does the ad use this emotion in an argument?

---

slated for reduction or elimination as component parts of *Washington*; he also encouraged these same people to talk about favored programs, those Republicans may want to expand, as *government*. Listen to his explanation:

> Most Americans appreciate their local government. It picks up their trash, cleans their streets, and provides police and transportation services. Local government is okay because they often know their locally elected representatives and can visit, call, or otherwise yell at them if something goes wrong.
>
> *"Washington"* is the governmental problem. *"Washington"* spending, *"Washington"* waste, *"Washington"* taxation, *"Washington"* bureaucracy, *"Washington"* rules, and *"Washington"* regulations [. . .] So if you're an advocate of *"less"* government, better to use the language of *"making Washington accountable"* or *"making Washington more effective"* than arguing over the proper size of government (*Words that Work: It's Not What you say, It's What People Hear* [New York: Hyperion, 2007], pp. 279–280).

Following Luntz's advice, politicians have consistently invoked *Washington* when they want people to associate bad experiences and negative emotions with particular federal programs. Luntz's counterpart on the left, cognitive scientist George Lakoff, has recommended that

Democrats find frames for their own use. For instance, Lakoff recommends that Democrats talk about "taxes" as "citizenship dues," a positive frame, rather than as a "burden," a negative though more common frame. (See Lakoff's *Moral Politics*, 2002 and *Don't Think of an Elephant*, 2004).

These examples and the recent efforts to import cognitive science and linguistics theory into rhetorical analysis bring us back to a central insight offered by classical rhetoricians: To move people, you should show them *pathemata*. One kind of *pathema* is the vivid representation (the detailed description or the realistic video) that incites the audience's imagination. We might call these *images*. Another kind is the symbol (a word, a brand, a monument, an historical event) that ties into a network of affects, behaviors, and experiences. We might call these *values*.

ANALYZING EMOTIONAL REPERTOIRES

What we've said so far should keep you very busy. However, we have one more analytic concept to present. The methods of analysis presented so far tend to privilege the single discourse, prompting the analyst to wonder what emotional appeals are important to this argument. To conclude the theoretic portion of this chapter, we will introduce a concept that extends beyond the scope of a particular argument. Following the lead of contemporary rhetorical theorists, we offer some pointers for analyzing and discussing related systems of feeling as they circulate in a given culture and as they contribute to particular efforts at persuasion. To do so, we must introduce one last term—the *emotional repertoire*.

We add this term in an effort to capture an especially difficult concept. We are talking about a relatively stable range of emotions shared by a large group of people and often in response to situations or objects that these people all encounter in their public lives. An emotional repertoire not only includes a range of feelings but also a behavioral script. (We borrow the term *emotional repertoire* from Barbara Koziak who develops this notion while reflecting on Aristotelian rhetorical theory in *Retrieving Political Emotion: Thumos, Aristotle, and Gender*, 1999. Others have discussed something similar under the names *structure of feeling* [Raymond Williams] and *affective archive* [Ann Cvetkovich].) Cultures tend to approve of and encourage both emotions and behaviors related to these emotions. Though there is substantial evidence to show that certain emotions, such as happiness, sadness, anger, disgust, fear, contempt, and surprise, are universal, there is also substantial evidence to suggest that these emotions and many others get constructed in different ways by different cultures. Even more remarkable are the various behaviors associated with these emotions. Sadness in American culture is associated with a stoic outward appearance and a perseverance in one's responsibilities—the proverbial stiff upper lip. In other cultures, sadness is associated with dramatic crying or extended periods of withdrawal.

Anger is likewise a commonly felt emotion. While anger may be universal, our thoughts about and manners of expressing anger differ across cultures. The ancient Greeks thought anger was a positive experience that should be relished. Homer, in the *Iliad* (18.109), described anger as "a thing much sweeter than honey in the throat." Ancient Greek anger was often tied to habitual enactment of revenge. Twenty-first-century Americans, on the other hand, think of anger as a destructive emotion, something to be suppressed, not enjoyed. Many angry Americans try to control themselves rather than indulge in revenge or retaliation. This is not to say that every ancient Greek loved to feel angry or that all twenty-first-century Americans try to control their rage. But we can safely say that the ancient Greeks had a different repertoire for anger and a different behavior typically included in the emotion. They could distinguish several types of anger; they felt that anger was wholly appropriate in many circumstances; and they willfully indulged in angry behaviors, such as revenge. Next, we more fully explore the notion of an emotional repertoire while analyzing the VW "Why" advertisement.

SAMPLE ANALYSIS: EMOTIONAL REPERTOIRES INVOKED BY TWO PRINT ADS

For the rhetorical analyst, the notion of an emotional repertoire opens up new possibilities. We are no longer confined to the single text or to its range of emotional proofs. Just as analysis of logical appeals (enthymemes and their presuppositions) in one argument can begin an investigation of a broader ideology, so can analysis of emotional proofs in an argument begin an investigation of a broader emotional repertoire.

WRITE AN ANALYSIS

To convincingly make the case for an emotional repertoire, you have to provide a series of rhetorical analyses, demonstrating over and over again that rhetors consistently appeal to the same feelings, the same interpretations, and the same behaviors in similar circumstances and for similar purposes. Like the effort to establish that an ideology exists and is rhetorically pervasive, such an argument may lie beyond the scope of a single analysis or a brief analytic paper. If you are interested in writing such an analysis, we recommend that you begin with a single analysis of a particular pathetic appeal and then expand your analysis. Look for other texts that present similar pathetic appeals, thus constructing (and expanding) an emotional repertoire. Upon completing your analysis of a single pathetic appeal, you might ask what other persuasive efforts resemble the one you've just discussed. What do these rhetorical efforts and rhetorical situations share?

You can also write an analysis of a commonly felt emotion, something people already experience together and in public circumstances. Take school pride, for instance. There is certainly an affective dimension to this condition (people feel strong, self-assured, powerful), just as there is a bodily disposition (biologists notice that animals, like humans, adopt a common comportment when feeling victorious—head high, chest thrust out). And there is an interpretive dimension as well. To feel school pride, one must believe that his or her school is good if not better than another (or all others) for some reason. But this emotion gets invoked in a variety of arguments and situations. Fight songs at football games invoke school pride to incite cheering. Singing the alma mater at graduation ceremonies invokes school pride to encourage a lasting bond with (and perhaps to solicit alumni contributions from) graduates. Write an analysis of two or three pathetic appeals to the same emotional repertoire in the interest of exploring its range.

In the interest of demonstrating the possibility here, we turn to the two advertisements reprinted in this book's appendices.

A brief glance at these two advertisements reveals that they engage the viewer's emotions in very different ways. In this analysis, we will focus our attention on the ads' visual images, treating them as *pathemata* that invoke certain affects and interpretations in the intended audience's psyche. These responses belong to broader emotional repertoires that were common in mid-twentieth-century American consumer culture.

Let's begin with the images in the Chrysler ad. Three visually dynamic stylized images of different vehicles dominate the ad, while four smaller images focus on specific features, such as the pushbutton dash or the automatic door locks switch. Close attention to these images reveals that they're very clean—probably artistically touched up photographs—creating a realistic effect without risking the grainy imperfections common to photographs before digital manipulation. These crisp images appear more lively, more vivid (even though they're not, technically, live). The three images also depict variety by showing three different models with noticeably different features in three identifiably different colors. All of this requests a heightened affective engagement from the viewer, insisting that we get excited about the variety before us, the technological wonder of a modern dashboard, the gleaming chrome trim, the tail lights that resemble rockets, and the fenders that appear to cut through the air like a shark's fin slices through water.

Each car is positioned on an angle, allowing the viewer to see two sides and therefore more of the product's sleek details. The three images of the vehicles themselves reinforce this sense of excitement and motion by showing the cars from the front, from the side, or from the back as if they were driving toward, past, or away from us. This sense of motion is reinforced by the lighting in each image. Long white lines of refracted light bounce off the cars' highly polished surfaces. These arrowlike reflections imply that the vehicles are racing along, an implication underscored by sharp fenders and forward-leaning grilles that seem aggressively to confront the air. Some of the images even attempt to recreate motion in a static format. Children in one station wagon happily look out, perhaps gazing at some roadside attraction or national landmark as it recedes on the rear horizon. We see a gloved hand actuating the door lock lever. Arrows show that the rear window raises and lowers at the touch of a button. A detailed cutaway image shows how to open the rear door and lift the floor panel to access a secure luggage compartment. In all, this ad's images try to create a certain affect in the viewer—excitement—by vividly representing motion.

These images tie this affect to an interpretation by including certain kinds of people interacting with the product in certain ways. The people are all quite obviously members of one family or another. No children appear without a mother or father. In one image, for example, a little girl clutches her stuffed teddy bear and playfully flirts with her mother through the side window. Thus an interpretation is formed: "These are family-friendly vehicles." The body text underscores this interpretation by explaining that Plymouth designers "know what parents are up against" so they built a car to remind parents of "how happy" they should be "to have a family of kids—even on a long haul." (Such a message is particularly kairotic in this issue of *Life*, which features a story about road trips in the southeastern United States.) By tying the affective component (excitement) to the interpretation (these are family-friendly vehicles), the images in this ad make an emotional appeal.

What does any of this have to do with an emotional repertoire? Like rhetorical analyses of ideologies, rhetorical analyses of emotional repertoires must begin with specific texts, teasing out the affective and interpretive dimensions of their emotional appeals and claiming that these pathetic arguments are not peculiar to this one discourse. So far, we have looked carefully at the visual imagery in the Chrysler ad, and we've claimed that these images invoke a sense of excitement to convince American families that they should purchase and enjoy this brand of car. As it turns out, we are not immediately interested in this ad's appeal to an emotional repertoire. Rather, we want to investigate a different emotional repertoire that appeared on the American consumer landscape in the early 1960s. We choose to do so by comparing the emotional appeals in the VW and the Chrysler ads. By offering such a *comparative analysis*, we hope to model one more way to investigate broad rhetorical trends in dialogue with one another.

Glancing at the three images of VW Beetles alongside the images of the Chrysler station wagons, many stark differences become apparent. The Chrysler ad showcases three different cars from flattering, exciting angles that imply motion and that maximize the amount of the vehicle shown. The images themselves take up the majority of the ad's two pages. The three images of VW Beetles, on the other hand, take up barely a fifth of the ad's space, and they give the viewer one very uninteresting and unflattering angle from which to inspect these nearly identical cars. Other than the different license plate numbers, a viewer is hard pressed to find any differences among the three VWs. The Volkswagens do not seem to be in motion—they boast no long lines implying progress, and they are all absent any people (passengers or drivers). They seem to be parked in front of us. Moreover, these are not crisp, clean images. They are grainy photographs. If the pictures of the Chrysler station wagons got us excited, it seems reasonable to say that the VW images ask us to feel very little about these cars. We become, upon viewing these images, affectively disinvested.

How can a lack of excitement be part of a pathetic appeal? If we can make the case that this ad's effort to suppress affect is part of a broader emotional repertoire and tied to an interpretation, it seems entirely reasonable to say that the marketers at Doyle Dane Bernbach were trying to make something persuasive out of such a *cool* feeling. Following a number of critics, we contend that consumer culture in the early twentieth century was built around a pervasive and excessive excitement, a hypertrophy of affect. Advertisements asked people to get emotional about everything from cars to soup. This resulted in some hyperbolic rhetoric, certainly, and it also contributed to a counterculture that refused to care about much of anything. When mid-twentieth-century jazz musicians decided to forego a high-energy big-band sound and shift toward smaller groups and less intense performances, they purposefully moved away from "hot" swing, a la Louis Armstrong, and toward "cool" jazz, a la Charlie Parker. Similarly, in advertising, we find an effort to get away from the affective intensity found in the Chrysler ad and to engage consumers in a *cool* register that would appeal to baby boomers raised on and cynical toward the bombast washing over them every time they opened a magazine or turned on the television.

The VW images are everything that the Chrysler images are not—uninteresting, uniform, unflatteringly realistic, static, small, and positioned so that the reader's eye neither moves toward nor fixates on them. Such a persuasive effort participates in the *cool* emotional repertoire developing in American popular and consumer culture during the early 1960s. It appealed to an audience of young people wanting to reject the high-energy consumerism that their parents adored during the post-war years. If cool is the affective component of this pathetic appeal, then we must ask what the interpretive component is. To find it, a reader must consult the text immediately below these images and toward the bottom of the page. Rather than selling emotional investment, this text promises low gas mileage, reliability, and inexpensive, infrequent maintenance. We are told that the VW Beetle gets good gas mileage, is cheap, and will rarely break down, unlike other cars, presumably those bejeweled with a host of features. The interpretation: "This is a practical, inexpensive car." When tied to the images' serene affective resonance, this interpretation comes together in an emotional appeal to consumer cool, which contrasts nicely with any affectively intense advertisement.

Therefore, we can say that cool is an emotional repertoire tied to an historical and geographic kairos (mid- to late-twentieth-century America), to a set of social developments (counterculture, consumer and popular culture, and particularly advertising), and to a given audience

METHODS OF ANALYSIS

In Chapter 6, we explained that those interested in writing ideological analyses should consider building on the work of others in order to extend or contest assertions about what logos appeals persist as ideologies. We recommend a similar method when attempting to locate an emotional repertoire. Learn what others have said about a commonly felt emotion or a range of emotions. For instance, we consulted several works on cool before attempting to write our analysis. Frederic Jameson famously argued that the "postmodern condition," his shorthand term for a host of cultural developments after 1950, can be characterized by what he calls a "waning of affect," the same cool feeling that we describe in "Why." (See Jameson's *Postmodernism, or, The Cultural Logic of Late Capitalism* [Durham: Duke UP, 1991].) Alan Liu argues that cool pervades several developments in "post-fordist" culture, labor, and society, including the aesthetics of online communication and the affective dimension of working in high-technology environments. (See Liu's *The Laws of Cool: Knowledge Work and the Culture of Information* [Chicago: University of Chicago Press, 2004].) Perhaps most immediately relevant to our analysis of "Why," Thomas Frank maintains that U.S. advertising in the early 1960s was overrun by a creative revolution invested in cool consumerism. Frank pays specific attention to the DDB Volkswagen ads that we discuss in this chapter. (See Frank's *The Conquest of Cool: Business Culture, Counterculture, and the Rise of Hip Consumerism* [Chicago: University of Chicago Press, 1997].)

(baby boomers). Of course, to make this argument even more convincing, we would have to analyze several other cool texts to see if they consistently relate to consumer culture and advertising. This comparison, like our brief efforts at analyzing an ideology in several discourses (Chapter 6), begins, but by no means completes, the discussion of emotional repertoire and its rhetorical potential.

QUESTIONS FOR ANALYSIS

The first step to any close analysis of a pathetic appeal is identification of the appeal, something we briefly touched on in Chapter 3. You must ask yourself what the rhetor expects the audience to feel when reading, seeing, or hearing X. Once you've answered that question and provided evidence to support your claim, then you can begin to explain how the effort achieved its end. Once you're able to identify and describe a pathetic appeal with some specificity—to say what emotion gets evoked and to what purpose—you're ready to dissect the pathetic appeal itself. The following questions should help you to label the pathetic appeal's parts and to explain how these parts interact:

- Finding *images*: Are there any detailed (particularly visual) descriptions? Any especially realistic scenes or images? If there are particularly detailed descriptions or realistic scenes, what does the rhetor want the audience to feel when reading or seeing them—fear, discomfort, revulsion, affection, joy, sorrow? If there are particularly detailed descriptions, what stylistic devices does the rhetor use to lay this material before the audience's senses—lots of adjectives, metaphors, alliteration, cacophony, onomatopoeia? Are there any detailed, especially memorable, lively, or graphic images or video segments? If there are particularly graphic images or video segments, what focuses the audience's attention here and not elsewhere—contrast, bright colors, lighting, angle, free camera cinematography? Are there any noticeable aural effects (music, sound effects, ambient noise, changes in vocal intonation) that might make the audience feel a certain way?

- Finding *values*: Are there any abstract ideas, terms, or icons that will likely resonate with a certain population in a certain way? What are these people likely to feel when they hear this term, think this idea, or see this icon? What makes the audience associate these terms, this idea, or this icon with such feelings? If there are ideas, terms, or icons whose emotional resonance cannot be explained by relating them to something the audience has experienced or lived, then how does the rhetor associate this idea, term, or icon with other things that the audience likely cares about? Are there any frames or value-heavy definitions invoked to encourage the audience to feel a certain way about a specific policy, event, person, place? Is there a value-heavy definition or metaphor in the argument?

- Separating the *affect*, the *behavior*, and the *interpretation*: What does this image or value ask the audience to feel? To do? To believe? How do these feelings, behaviors, and beliefs fit together into a single emotional response?

- Finding the *emotional repertoire*: What other arguments ask the audience to feel the same way in response to similar things? Why is this audience likely to share these emotional responses to these common experiences, symbols, ideas, or situations?

8

Habit (Ethos Revisited)

If there are two words that are likely to make an audience skeptical, they are "trust me." Whenever anyone requests your trust, you begin to wonder about that person's trustworthiness. Why do you have to tell me to trust you? Shouldn't I be able to judge based on the argument's merits? We don't discourage this reaction. But we also encourage you to notice how important trust can be when judging and persuading. Without earning an audience's trust, a rhetor will not likely convince anyone of anything.

Classical thinkers were quite aware of how important trust could be in any rhetorical situation. They spoke at length of ethical appeal. Isocrates contended that character is the strongest source of persuasion. Aristotle said that if the rhetor could not forge an ethical connection with the audience, then he would never move them rationally or emotionally. Cicero likewise maintained that a rhetor's character is central to his persuasive potential. Finally, Quintilian put moral character at the center of rhetorical education. He wrote an entire book (in twelve volumes) about how to make citizens virtuous, how to make orators trustworthy. Every one of these men would insist that the audience must feel a moral and ethical connection to the rhetor.

In the twentieth century, the rhetorical theorist perhaps most preoccupied with trust is Kenneth Burke, who maintained that ethical appeal lays the foundation for all other communication. Burke insisted that rhetoric does not ultimately aim at persuasion but rather at identification, a sense that the listener and the audience are consubstantial in their motives. Burke wrote extensive theoretic arguments about the centrality of identification, offering us a convincing case for the importance of ethos. We will have more to say about Burke and identification later in this chapter. Before we venture into rhetorical theory or analysis, however, we will address two questions in a brief digression: Why did ancient rhetoricians emphasize about ethical appeal? And why do modern rhetoricians have such a hard time grasping the concept?

ETHOS AND THE *PSYCHE*

Let's begin to explain the modern inability to grasp the ancient concept of ethos by noticing that the contemporary word *ethics* derives from the Greek *ethos*. You are, no doubt, familiar with the English term. An ethic is a valued manner of getting along with others. It is unethical to lie when negotiating a sale because, according to a commonly accepted business ethic, honesty is a valued manner of treating other people when negotiating contracts. Furthermore, a person of sound ethics is also a person of respectable character. When making an ethos appeal, the rhetor asks for the audience's trust based on his/her character—the rhetor demonstrates that s/he is a person of sound character by addressing the audience in a way that they will likely appreciate.

That's enough of our modern take on ethical appeal. Let's take a quick trip through the classically Greek understanding of ethos, beginning with Homer's *Iliad*. Several of the major characters in this epic deliver long speeches in which they enact public roles associated with certain characteristics. Achilles, for instance, behaves as a warrior—impetuous, rash, but also brave and honorable. Agamemnon behaves as a king—noble and fair-minded, but sometimes proud. Among preliterate Greeks, the poem was performed. Audience members would either witness or themselves enact these speeches, for a moment becoming or witnessing an ethos. To read as Achilles is, for the moment, to become a warrior. To listen to a poet performing Achilles's orations is, momentarily, to be confronted with a respected character type. The poem's continued performance in public circumstances served an important social function. By repeating the poem orally, people reminded themselves of and maintained the character traits that ancient Greek society shared and valued. Poetry reminded ancient Greek society of their ethics. Today, we see a similar function performed by politicians, military heroes, and celebrities who perform for us the characters of admirable people, thus filling our public spaces with *ethe* (the plural of *ethos*) that we can imitate—the reserved and deliberate politician, the humble war hero, the self-effacing and philanthropic movie star.

In sum, for the ancient Greeks, an ethical appeal was understood as an effort to inhabit a moral character that others should recognize, admire, and imitate. The orator, for instance, could gain the audience's trust by becoming the noble warrior in circumstances of foreign aggression. Of course, persuasive enactment of this character may require some credentials. It would help if the audience knew the rhetor as a noble warrior. But such *situated ethos* was not (and is not) necessary. One can act like a noble warrior (as do many American political leaders who have little or no military experience) and still win the audience's trust and admiration.

At this point, you might object, "But isn't that lying about who we really are?" Such an objection points to one of the central differences between ancient Greek and modern Western thought. As moderns, we tend to think of ourselves as individuals with identities and personalities that do not depend upon the *ethe* circulating in our public spaces. Therefore, when we admire a person's character (his or her ethics), we imagine that the person (and not the role) deserves our praise. We also imagine that the person has become this way and will continue to be this way regardless of circumstances. The ancient Greeks saw things a bit differently. They praised virtue in the performance, not in the individual. The warrior *role* (*ethos*) deserves our praise, and the individual is only praiseworthy if and when s/he performs the role acceptably.

Plato offers the first Western effort at imagining an identity that can be separated from a public performance. Prior to Plato's effort at theorizing a *psyche*, however, no such belief can be found among the ancient Greeks. It seems likely that they did not separate their identities from the characters that they performed in public life. The role(s) they performed in public were what they really were; in private, at home, in solitude, they were nothing. (The word for the private individual was *idiotes*, from which we derive the word *idiot*; it was not a term of respect.) The ancient Greek citizen *became somebody* by performing a public role. Likewise, the ancient Greek poet reciting Achilles's speech, thus, *became Achilles* (or the noble warrior) for a little while. (For a fuller treatment of the ancient Greek sense of *ethos*, see Eric Havelock's *Preface to Plato*, 1963.)

The sophists, some of the first Greek rhetoricians, even had a term for the public actor able to inhabit an array of *ethe*. They didn't call this person duplicitous. In fact, they thought such a rhetor had a special excellence—*metis*. The rhetor possessed of metis has learned many different characters and has learned how to perform these roles in the appropriate situations. To explore the differences between the sophist's notion of metis and the modern notion of the psyche, consider the case of Kaycee Nicole Swenson. Between 1999 and 2001, this young Kansas woman, who was suffering from leukemia, wrote a weblog that captivated readers across the nation. People sympathized with Kaycee, conversed with her online, and sent her positive messages. Only after Kaycee died, from a reported aneurysm, did readers learn that the entire thing (including Kaycee herself) was a fiction perpetrated by the real author, Debbie Swenson. Many, of course, were outraged. They called the blog a hoax and assaulted the actual rhetor with accusations of fraud. Debbie Swenson immediately lost her credibility. People insisted that she had misrepresented her psyche. Would a sophist retort that Debbie was filled with metis?

This case highlights not only our modern beliefs about the psyche, but it also demonstrates how contemporary media disrupt these beliefs every day. Online environments allow—even encourage—us to play with our *ethe*. We create personas on Facebook, identities on blogs, and avatars in *Second Life*. Like the ancient Greeks listening to and reciting Homeric poetry, we morph out of one ethos and into another, and we don't worry about dishonesty. Way back in the mid-1990s, Sherry Turkle, an expert on digital communication, argued that online environments encourage people to play with identity. (See Turkle's *Life on the Screen: Identity in the Age of the Internet*, 1997.) If we're not disturbed by someone becoming a fuzzy rabbit with a machine gun in an online café, then why should we be upset about a Kansas woman becoming a terminally ill leukemia patient? Like the ancient Greeks, we might conclude that the quality of the ethical appeal cannot be separated from the substance. Who cares if you're not really a bunny with an AK-47, so long as you can convincingly behave like one? Once we stop worrying about the psyche's genuine representation, we can start analyzing ethical appeals.

ETHICAL APPEAL AND IDENTIFICATION

While the previous discussion illuminates the classical conception of ethos, it doesn't help us to understand what happens, psychologically and socially, when an audience is moved by an ethical appeal. If a logical appeal encourages us to think in a prescribed manner, if a pathos appeal petitions us to feel a certain emotion, does an ethos appeal suggest that we become a certain character? If I find a performance of the warrior ethos convincing or trustworthy, do I myself become a warrior? Not exactly. To best answer these questions, we turn, not to the ancients, but to the contemporary rhetorical theorist, Kenneth Burke.

Burke placed ethos in a very privileged position. In fact, he developed a new term to describe what happens when an audience is moved by an ethical appeal: *identification*. According to Burke, when an audience identifies with a rhetor, they imagine themselves as *consubstantial*. "In being identified with B, A is 'substantially one' with a person other than himself. Yet at the same time he remains unique, an individual locus of motives. Thus he is both joined and separate, at once a distinct substance and consubstantial with another" (*A Rhetoric of Motives* [Berkeley: University of California Press, 1969], p. 21). Furthermore, Burke insisted that identification with one person or group required "division" from another. To identify with one character or community is to separate oneself from another character or community. Finally, Burke insisted that humans feel the need to identify with one another even though they can never completely fulfill that desire. We're not body-snatchers. We cannot become completely consubstantial with another person—if we could, there would be no strife and no rhetoric—so we will always try to move and to be moved ethically, and we will ultimately fail in this effort.

Let's apply Burke's three principles of identification—to identify is to feel consubstantial; to identify with one is to divide from another; identification is never complete but always desired—to an ethical appeal that the ancients would certainly recognize: a "correct" style.

While most people aspire to speak correctly, there are many ways to perform this virtue, many ways to enact this ethical appeal. Consider two—hypercorrection and the occasional but disregarded error. Hypercorrection is often found among social climbers (the lower-middle-class bureaucrat, for instance). Many people have learned to speak so carefully and so correctly that they rarely transgress the rules of proper grammar, making for an unusually stilted speech that some would judge as trying too hard. We often feel that they're putting on airs to impress, even if that's not their conscious motive. In sum, we are not moved because we do not feel consubstantial with the speakers—we don't feel like we share their motives. We aim to speak correctly because correct speech is part of an educated ethos that we value and that we want to repeat. Moreover, we believe that we should take our audience seriously and address them as educated people who can understand and appreciate correct speech. The hypercorrect speaker, on the other hand, seems motivated by social aspiration. S/he wants status, not consubstantiality. And she wants to impress us, not to address us seriously as educated and thoughtful listeners.

Now, consider another performance of a correct style. Many people who already have social privilege—who are educated—indulge in an occasional grammatical transgression without noting its presence. The ability to casually insert a "y'all" or a "he don't" into an otherwise steady stream of correct English tells us that the speaker isn't worried about social rank. The otherwise correct style tells us that the speaker is motivated by a desire to speak correctly—to take us seriously—while the disregarded error tells us that s/he's not motivated by status. (For more on hypercorrection and occasional error, see Pierre Bourdieu's "The Production and Reproduction of Legitimate Language" in *Language and Symbolic Power*, 1981.) Finally, when moved by the correct style peppered with an occasional error, we identify with the speaker while dividing ourselves from social climbers and their hypercorrect style. And even though we identify with the correct speaker who indulges in a salty expression, we never feel like we, ourselves, have become such a patrician rhetor. We always feel a little removed, a little incorrect, ourselves. This, perhaps, is why social privilege is often admired but rarely felt. Burke said as much when he insisted that the "mystery" of rhetoric (and the impossibility of identification) explains more than the "class motive" (*A Rhetoric of Motives*, p. 273). Differences of social status matter. We are no doubt separated by wealth and by rank. But the more important—the ultimately motivating—distances among people are created by our desire and our consummate inability to become one another. That condition, according to Burke, leads to rhetoric.

WHAT MAKES AN ETHICAL APPEAL? HABITS

We hope that the foregoing pages help you to better understand *ethos* and to see why some modern rhetoricians stress its importance. We also hope that this discussion will illuminate what happens to an audience when they are moved by an ethical appeal. But we recognize that you will need something more, something else, in order to analyze ethical appeals yourself. What should the rhetorical analyst examine when trying to locate and explicate ethos in a discourse? Ancient rhetors attended to introductions and style largely because these two features present ideal opportunities to show the audience an admirable ethos. In the introductory paragraph of King's "Letter," as we mentioned much earlier, King presents details about his life to establish a character whom we should respect (a professional minister) and to show that he has our best interests at heart (he is a fair-minded person who likewise seeks a patient and reasonable audience). King's style of writing also presents his ministerial ethos by occasionally echoing the King James translation of the Old Testament and by alluding continually to other biblical verses.

But we find this attention to style and to introductions somewhat limiting. For this reason, we encourage you to look for something else—habits. And we'll begin with a simple definition: *Habits* are naturalized behaviors, things we do so often that we don't think about them and don't immediately notice them. Our understanding of habit derives in part from Aristotle, who argued that every living creature has a *hexis*, a set of habitualized manners. In the *Nichomachean Ethics* (1103a33–b25), Aristotle argued that people are influenced both by their innate dispositions and by their habits. Innate dispositions are the givens of human behavior—the biological preconditions that shape our psyches. Habits are what people, in their purposeful efforts at cooperation, construct on top of their innate dispositions. Politics, according to Aristotle, is the effort to instill virtuous habits of human interaction through institutions. Rhetoric is the first ancillary art to politics. When we can't ensure virtuous behavior through courts and laws, we seek to instill virtuous behavior through education in the habits of virtuous cooperation. We can't make people behave politely by threatening police action, but we can encourage polite behavior by cultivating certain habits in discourse.

A collection of habits (a *hexis*), when taught and learned, can lead people to behave ethically. To put this another way, communities develop and judge ethical behaviors by learning habitually to embody a hexis. *Hexeis* (the plural of hexis) that comprise a community's *ethe* are developed and maintained in social circumstances where people come together based on common beliefs, common feelings, and common behavioral dispositions. Thus, the hexis has an ethical rhetorical dimension.

We admit that Aristotle's (and our) treatment of habit and hexis is quite abstract. So, in an effort to clarify, we'll return to our example of correct speech (a hexis) along with our brief treatment of two manners of speaking correctly (two habits). While we can and often do create elaborate conscious arguments about why a given set of speech patterns is correct, in the moment of judgment, we are more inclined to rely on our own hexis, our habituated sense of what correct speech should sound like. For this reason, if pressed, most people will insist that a word or verb conjugation is used correctly because it sounds right, not because the Oxford English Dictionary defines the term in a specific way or because the subjunctive mood must be conjugated like the past plural form of the verb. We measure by our habits, not our rules. Based on these habits, we make judgments about the speaker's character. For example, we might say that, based on his language use, this person must be "trying too hard" or "properly educated but not pretentious." These are both ethical judgments that reflect a psychological condition. If we feel that the speaker is trying too hard, we do not identify with what we perceive to be his or her motives. If we feel that the speaker is educated but not pretentious, we do identify. In either case, we are moved by this person's habits and by our own habituated sense of ethical behavior.

AN ANALYTIC VOCABULARY: HABIT, THE HABITUS, AND THE SOCIAL FIELD

Attention to habit focuses rhetorical analysis on routine and quotidian behaviors. To look at habit, however, we must distinguish between the little idiosyncrasies that everyone possesses, and the habituated actions that we share and that we pass along to others in our social environments. Consider a fairly mundane behavior, for instance—buttoning your coat.

Many of us prefer to begin buttoning our coats at the bottom, while others prefer to begin buttoning from the top. Certainly there are those who start somewhere in the middle, and a reckless few who go without buttoning at all. Such behaviors are peculiar to individual people. They bear little significance because they have no social purpose. They don't tell us anything about the person's character. These are habits. We can suppose a world where whole nations are divided according to the places at which citizens begin to button their coats—a continent fractured into top-buttoners, bottom-buttoners, and a militant rebel nation of mountain-dwelling middle-buttoners. But we can also say that this situation exists only in the most fantastic literary imaginations. Or does it?

A careful observer will notice that Americans do divide themselves according to how they button their coats. Women button their coats to the left, and men button their coats to the right. These individual habits are acquired largely because women's and men's coats are made differently, with the buttons positioned on different sides of the garment. If you are male, then you are probably in the habit of using your left hand to unbutton your coats and shirts. You probably also do this without consciously thinking of your gender, even though your habit will indicate to others that you are male. At this point, we are no longer looking at an idiosyncratic behavior. We are looking at a shared, subconsciously maintained behavior that reveals something important about the person's character. This is a *habitus*.

A habitus is a set of socially significant behaviors that people learn, repeat, and recognize, often without conscious awareness of their recognition and repetition. A habitus is not made up of one single habitualized behavior. If we are to imagine a gendered habitus, for instance, we must go beyond the distinction between left-coat buttoners and right-coat buttoners. Such a gendered habitus in America must include a host of habituated behaviors that mark us as males or females. These include such learned and repeated actions as the different ways people throw a ball, the different ways they cross their legs while sitting, the different ways they flirt, even the different ways that they approach conversation. (Are you in the habit of imagining a conversation as an exercise in sharing thoughts or as a way to solve problems?) These behaviors have moral and ethical overtones. A "masculine" man will converse in a certain manner. A "feminine" woman will flirt in specific ways. People's habits will be shaped by the dominant habitus in a given society, just as people's behaviors will mark them as belonging to specific groups. Our evaluation of particular individuals often depends upon their ability to display the habitualized behaviors associated with an ethos that we appreciate. For example, you may have overheard or been the object of comments like, "She sits like a lady, with her feet crossed at the ankles," or "He stands like a man, with his shoulders square, back straight, and chest out." (Note: We present this rather simplistic example simply to illustrate. Anyone who reflects on the matter will quickly realize that in the United States today, there are multiple gendered habituses, each with its own norms of judgment and behavior.)

The last element in our equation is the *field*. If a habit is an idiosyncratic behavior, and a habitus is a range of interrelated, socially significant behaviors, then a *field* is the place (the scene) where people evaluate and acquire their individual habits by encountering the dominant habitus. The field, in short, is where people learn, recognize, and repeat certain symbolically important habits. To return to our earlier example, the habit is the direction from which people button their coats; the habitus is the gendered division between left-buttoners (women) and right-buttoners (men); a field is any place where particular people acquire and learn to recognize these behaviors. A habitus often persists and structures behaviors across a series of fields. The gendered habitus traverses a variety of fields including coat stores, the fashion-design industry and those embarrassing moments as we exit a party, grabbing the wrong coat only to find that it buttons from the wrong side.

WRITE AN ANALYSIS

The habits associated with gender are constantly tested in a variety of fields—when women wear clothes typically associated with men or vice-versa (the sartorial field) or when men become stay-at-home parents or adopt behaviors typically associated with a feminine caregiver (the domestic field).

Write an analysis of how two people, in their subtle habits of dress, performed two different feminine habituses in public circumstances. The subject of such an analysis can come from the 2008 presidential election. Both Hillary Clinton and Sarah Palin pursued the presidency that year, each dressing in ways that reinforced separate habitualized norms of feminine dress. Clinton wore brightly colored pantsuits, while Palin often wore skirts and jackets. Clinton wore her hair short, while Palin kept hers long and often in a beehive. Clinton wore low heels, while Palin wore high heels. In each subtle gesture, these two women dressed in a separate feminine style. Analyzing their habits of dress, explain how Clinton and Palin embodied different feminine habituses. Can you explain why the ethos demonstrated by Clinton's feminine habitus appealed to and garnered votes from some women and why Palin's ethos appealed to and garnered more support from men than women?

We borrow the vocabulary of *habit, habitus,* and *field* from anthropology, particularly from the works of Marcel Mauss and Pierre Bourdieu. We adapt this vocabulary to rhetorical analysis because it allows us to discuss socially symbolic behavior and particular scenes when people learn, enact, and reproduce the naturalized dispositions that make them who they are. This vocabulary allows a more nuanced discussion of ethos by attending to the elements of a successful ethical appeal. Most importantly, this vocabulary allows us to look in a variety of places and at a variety of things. Ethos no longer seems confined to introductions or to style. It can be written on our very bodies, just as it can be read in our most naturalized gestures. In a sense, everything that people do for other people has an ethical quality insofar as the behavior reflects the rhetor's character.

To illustrate the versatility of this vocabulary, we'll encourage you to consider a not-so-intuitive example. The Starbucks chain of coffeehouses typically features stores that resemble one another in a variety of ways. The counter is located at a distance from the entrance, requiring you to walk through a set of tables and usually a crowd of people to buy anything. Therefore, part of your coffee experience includes walking among other people who are doing various things—studying, chatting, and so forth. These behaviors ask you to habitually associate the act of coffee drinking with socializing, with intense study, with out-of-the-office work. The tables themselves are typically mobile, allowing people to change their environment. They can sit in large groups or as individuals at small tables. There are often comfortable, overstuffed chairs where people can relax. Electrical outlets and Internet access abound, allowing people to take out their laptops for online work (or play). In sum, the stores' layout encourages people to stay, drink coffee (or some other beverage), and do other things. It encourages them to structure their habits of consumption in a particular way.

Prior to the early 1990s, U.S. residents did not habitually stay in the places where they purchased or drank coffee. Coffeehouse culture was associated with Europe, not with America. Coffee vendors tended to sell the "to go" cup at a window or at a counter. Scott Bedbury, who became an advertising and marketing executive at Starbucks in 1994, decided to change the American coffee habitus by creating warm, inviting places where people not only buy coffee but also stay to do other things. Bedbury aimed to change the coffeehouse experience by reworking every aspect of Starbucks' marketing—store design, logo, and product placement. He also aimed to change Starbucks's ethos—he wanted to make Starbucks the coffeehouse corporation. (See Scott Bedbury's *New Brand World* [2002] for a fuller discussion.) Most of the elements just mentioned, and many others not mentioned at all, were meticulously designed to change people's *habits* and thus to alter the coffeehouse *habitus* by changing the *field*—the coffeehouse itself. It would be hard to say that Bedbury and his Starbucks marketing team single handedly changed U.S. coffeehouse culture. After all, many present-day Starbucks stores now feature or are restricted to drive-through sales. But we can't deny that a very different coffeehouse ethos thrives today in part because Starbucks (and others) created spatial arrangements to change people's habits. And many consumers trust the Starbucks corporation because they admire the coffeehouse ethos. Next time you decide to study at a local coffeehouse, we encourage you to consider how the store's architectural layout persuades you to identify with the place's ethos. Are the walls painted a soothing cream with green accents? Do local artists' works adorn the walls? Is there a shabby, but nevertheless comfortable, couch behind a well-worn, knee-high table where you can rest your laptop? We'll also encourage you to consider how all of these devices affect your sense of the store's credibility. Do you think that they make good coffee (that you can trust their product) because the store has a coffeehouse ethos?

THE IRONIC HABITUS AND THE "WHY" AD

To further explore the advantage of tracing a habitus across a range of fields, we return to the VW "Why" ad. "Why" belongs to a significant series in advertising history. Among other things, all of the "Think Small" ads (including "Why") pioneered a form of ethical appeal. The marketers assembling and circulating this advertisement tried to identify with the audience by enacting an ironic disposition toward consumption, what we will call an *ironic habitus*. Since the 1960s, ethos has become increasingly important to U.S. advertising. "Image" ads and "branding" both sell a product based on the company's ethical appeal to a lifestyle. As we've mentioned already, the baby boomers grew up in a media-saturated environment, accosted at every corner by a hyperbolic rhetoric trying to sell them something. They quickly became jaded. Doyle Dane and Bernbach were aware of this developing ironic habitus, and they appealed to it consciously through a number of rhetorical devices.

Notice that our analysis returns to a discussion of style (as explored in Chapter 5) but with a broader scope allowed by this chapter's new vocabulary. We're looking closely at rhetorical style, using analytic methods explored in Chapter 5, while adding an attention to broader cultural forces (such as a habitus). Even though we're employing more contemporary methods of rhetorical analysis, we can't forget the classical material covered in earlier chapters.

Let's begin with *parody*, the broad-scale effort to mimic and therefore to mock another widely known form of art or, in this case, advertisement. Parody is both a stylistic element and a habit. Those who identify with an ironic habitus will recognize and appreciate a rhetor who speaks in a parodic style. "Why" parodies car advertisements in a variety of ways, repeating key elements such as the picture of the vehicle, the text explaining its advantages and features. But the images, as we've noted previously, are especially unflattering. Thus, while repeating many of the generic features found in a car ad, "Why" mocks these features by performing them in unexpected ways. Like any good parody, "Why" calls attention to features that might pass unnoticed in the genre getting spoofed. After closely analyzing the layout of this VW ad, it's hard to look at the Chrysler ad, contained in this same magazine, without noticing and then becoming a bit wary of its smooth layout, eye-catching images, and evenly formatted text. The difference between the VW and the Chrysler ads should also help us to understand the implied audience's psychological reaction. If the reader identifies with an ironic habitus, as performed in the VW ad, then s/he will separate herself or himself from the sincere, however bombastic, ethos of the Chrysler ad.

In addition to the ironic habitus of its parodic style, "Why" exhibits other habits that the audience could identify as part of the ironic habitus. The ad habitually takes notice of and apologizes for itself. Though pronouncing the car's features (dependability and affordability), the text is simultaneously self-effacing. The VW copywriters are deeply aware of, ironically distanced from, and even critical of their effort at selling. Sentences are often so informal and incomplete as to sound almost indifferent: "Depends on how you drive it. And where." "Lower insurance rates in many states. Practically no oil between changes. And no anti-freeze." As anyone who's ever stepped onto an auto dealer's showroom knows, the enthusiastic salesperson speaks mellifluously and unhaltingly to prevent the consumer from responding or even carefully considering the pitch. "Why's" off-hand style (marked by short sentences and sparing conjunctions) indicates to the reader that, though the speaker is selling something, s/he doesn't really believe in the act of selling. The rhetor does not seem to be motivated by the sale.

Another rhetorical device, another habit, displays an ironic habitus to the audience—*concession*. We're told, "Driven by a pro in an economy run, a stock Volkswagen will average close to 50 miles per gallon. But for everyday driving, figure on getting about 32 mpg with a Volkswagen." The rhetor concedes that people should not take many of the claims found in automobile ads at face value. The rhetor even admits that Volkswagen has offered some doubtful statements about the vehicle's performance.

WRITE AN ANALYSIS

Analyze another series of car advertisements marked by an ironic habitus. In 1991, Subaru hired Wieden & Kennedy to produce a series of ads, all identifying their product with an ironic ethos that the audience, they assumed, already appreciated. One commercial, for instance, proclaimed, "A car is just a car. It won't make you handsome or prettier, and if it improves your standing with your neighbors, then you live among snobs." In his book *Where the Suckers Moon: The Life and Death of an Advertising Campaign* (1994), Randall Rothberg closely chronicles this campaign and its ultimate inability to generate sales. Analyze one or more of the ads to explain why the ethical appeal failed. Did these newer ads fail to present habits that the audience would associate with an ironic habitus? Did the audience in 1991 no longer identify with an ironic habitus (as they may have in 1960)? In the early 1990s, was the field of consumer culture no longer an accepted or appropriate place to perform an ironic habitus?

These three habits (parody, self-effacement, and concession) contribute to the ad's ironic ethical appeal. The rhetor says one thing (buy this car because the ad is convincing) while implying another (the whole advertising game is a bit ridiculous and unconvincing). If we were to analyze the ironic ethos while focusing on the ad's core enthymeme (you should buy a VW because it's dependable and affordable), we might conclude that the ethical appeal undercuts the logical appeal. If we identify with such an ironic habitus, we have no reason to believe any advertisement, no reason to make the inference that the above enthymeme presents. Focusing on the ironic habitus as an ethical appeal, however, we might conclude that the ad works primarily by identifying with an audience already alienated from consumer culture. Irony, therefore, is an appropriate manner of ethically identifying with the boomer generation. Furthermore, if ethos is the most important appeal in the ad, we might conclude that performing an ironic habitus makes the ad's core enthymeme more believable. If the audience already identifies with an ironic habitus, then they are likely to doubt any enthymeme whose conclusion encourages them to open their wallets. But, if the rhetor can frame a sales pitch with an extended effort to show that s/he is also aware of and skeptical toward advertising, then the audience might be more willing to trust the speaker. This trust leads the audience to entertain the cap to a presentational enthymeme: "But the figure of 32 miles per gallon has stood up over the years. And you can put these in your bankbook too."

This brief analysis not only demonstrates the value of focusing on ethical appeal but also the value of supplementing ethos with habit. A rhetorical analysis focused on ethos might touch upon the stylistic features that we discuss, but it might not mention issues of imagery or textual design. A vocabulary of habit, however, encourages the analyst to look everywhere. Each seemingly mundane and unremarkable detail has the ability to enact a disposition and thereby to invite the audience's identification. In the last paragraphs of this analysis, we point toward another advantage to this analytic method. So far, we have examined the ironic habitus and its rhetorical manifestation in one persuasive effort that belongs in one field (consumer culture), but we could easily extend this analysis to a range of persuasive efforts across a variety of fields. With the broad category of an ironic habitus in mind, we can scan the broad rhetorical horizon for similar efforts to identify with the audience.

In the field of contemporary political media, for instance, we might look at certain publications or broadcasts. *The Onion* is a bastion of stylistic parody (in print and more recently in web formats). Parodies of television news have likewise been around for some time. (*Not the Nine-O'Clock News* was produced by the British Broadcasting Corporation from 1979 to 1982. *Not Necessarily the News* ran on the U.S. Home Box Office from 1983 until 1990. Most recently, *The Daily Show* began on Comedy Central in 1996 and continues today. Comedy Central also broadcasts *The Colbert Report*, a parody of programs on Fox News.) Thus, we see the parodic habit in the news media field. And we can find similar habits of parody in the political field. When comedian Al Franken ran for the U.S. Senate in 2008, his flat monotone delivery and wry awareness of the news media's presence turned his entire campaign into a parody of other campaigns. Kinky Friedman's campaign for the governorship of Texas in 2006 was likewise habitually parodic in its insistence upon apparently serious policy solutions to illegal immigration and its invocation of slogans that mocked other campaign rhetoric. Friedman, for example, grew fond of saying, "I'm not pro-life, and I'm not pro-choice. I'm pro-football." Close rhetorical analysis of a range of persuasive efforts in contemporary politics can easily locate and dissect an ironic habitus in a field far removed from consumer culture. We just have to look for the habits of stylistic parody, self-effacement, and perhaps concession.

FOR FURTHER DISCUSSION

In our analysis of the VW ad, we focus on the ironic habitus in one field (advertising) while emphasizing certain habits of document design and rhetorical style. Others have described a similarly ironic habitus in other fields, such as U.S. politics. Neal Gabler's article "The Maverick and the Media" (*New York Times,* 26 Mar 2008) openly labels Senator John McCain (at the time running for president) the first "postmodern" politician because of McCain's ability to regard the media cynically and to appeal to the audience's sense that the entire political game deserves our skepticism. Read Gabler's article and discuss the subtle habits in McCain's presentation that might arise from such a habitus. Is McCain parodic or self-effacing in his presentation? Does he regularly make concessions about the nature of political campaigning? Are there other habits that might lead Gabler to identify McCain's ethos as ironic?

An ironic habitus can also be found in yet another field—contemporary American literature. Former poet laureate Billy Collins often parodies high-flown and metaphoric language in his own poems, such as "Litany," which begins with the declaration "You are the bread and the knife// the crystal goblet and the wine" but then cascades into a series of deflated exercises at metaphorically describing "you": "It is possible that you are the fish under the bridge. [. . .] It might interest you to know// speaking of the plentiful imagery of the world,// that I am the sound of rain on the roof. [. . .] But don't worry, I am not the bread and the knife." Thomas Pynchon's novels parody every writing style imaginable, from comic books to technical manuals. Searching for habitual stylistic parody across the fields of consumer culture, politics, and literary art, a trained rhetorical analyst could track an ironic habitus, a series of efforts to identify with an audience by embodying a detached and skeptical disposition. Perhaps this cynicism persists because subsequent generations (particularly the infamously apathetic and cynical Generation X) swam in the same saturated salesmanship that soaked their boomer parents. Perhaps further rhetorical analysis can lend support to or debunk our tenuous claims about a transgenerational ironic habitus. We leave these questions open; we are confident that a skilled analyst, equipped with the terms introduced by this chapter, can answer them and many others.

QUESTIONS FOR ANALYSIS: ETHOS AND IDENTIFICATION

- Does the rhetor already have a status among the audience?
  - Will these people know who the rhetor is initially, and, if not, how does the rhetor reveal his or her standing in the community?
  - Will these people respect or trust the rhetor based on their knowledge of his or her position?
  - How does the rhetor's status affect the audience's willingness to trust, believe, or identify with him or her?
- Does the rhetor say or present anything in the introduction that reveals a certain character to the audience?
  - Is there any explicit mention of the rhetor's profession, character, or life story?

- Does the rhetor explain how he or she came upon the information (the artistic or the inartistic proof) that will be presented in this argument?
- Does the rhetor try to show that he or she shares with the audience a background or a set of values?
- Does the rhetor's style indicate anything about his or her character?
  - Are there recurrent patterns in the rhetor's syntax that the audience might connect with a type of speaker?
  - Does the rhetor use key words to show a certain background, knowledge, or set of beliefs and values?
  - Does the rhetor depend upon certain figures or tropes that the audience will relate to a known and/or revered character type?
  - Does the rhetor rely on a stylistic register (moderate, lyrical, plain) that the audience often hears among certain types of people?
  - Does the rhetor speak in a dialect or a professional jargon that the audience will know or connect with a character type?
  - If there is a visual component to the text (textual design, layout, or images), do these visuals convey a certain character type and how?

QUESTIONS FOR ANALYSIS: HABIT, HABITUS, AND FIELD

- What subtle and embodied gestures are evident in this presentation?
  - How does the rhetor carry his or herself?
  - What are the rhetor's habits of speech (writing) and motion?
  - How is the rhetor dressed?
- How do these subtle and embodied gestures get presented, and how do they relate to one another?
  - Are there specific acts that make these habits particularly evident, or could they find expression in nearly any social interaction?
  - Is there a common thread (such as a fastidious attention to detail) running through all of these habits?
- Who else shares these embodied gestures?
  - Can you attribute the rhetor's habits to a recognizable gender?
  - Can you attribute the rhetor's habits to a recognizable ethnicity?

- Can you find other people who speak, dress, or act similarly in a given geographic area?
- Are the rhetor's habits peculiar to a form of religious worship?
- Are the rhetor's habits common among people in a specific social or economic class?
- Are the rhetor's habits common to people living in a given historical moment?

- How can you characterize the collection of habits that this speaker shares with an identifiable group?
  - Is there a disposition (enthusiastic, aloof, cautious), a nationality (U.S. citizen, Mexican, Indonesian), a gender (masculine, feminine), and so forth whose adherents would behave in a similar fashion?
  - Upon seeing someone with these habits, how would an audience describe their possessor?

- Where and how is one likely to see these habits displayed?
  - In how many noticeably different social spaces would an audience be able to say that this person is X?
  - Across two (or more) different spaces, how do these habits get similarly or differently performed?

Appendix A

Martin Luther King, Jr.'s "Letter from Birmingham Jail"

The following statement by eight white Alabama clergymen, reprinted by the American Friends Service Committee, prompted King's "Letter from Birmingham Jail."

April 12, 1963

1 We the undersigned clergymen are among those who, in January, issued "An Appeal for Law and Order and Common Sense," in dealing with racial problems in Alabama. We expressed understanding that honest convictions in racial matters could properly be pursued in the courts, but urged that decisions of those courts should in the meantime be peacefully obeyed.

2 Since that time there had been some evidence of increased forebearance and a willingness to face facts. Responsible citizens have undertaken to work on various problems which cause racial friction and unrest. In Birmingham, recent public events have given indication that we will have opportunity for a new constructive and realistic approach to racial problems.

3 However, we are now confronted by a series of demonstrations by some of our Negro citizens, directed and led in part by outsiders. We recognize the natural impatience of people who feel that their hopes are slow in being realized. But we are convinced that these demonstrations are unwise and untimely.

4 We agree rather with certain local Negro leadership which has called for honest and open negotiation of racial issues in our area. And we believe this kind of facing of issues can best be accomplished by citizens of our own metropolitan area, white and Negro, meeting with their knowledge and experience of the local situation. All of us need to face that responsibility and find proper channels for its accomplishment.

5   Just as we formerly pointed out that "hatred and violence have no sanction in our religious and political traditions," we also point out that such actions as incite to hatred and violence, however technically peaceful those actions may be, have not contributed to the resolution of our local problems. We do not believe that these days of new hope are days when extreme measures are justified in Birmingham.

6   We commend the community as a whole, and the local news media and law enforcement officials in particular, on the calm manner in which these demonstrations have been handled. We urge the public to continue to show restraint should the demonstrations continue, and the law enforcement officials to remain calm and continue to protect our city from violence.

7   We further strongly urge our own Negro community to withdraw support from these demonstrations, and to unite locally in working peacefully for a better Birmingham. When rights are consistently denied, a cause should be pressed in the courts and in negotiations among local leaders, and not in the streets. We appeal to both our white and Negro citizenry to observe the principles of law and order and common sense.

Signed by:

C.C.J. Carpenter, D.D., LL.D., Bishop of Alabama

Joseph A Durick, D.D., Auxiliary Bishop, Diocese of Mobile-Birmingham

Rabbi Milton L. Grafman, Temple Emanu-El, Birmingham, Alabama

Bishop Paul Hardin, Bishop of the Alabama-West Florida Conference of the Methodist Church

Bishop Nolan B. Harmon, Bishop of the North Alabama Conference of the Methodist Church

George M. Murray, D.D., LL.D., Bishop Coadjutor, Episcopal Diocese of Alabama

Edward V. Ramage, Moderator, Synod of the Alabama Presbyterian Church in the United States

Earl Stallings, Pastor, First Baptist Church, Birmingham, Alabama

LETTER FROM BIRMINGHAM JAIL
by
Martin Luther King, Jr.

April 16, 1963

MY DEAR FELLOW CLERGYMEN:

1   While confined here in the Birmingham city jail, I came across your recent statement calling my present activities "unwise and untimely." Seldom do I pause to answer criticism of my work and ideas. If I sought to answer all the criticisms that cross my desk, my secretaries would have little time for anything other than such correspondence in the course of the day, and I would have no time for constructive work. But since I feel that you are men of genuine good will and that your criticisms are sincerely set forth, I want to try to answer your statements in what I hope will be patient and reasonable terms.

2   I think I should indicate why I am here in Birmingham, since you have been influenced by the view which argues against "outsiders coming in." I have the honor of serving as president of the Southern Christian Leadership Conference, an organization operating in every southern state, with headquarters in Atlanta, Georgia. We have some eighty-five affiliated organizations across the South, and one of them is the Alabama Christian Movement for Human Rights. Frequently we share staff, educational and financial resources with our affiliates. Several months ago the affiliate here in Birmingham asked us to be on call to engage in a nonviolent direct-action program if such were deemed necessary. We readily consented, and when the hour came we lived up to our promise. So I, along with several members of my staff, am here because I was invited here. I am here because I have organizational ties here.

3   But more basically, I am in Birmingham because injustice is here. Just as the prophets of the eighth century B.C. left their villages and carried their "thus saith the Lord" far beyond the boundaries of their home towns, and just as the Apostle Paul left his village of Tarsus and carried the gospel of Jesus Christ to the far corners of the Greco-Roman world, so am I compelled to carry the gospel of freedom beyond my own home town. Like Paul, I must constantly respond to the Macedonian call for aid.

4   Moreover, I am cognizant of the interrelatedness of all communities and states. I cannot sit idly by in Atlanta and not be concerned about what happens in Birmingham. Injustice anywhere is a threat to justice everywhere. We are

caught in an inescapable network of mutuality, tied in a single garment of destiny. Whatever affects one directly, affects all indirectly. Never again can we afford to live with the narrow, provincial "outside agitator" idea. Anyone who lives inside the United States can never be considered an outsider anywhere within its bounds.

5   You deplore the demonstrations taking place In Birmingham. But your statement, I am sorry to say, fails to express a similar concern for the conditions that brought about the demonstrations. I am sure that none of you would want to rest content with the superficial kind of social analysis that deals merely with effects and does not grapple with underlying causes. It is unfortunate that demonstrations are taking place in Birmingham, but it is even more unfortunate that the city's white power structure left the Negro community with no alternative.

6   In any nonviolent campaign there are four basic steps: collection of the facts to determine whether injustices exist; negotiation; self-purification; and direct action. We have gone through all these steps in Birmingham. There can be no gainsaying the fact that racial injustice engulfs this community. Birmingham is probably the most thoroughly segregated city in the United States. Its ugly record of brutality is widely known. Negroes have experienced grossly unjust treatment in the courts. There have been more unsolved bombings of Negro homes and churches in Birmingham than in any other city in the nation. These are the hard, brutal facts of the case. On the basis of these conditions, Negro leaders sought to negotiate with the city fathers. But the latter consistently refused to engage in good-faith negotiation.

7   Then, last September, came the opportunity to talk with leaders of Birmingham's economic community. In the course of the negotiations, certain promises were made by the merchants — for example, to remove the stores' humiliating racial signs. On the basis of these promises, the Reverend Fred Shuttlesworth and the leaders of the Alabama Christian Movement for Human Rights agreed to a moratorium on all demonstrations. As the weeks and months went by, we realized that we were the victims of a broken promise. A few signs, briefly removed, returned; the others remained.

8   As in so many past experiences, our hopes bad been blasted, and the shadow of deep disappointment settled upon us. We had no alternative except to prepare for direct action, whereby we would present our very bodies as a means of laying our case before the conscience of the local and the national community. Mindful of the difficulties involved, we decided to undertake a

process of self-purification. We began a series of workshops on nonviolence, and we repeatedly asked ourselves: "Are you able to accept blows without retaliating?" "Are you able to endure the ordeal of jail?" We decided to schedule our direct-action program for the Easter season, realizing that except for Christmas, this is the main shopping period of the year. Knowing that a strong economic-withdrawal program would be the by-product of direct action, we felt that this would be the best time to bring pressure to bear on the merchants for the needed change.

9   Then it occurred to us that Birmingham's mayoralty election was coming up in March, and we speedily decided to postpone action until after election day. When we discovered that the Commissioner of Public Safety, Eugene "Bull" Connor, had piled up enough votes to be in the run-off we decided again to postpone action until the day after the run-off so that the demonstrations could not be used to cloud the issues. Like many others, we waited to see Mr. Connor defeated, and to this end we endured postponement after postponement. Having aided in this community need, we felt that our direct-action program could be delayed no longer.

10   You may well ask: "Why direct action? Why sit-ins, marches and so forth? Isn't negotiation a better path?" You are quite right in calling, for negotiation. Indeed, this is the very purpose of direct action. Nonviolent direct action seeks to create such a crisis and foster such a tension that a community which has constantly refused to negotiate is forced to confront the issue. It seeks so to dramatize the issue that it can no longer be ignored. My citing the creation of tension as part of the work of the nonviolent-resister may sound rather shocking. But I must confess that I am not afraid of the word "tension." I have earnestly opposed violent tension, but there is a type of constructive, nonviolent tension which is necessary for growth. Just as Socrates felt that it was necessary to create a tension in the mind so that individuals could rise from the bondage of myths and half-truths to the unfettered realm of creative analysis and objective appraisal, so must we see the need for nonviolent gadflies to create the kind of tension in society that will help men rise from the dark depths of prejudice and racism to the majestic heights of understanding and brotherhood.

11   The purpose of our direct-action program is to create a situation so crisis-packed that it will inevitably open the door to negotiation. I therefore concur with you in your call for negotiation. Too long has our beloved South land been bogged down in a tragic effort to live in monologue rather than dialogue.

12   One of the basic points in your statement is that the action that I and my associates have taken in Birmingham is untimely. Some have asked: "Why didn't you give the new city administration time to act?" The only answer that I can give to this query is that the new Birmingham administration must be prodded about as much as the outgoing one, before it will act. We are sadly mistaken if we feel that the election of Albert Boutwell as mayor will bring the millennium to Birmingham. While Mr. Boutwell is a much more gentle person than Mr. Connor, they are both segregationists, dedicated to maintenance of the status quo. I have hope that Mr. Boutwell will be reasonable enough to see the futility of massive resistance to desegregation. But he will not see this without pressure from devotees of civil rights. My friends, I must say to you that we have not made a single gain in civil rights without determined legal and nonviolent pressure. Lamentably, it is an historical fact that privileged groups seldom give up their privileges voluntarily. Individuals may see the moral light and voluntarily give up their unjust posture; but, as Reinhold Niebuhr has reminded us, groups tend to be more immoral than individuals.

13   We know through painful experience that freedom is never voluntarily given by the oppressor; it must be demanded by the oppressed. Frankly, I have yet to engage in a direct-action campaign that was "well timed" in the view of those who have not suffered unduly from the disease of segregation. For years now I have heard the word "Wait!" It rings in the ear of every Negro with piercing familiarity. This "Wait" has almost always meant "Never." We must come to see, with one of our distinguished jurists, that "justice too long delayed is justice denied."

14   We have waited for more than 340 years for our constitutional and God-given rights. The nations of Asia and Africa are moving with jetlike speed toward gaining political independence, but we still creep at horse-and-buggy pace toward gaining a cup of coffee at a lunch counter. Perhaps it is easy for those who have never felt the stinging dark of segregation to say, "Wait." But when you have seen vicious mobs lynch your mothers and fathers at will and drown your sisters and brothers at whim; when you have seen hate-filled policemen curse, kick and even kill your black brothers and sisters; when you see the vast majority of your twenty million Negro brothers smothering in an airtight cage of poverty in the midst of an affluent society; when you suddenly find your tongue twisted and your speech stammering as you seek to explain to your six-year-old daughter why she can't go to the public amusement park that has just been advertised on television, and see tears welling up in her eyes when she is told

that Funtown is closed to colored children, and see ominous clouds of inferiority beginning to form in her little mental sky, and see her beginning to distort her personality by developing an unconscious bitterness toward white people; when you have to concoct an answer for a five-year-old son who is asking: "Daddy, why do white people treat colored people so mean?"; when you take a cross-county drive and find it necessary to sleep night after night in the uncomfortable corners of your automobile because no motel will accept you; when you are humiliated day in and day out by nagging signs reading "white" and "colored"; when your first name becomes "nigger," your middle name becomes "boy" (however old you are) and your last name becomes "John," and your wife and mother are never given the respected title "Mrs."; when you are harried by day and haunted by night by the fact that you are a Negro, living constantly at tiptoe stance, never quite knowing what to expect next, and are plagued with inner fears and outer resentments; when you are forever fighting a degenerating sense of "nobodiness" then you will understand why we find it difficult to wait. There comes a time when the cup of endurance runs over, and men are no longer willing to be plunged into the abyss of despair. I hope, sirs, you can understand our legitimate and unavoidable impatience.

15   You express a great deal of anxiety over our willingness to break laws. This is certainly a legitimate concern. Since we so diligently urge people to obey the Supreme Court's decision of 1954 outlawing segregation in the public schools, at first glance it may seem rather paradoxical for us consciously to break laws. One may well ask: "How can you advocate breaking some laws and obeying others?" The answer lies in the fact that there are two types of laws: just and unjust. I would be the first to advocate obeying just laws. One has not only a legal but a moral responsibility to obey just laws. Conversely, one has a moral responsibility to disobey unjust laws. I would agree with St. Augustine that "an unjust law is no law at all."

16   Now, what is the difference between the two? How does one determine whether a law is just or unjust? A just law is a man-made code that squares with the moral law or the law of God. An unjust law is a code that is out of harmony with the moral law. To put it in the terms of St. Thomas Aquinas: An unjust law is a human law that is not rooted in eternal law and natural law. Any law that uplifts human personality is just. Any law that degrades human personality is unjust. All segregation statutes are unjust because segregation distorts the soul and damages the personality. It gives the segregator a false sense of superiority and the segregated a false sense of inferiority. Segregation, to use the terminology

of the Jewish philosopher Martin Buber, substitutes an "I it" relationship for an "I-thou" relationship and ends up relegating persons to the status of things. Hence segregation is not only politically, economically and sociologically unsound, it is morally wrong and awful. Paul Tillich said that sin is separation. Is not segregation an existential expression of man's tragic separation, his awful estrangement, his terrible sinfulness? Thus it is that I can urge men to obey the 1954 decision of the Supreme Court, for it is morally right; and I can urge them to disobey segregation ordinances, for they are morally wrong.

17 Let us consider a more concrete example of just and unjust laws. An unjust law is a code that a numerical or power majority group compels a minority group to obey but does not make binding on itself. This is difference made legal. By the same token, a just law is a code that a majority compels a minority to follow and that it is willing to follow itself. This is sameness made legal.

18 Let me give another explanation. A law is unjust if it is inflicted on a minority that, as a result of being denied the right to vote, had no part in enacting or devising the law. Who can say that the legislature of Alabama which set up that state's segregation laws was democratically elected? Throughout Alabama all sorts of devious methods are used to prevent Negroes from becoming registered voters, and there are some counties in which, even though Negroes constitute a majority of the population, not a single Negro is registered. Can any law enacted under such circumstances be considered democratically structured?

19 Sometimes a law is just on its face and unjust in its application. For instance, I have been arrested on a charge of parading without a permit. Now, there is nothing wrong in having an ordinance which requires a permit for a parade. But such an ordinance becomes unjust when it is used to maintain segregation and to deny citizens the First Amendment privilege of peaceful assembly and protest.

20 I hope you are able to see the distinction I am trying to point out. In no sense do I advocate evading or defying the law, as would the rabid segregationist. That would lead to anarchy. One who breaks an unjust law must do so openly, lovingly, and with a willingness to accept the penalty. I submit that an individual who breaks a law that conscience tells him is unjust and who willingly accepts the penalty of imprisonment in order to arouse the conscience of the community over its injustice, is in reality expressing the highest respect for law.

21 Of course, there is nothing new about this kind of civil disobedience. It was evidenced sublimely in the refusal of Shadrach, Meshach and Abednego to obey the laws of Nebuchadnezzar, on the ground that a higher moral law was

at stake. It was practiced superbly by the early Christians, who were willing to face hungry lions and the excruciating pain of chopping blocks rather than submit to certain unjust laws of the Roman Empire. To a degree, academic freedom is a reality today because Socrates practiced civil disobedience. In our own nation, the Boston Tea Party represented a massive act of civil disobedience.

22   We should never forget that everything Adolf Hitler did in Germany was "legal" and everything the Hungarian freedom fighters did in Hungary was "illegal." It was "illegal" to aid and comfort a Jew in Hitler's Germany. Even so, I am sure that, had I lived in Germany at the time, I would have aided and comforted my Jewish brothers. If today I lived in a Communist country where certain principles dear to the Christian faith are suppressed, I would openly advocate disobeying that country's anti religious laws.

23   I must make two honest confessions to you, my Christian and Jewish brothers. First, I must confess that over the past few years I have been gravely disappointed with the white moderate. I have almost reached the regrettable conclusion that the Negro's great stumbling block in his stride toward freedom is not the White Citizen's Councilor or the Ku Klux Klanner, but the white moderate, who is more devoted to "order" than to justice; who prefers a negative peace which is the absence of tension to a positive peace which is the presence of justice; who constantly says: "I agree with you in the goal you seek, but I cannot agree with your methods of direct action"; who paternalistically believes he can set the timetable for another man's freedom; who lives by a mythical concept of time and who constantly advises the Negro to wait for a "more convenient season." Shallow understanding from people of good will is more frustrating than absolute misunderstanding from people of ill will. Lukewarm acceptance is much more bewildering than outright rejection.

24   I had hoped that the white moderate would understand that law and order exist for the purpose of establishing justice and that when they fail in this purpose they become the dangerously structured dams that block the flow of social progress. I had hoped that the white moderate would understand that the present tension in the South is a necessary phase of the transition from an obnoxious negative peace, in which the Negro passively accepted his unjust plight, to a substantive and positive peace, in which all men will respect the dignity and worth of human personality. Actually, we who engage in nonviolent direct action are not the creators of tension. We merely bring to the surface the hidden tension that is already alive. We bring it out in the open, where it can be seen and dealt with. Like

a boil that can never be cured so long as it is covered up but must be opened with all its ugliness to the natural medicines of air and light, injustice must be exposed, with all the tension its exposure creates, to the light of human conscience and the air of national opinion before it can be cured.

25   In your statement you assert that our actions, even though peaceful, must be condemned because they precipitate violence. But is this a logical assertion? Isn't this like condemning a robbed man because his possession of money precipitated the evil act of robbery? Isn't this like condemning Socrates because his unswerving commitment to truth and his philosophical inquiries precipitated the act by the misguided populace in which they made him drink hemlock? Isn't this like condemning Jesus because his unique God-consciousness and never-ceasing devotion to God's will precipitated the evil act of crucifixion? We must come to see that, as the federal courts have consistently affirmed, it is wrong to urge an individual to cease his efforts to gain his basic constitutional rights because the quest may precipitate violence. Society must protect the robbed and punish the robber.

26   I had also hoped that the white moderate would reject the myth concerning time in relation to the struggle for freedom. I have just received a letter from a white brother in Texas. He writes: "All Christians know that the colored people will receive equal rights eventually, but it is possible that you are in too great a religious hurry. It has taken Christianity almost two thousand years to accomplish what it has. The teachings of Christ take time to come to earth." Such an attitude stems from a tragic misconception of time, from the strangely rational notion that there is something in the very flow of time that will inevitably cure all ills. Actually, time itself is neutral; it can be used either destructively or constructively. More and more I feel that the people of ill will have used time much more effectively than have the people of good will. We will have to repent in this generation not merely for the hateful words and actions of the bad people but for the appalling silence of the good people. Human progress never rolls in on wheels of inevitability; it comes through the tireless efforts of men willing to be co-workers with God, and without this hard work, time itself becomes an ally of the forces of social stagnation. We must use time creatively, in the knowledge that the time is always ripe to do right. Now is the time to make real the promise of democracy and transform our pending national elegy into a creative psalm of brotherhood. Now is the time to lift our national policy from the quicksand of racial injustice to the solid rock of human dignity.

27   You speak of our activity in Birmingham as extreme. At first I was rather disappointed that fellow clergymen would see my nonviolent efforts as those of an

extremist. I began thinking about the fact that I stand in the middle of two opposing forces in the Negro community. One is a force of complacency, made up in part of Negroes who, as a result of long years of oppression, are so drained of self-respect and a sense of "somebodiness" that they have adjusted to segregation; and in part of a few middle class Negroes who, because of a degree of academic and economic security and because in some ways they profit by segregation, have become insensitive to the problems of the masses. The other force is one of bitterness and hatred, and it comes perilously close to advocating violence. It is expressed in the various black nationalist groups that are springing up across the nation, the largest and best-known being Elijah Muhammad's Muslim movement. Nourished by the Negro's frustration over the continued existence of racial discrimination, this movement is made up of people who have lost faith in America, who have absolutely repudiated Christianity, and who have concluded that the white man is an incorrigible "devil."

28   I have tried to stand between these two forces, saying that we need to emulate neither the "do-nothingism" of the complacent nor the hatred and despair of the black nationalist. For there is the more excellent way of love and nonviolent protest. I am grateful to God that, through the influence of the Negro church, the way of nonviolence became an integral part of our struggle.

29   If this philosophy had not emerged, by now many streets of the South would, I am convinced, be flowing with blood. And I am further convinced that if our white brothers dismiss as "rabble-rousers" and "outside agitators" those of us who employ nonviolent direct action, and if they refuse to support our nonviolent efforts, millions of Negroes will, out of frustration and despair, seek solace and security in black-nationalist ideologies—a development that would inevitably lead to a frightening racial nightmare.

30   Oppressed people cannot remain oppressed forever. The yearning for freedom eventually manifests itself, and that is what has happened to the American Negro. Something within has reminded him of his birthright of freedom, and something without has reminded him that it can be gained. Consciously or unconsciously, he has been caught up by the Zeitgeist, and with his black brothers of Africa and his brown and yellow brothers of Asia, South America and the Caribbean, the United States Negro is moving with a sense of great urgency toward the promised land of racial justice. If one recognizes this vital urge that has engulfed the Negro community, one should readily understand why public demonstrations are taking place. The Negro has many pent-up resentments

and latent frustrations, and he must release them. So let him march; let him make prayer pilgrimages to the city hall; let him go on freedom rides—and try to understand why he must do so. If his repressed emotions are not released in nonviolent ways, they will seek expression through violence; this is not a threat but a fact of history. So I have not said to my people: "Get rid of your discontent." Rather, I have tried to say that this normal and healthy discontent can be channeled into the creative outlet of nonviolent direct action. And now this approach is being termed extremist.

31   But though I was initially disappointed at being categorized as an extremist, as I continued to think about the matter I gradually gained a measure of satisfaction from the label. Was not Jesus an extremist for love: "Love your enemies, bless them that curse you, do good to them that hate you, and pray for them which despitefully use you, and persecute you." Was not Amos an extremist for justice: "Let justice roll down like waters and righteousness like an ever-flowing stream." Was not Paul an extremist for the Christian gospel: "I bear in my body the marks of the Lord Jesus." Was not Martin Luther an extremist: "Here I stand; I cannot do otherwise, so help me God." And John Bunyan: "I will stay in jail to the end of my days before I make a butchery of my conscience." And Abraham Lincoln: "This nation cannot survive half slave and half free." And Thomas Jefferson: "We hold these truths to be self-evident, that all men are created equal . . ." So the question is not whether we will be extremists, but what kind of extremists we will be. Will we be extremists for hate or for love? Will we be extremists for the preservation of injustice or for the extension of justice? In that dramatic scene on Calvary's hill three men were crucified. We must never forget that all three were crucified for the same crime—the crime of extremism. Two were extremists for immorality, and thus fell below their environment. The other, Jesus Christ, was an extremist for love, truth and goodness, and thereby rose above his environment. Perhaps the South, the nation and the world are in dire need of creative extremists.

32   I had hoped that the white moderate would see this need. Perhaps I was too optimistic; perhaps I expected too much. I suppose I should have realized that few members of the oppressor race can understand the deep groans and passionate yearnings of the oppressed race, and still fewer have the vision to see that injustice must be rooted out by strong, persistent and determined action. I am thankful, however, that some of our white brothers in the South have grasped the meaning of this social revolution and committed themselves to it. They are still too few in quantity, but they are big in quality. Some—such as

Ralph McGill, Lillian Smith, Harry Golden, James McBride Dabbs, Ann Braden and Sarah Patton Boyle—have written about our struggle in eloquent and prophetic terms. Others have marched with us down nameless streets of the South. They have languished in filthy, roach-infested jails, suffering the abuse and brutality of policemen who view them as "dirty nigger lovers." Unlike so many of their moderate brothers and sisters, they have recognized the urgency of the moment and sensed the need for powerful "action" antidotes to combat the disease of segregation.

33   Let me take note of my other major disappointment. I have been so greatly disappointed with the white church and its leadership. Of course, there are some notable exceptions. I am not unmindful of the fact that each of you has taken some significant stands on this issue. I commend you, Reverend Stallings, for your Christian stand on this past Sunday, in welcoming Negroes to your worship service on a non segregated basis. I commend the Catholic leaders of this state for integrating Spring Hill College several years ago.

34   But despite these notable exceptions, I must honestly reiterate that I have been disappointed with the church. I do not say this as one of those negative critics who can always find something wrong with the church. I say this as a minister of the gospel, who loves the church; who was nurtured in its bosom; who has been sustained by its spiritual blessings and who will remain true to it as long as the cord of life shall lengthen.

35   When I was suddenly catapulted into the leadership of the bus protest in Montgomery, Alabama, a few years ago, I felt we would be supported by the white church. I felt that the white ministers, priests and rabbis of the South would be among our strongest allies. Instead, some have been outright opponents, refusing to understand the freedom movement and misrepresenting its leader era; all too many others have been more cautious than courageous and have remained silent behind the anesthetizing security of stained-glass windows.

36   In spite of my shattered dreams, I came to Birmingham with the hope that the white religious leadership of this community would see the justice of our cause and, with deep moral concern, would serve as the channel through which our just grievances could reach the power structure. I had hoped that each of you would understand. But again I have been disappointed.

37   I have heard numerous southern religious leaders admonish their worshipers to comply with a desegregation decision because it is the law, but I have longed to hear white ministers declare: "Follow this decree because integration is morally right and because the Negro is your brother." In the midst of blatant injustices

inflicted upon the Negro, I have watched white churchmen stand on the sideline and mouth pious irrelevancies and sanctimonious trivialities. In the midst of a mighty struggle to rid our nation of racial and economic injustice, I have heard many ministers say: "Those are social issues, with which the gospel has no real concern." And I have watched many churches commit themselves to a completely other worldly religion which makes a strange, un-Biblical distinction between body and soul, between the sacred and the secular.

38   I have traveled the length and breadth of Alabama, Mississippi and all the other southern states. On sweltering summer days and crisp autumn mornings I have looked at the South's beautiful churches with their lofty spires pointing heavenward. I have beheld the impressive outlines of her massive religious-education buildings. Over and over I have found myself asking: "What kind of people worship here? Who is their God? Where were their voices when the lips of Governor Barnett dripped with words of interposition and nullification? Where were they when Governor Walleye gave a clarion call for defiance and hatred? Where were their voices of support when bruised and weary Negro men and women decided to rise from the dark dungeons of complacency to the bright hills of creative protest?"

39   Yes, these questions are still in my mind. In deep disappointment I have wept over the laxity of the church. But be assured that my tears have been tears of love. There can be no deep disappointment where there is not deep love. Yes, I love the church. How could I do otherwise? I am in the rather unique position of being the son, the grandson and the great-grandson of preachers. Yes, I see the church as the body of Christ. But, oh! How we have blemished and scarred that body through social neglect and through fear of being nonconformists.

40   There was a time when the church was very powerful—in the time when the early Christians rejoiced at being deemed worthy to suffer for what they believed. In those days the church was not merely a thermometer that recorded the ideas and principles of popular opinion; it was a thermostat that transformed the mores of society. Whenever the early Christians entered a town, the people in power became disturbed and immediately sought to convict the Christians for being "disturbers of the peace" and "outside agitators." But the Christians pressed on, in the conviction that they were "a colony of heaven," called to obey God rather than man. Small in number, they were big in commitment. They were too God intoxicated to be "astronomically intimidated." By their effort and example they brought an end to such ancient evils as infanticide and gladiatorial contests.

41   Things are different now. So often the contemporary church is a weak, ineffectual voice with an uncertain sound. So often it is an archdefender of the status quo. Far from being disturbed by the presence of the church, the power structure of the average community is consoled by the church's silent—and often even vocal sanction—of things as they are.

42   But the judgment of God is upon the church as never before. If today's church does not recapture the sacrificial spirit of the early church, it will lose its authenticity, forfeit the loyalty of millions, and be dismissed as an irrelevant social club with no meaning for the twentieth century. Every day I meet young people whose disappointment with the church has turned into outright disgust.

43   Perhaps I have once again been too optimistic. Is organized religion too inextricably bound to the status quo to save our nation and the world? Perhaps I must turn my faith to the inner spiritual church, the church within the church, as the true ekklesia and the hope of the world. But again I am thankful to God that some noble souls from the ranks of organized religion have broken loose from the paralyzing chains of conformity and joined us as active partners in the struggle for freedom. They have left their secure congregations and walked the streets of Albany, Georgia, with us. They have gone down the highways of the South on tortuous rides for freedom. Yes, they have gone to jail with us. Some have been dismissed from their churches, have lost the support of their bishops and fellow ministers. But they have acted in the faith that right defeated is stronger than evil triumphant. Their witness has been the spiritual salt that has preserved the true meaning of the gospel in these troubled times. They have carved a tunnel of hope through the dark mountain of disappointment.

44   I hope the church as a whole will meet the challenge of this decisive hour. But even if the church does not come to the aid of justice, I have no despair about the future. I have no fear about the outcome of our struggle in Birmingham, even if our motives are at present misunderstood. We will reach the goal of freedom in Birmingham and all over the nation, because the goal of America is freedom. Abused and scorned though we may be, our destiny is tied up with America's destiny. Before the pilgrims landed at Plymouth, we were here. Before the pen of Jefferson etched the majestic words of the Declaration of Independence across the pages of history, we were here. For more than two centuries our forebears labored in this country without wages; they made cotton king; they built the homes of their masters while suffering gross injustice and shameful humiliation—and yet out of a bottomless vitality they continued to

thrive and develop. If the inexpressible cruelties of slavery could not stop us, the opposition we now face will surely fail. We will win our freedom because the sacred heritage of our nation and the eternal will of God are embodied in our echoing demands.

45   Before closing I feel impelled to mention one other point in your statement that has troubled me profoundly. You warmly commended the Birmingham police force for keeping "order" and "preventing violence." I doubt that you would have so warmly commended the police force if you had seen its dogs sinking their teeth into unarmed, nonviolent Negroes. I doubt that you would so quickly commend the policemen if you were to observe their ugly and inhumane treatment of Negroes here in the city jail; if you were to watch them push and curse old Negro women and young Negro girls; if you were to see them slap and kick old Negro men and young boys; if you were to observe them, as they did on two occasions, refuse to give us food because we wanted to sing our grace together. I cannot join you in your praise of the Birmingham police department.

46   It is true that the police have exercised a degree of discipline in handling the demonstrators. In this sense they have conducted themselves rather "nonviolently" in public. But for what purpose? To preserve the evil system of segregation. Over the past few years I have consistently preached that nonviolence demands that the means we use must be as pure as the ends we seek. I have tried to make clear that it is wrong to use immoral means to attain moral ends. But now I must affirm that it is just as wrong, or perhaps even more so, to use moral means to preserve immoral ends. Perhaps Mr. Connor and his policemen have been rather nonviolent in public, as was Chief Pritchett in Albany, Georgia but they have used the moral means of nonviolence to maintain the immoral end of racial injustice. As T. S. Eliot has said: "The last temptation is the greatest treason: To do the right deed for the wrong reason."

47   I wish you had commended the Negro sit-inners and demonstrators of Birmingham for their sublime courage, their willingness to suffer and their amazing discipline in the midst of great provocation. One day the South will recognize its real heroes. They will be the James Merediths, with the noble sense of purpose that enables them to face jeering, and hostile mobs, and with the agonizing loneliness that characterizes the life of the pioneer. They will be old, oppressed, battered Negro women, symbolized in a seventy-two-year-old woman in Montgomery, Alabama, who rose up with a sense of dignity and with her people decided not to ride segregated buses, and who responded with

ungrammatical profundity to one who inquired about her weariness: "My feets is tired, but my soul is at rest." They will be the young high school and college students, the young ministers of the gospel and a host of their elders, courageously and nonviolently sitting in at lunch counters and willingly going to jail for conscience' sake. One day the South will know that when these disinherited children of God sat down at lunch counters, they were in reality standing up for what is best in the American dream and for the most sacred values in our Judaeo-Christian heritage, thereby bringing our nation back to those great wells of democracy which were dug deep by the founding fathers in their formulation of the Constitution and the Declaration of Independence.

48   Never before have I written so long a letter. I'm afraid it is much too long to take your precious time. I can assure you that it would have been much shorter if I had been writing from a comfortable desk, but what else can one do when he is alone in a narrow jail cell, other than write long letters, think long thoughts and pray long prayers?

49   If I have said anything in this letter that overstates the truth and indicates an unreasonable impatience, I beg you to forgive me. If I have said anything that understates the truth and indicates my having a patience that allows me to settle for anything less than brotherhood, I beg God to forgive me.

50   I hope this letter finds you strong in the faith. I also hope that circumstances will soon make it possible for me to meet each of you, not as an integrationist or a civil rights leader but as a fellow clergyman and a Christian brother. Let us all hope that the dark clouds of racial prejudice will soon pass away and the deep fog of misunderstanding will be lifted from our fear-drenched communities, and in some not too distant tomorrow the radiant stars of love and brotherhood will shine over our great nation with all their scintillating beauty.

Yours for the cause of Peace and Brotherhood,
Martin Luther King, Jr.

Appendix B

Chrysler Ad from April 25, 1960 Issue of *Life* Magazine

Appendix C

Volkswagen's "Why" Ad from April 25, 1960 Issue of *Life* Magazine

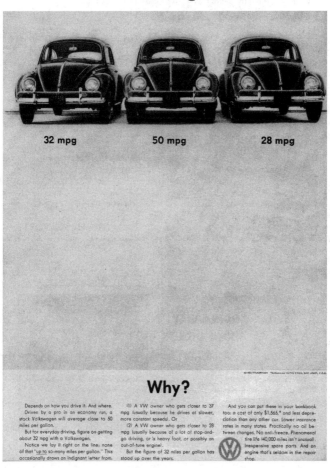

Works Cited

Page vi: From Wayne Booth, *Rhetoric of Rhetoric: The Quest for Effective Communication* (Malden MA: Blackwell, 2004), p. 109.

Page 3: From Kenneth Burke, *A Rhetoric of Motives* (Berkeley: University of California Press, 1969), p. 43.

Page 19: Mention of Steven Mailloux, Rhetorical Power (1989) and Mark Twain, *Huckleberry Finn*.

Page 25: From the *New York Times* "Opinion of the Week" survey, 5 May 1963.

Pages 25–26: From VW ads in the "Think Small" campaign, including "Think Small," "Lemon," "It's Ugly, But it Gets you There," "Has the Volkswagen Fad Died Out?"

Pages 39–43: Rebecca Reilly, "The Kairos of War." Reprinted with Permission.

Page 55: From jsmooth's "How to Tell People they Sound Racist" (*illdoctrine* 21 July 2008), which can still be viewed at: http://www.illdoctrine.com/2008/07/.

Pages 67–68: From jsmooth's "How to Tell People they Sound Racist" (*illdoctrine* 21 July 2008), which can still be viewed at: http://www.illdoctrine.com/2008/07/.

Pages 96–101: David Daniel, "Building An Electronic Empire with Argument," Reprinted with Permission. David's paper cites and describes the video game Mass Effect (2007).

Page 104: From Kenneth Burke, *Counter-Statement* (Berkeley: California, 1968), p.124.

Page 109: Discussion of Volkswagen "Think Small" commercial, which can still be viewed here: http://www.youtube.com/watch?v=qw2rRSLvIO0.

Page 111: From Martin Luther King, Jr.'s "I Have a Dream" speech discussed and reprinted. Entire speech can be read and viewed here: http://www.americanrhetoric.com/speeches/mlkihaveadream.htm.

Pages 132–135: Haley Faulkner, "Real Beauty, Real Form: An Analysis of Structure in the Dove 'Onslaught' Video." This analysis describes and quotes the "Onslaught" video, which can be viewed here: http://www.dove.us/#/features/videos/default.aspx[cp-documentid=7049579].

Page 146: From Edward Bulwer-Lytton, *Richelieu* (1839), 2.2, which can be read here: http://books .google.com/books?id=fVLrNin8pzwC&pg=PA102&dq=Edward+Bulwer-Lytton+Richelieu&hl=en&ei=_ TINTKqnGIK88gaz6-mNBw&sa=X&oi=book_result&ct=result&resnum=1&ved=0CCoQ6AEwAA#v= onepage&q&f=false.

Page 148: From Walt Whitman, "Vigil Strange I Kept on the Field one Night," which can be read here: http://books.google.com/books?id=FGDfs9AMY1cC&printsec=frontcover&dq=leaves+of+grass&cd=1#v=o nepage&q&f=false.

Page 148: From Abraham Lincoln, "Gettysburg Address," which can be read here: http://avalon.law .yale.edu/19th_century/gettyb.asp.

Page 149: From J. F. Kennedy's 1961 Inaugural Address, which can be read and watched here: http://www.americanrhetoric.com/speeches/jfkinaugural.htm.

Page 149: From Alexander Pope, *The Rape of the Lock*, which can be read here: http://books.google .com/books?id=9SwhAAAAMAAJ&dq=the+rape+of+the+lock&printsec=frontcover&source=bn&hl=en&ei =9DQNTLCqA8H38Aa-8aSRBw&sa=X&oi=book_result&ct=result&resnum=4&ved=0CC0Q6AEwAw#v= onepage&q&f=false.

Page 149: From W. B. Yeates, "Among School Children," which can be read here: http://rpo .library.utoronto.ca/poem/3354.html.

Page 150: From Abraham Lincoln's Second Inaugural Address, which can be read here: http://www .americanrhetoric.com/speeches/abrahamlincolnsecondinauguraladdress.htm.

Page 152: From the King James translation of the Book of Genesis 1.2–3, which can be read here: http://quod.lib.umich.edu/cgi/k/kjv/kjv-idx?type=DIV1&byte=1477.

Page 153: From W. H. Auden, Musée des Beaux Arts, which can be read here: http://www .poemhunter.com/poem/mus-eacute-e-des-beaux-arts/.

Pages 157–159: From Lincoln's "Gettysburg Address."

Pages 181–184: Tara Hall, "Clarity and Rhythm in a British PSA." Reprinted with Permission. The analysis references a short film by Peter Watkins-Hughes, which can be viewed at: http://www.youtube.com/watch?v=5ttNgZDZrul&has_verified=1.

Page 189: From the Declaration of Independence, which can be read here: http://www.ushistory.org/declaration/document/index.htm.

Page 198: From Kenneth Burke, *Rhetoric of Motives*, (Berkeley: University of California Press, 1969), p. 146.

Page 198: From Judith Butler, *Gender Trouble: Feminism and the Subversion of Identity*, (New York: Routledge, 1990), p. 10.

Page 198: From Friedrich Nietzsche, *Geneology of Morals XIII*, which can be read here: http://books.google.com/books?id=n4INAQAAIAAJ&printsec=frontcover&dq=genealogy+of+morals&source=bl&ots=EfdSOZJg4v&sig=cJ3460DEB9SYu5hNc1TFaUmVgko&hl=en&ei=75W4TLrUMsKAlAeI9ZHUDA&sa=X&oi=book_result&ct=result&resnum=3&ved=0CC0Q6AEwAg#v=onepage&q&f=false.

Page 212: From Joseph Ledoux, *The Emotional Brain: The Mysterious Underpinnings of Emotional Life* (New York: Simon and Schuster, 1996), p. 69.

Page 216: From George Campbell, *The Philosophy of Rhetoric, ed.* and intro. Lloyd F. Bitzer (Carbondale: Southern Illinois University Press, 1963), p. 73.

Pages 219–220: From Barack Obama's 2004 keynote address at the Democratic National Convention, which can be read and watched at: http://www.americanrhetoric.com/speeches/convention2004/barackobama2004dnc.htm.

Page 222: From Frank Lutz, *Words that Work: It's Not What you say, It's What People Hear*, (New York: Hyperion, 2007), pp. 279–80.

Page 236: From Kenneth Burke, *A Rhetoric of Motives* (Berkeley: University of California Press, 1969), p. 21.

Page 237: Ibid., p. 273.

Page 248: From Billy Collins, "Litany," which can be read here: http://www.americanpoems.com/poets/Billy-Collins/4367. Collins can be seen reading and commenting on "Litany" here: http://www.youtube.com/watch?v=56Iq3PbSWZY.

Credits

Text Credits

Page 251: "Letter from Eight Alabama Clergymen," Copyright, 2010, The Birmingham News. All rights reserved. Reprinted with permission.

Page 253: "Letter from Birmingham Jail." Reprinted by arrangement with The Heirs to the Estate of Martin Luther King Jr., c/o Writers House as agent for the proprietor New York, NY. Copyright 1963 Dr. Martin Luther King Jr; copyright renewed 1991 Coretta Scott King.

Photo Credits

Figure 3.1: Image Courtesy of the Advertising Archives.

Figure 6.4: From the Washington Post, © 2010 The Washington Post. All rights reserved. Used by permission and protected by the Copyright Laws of the United States. The printing, copying, redistribution, or retransmission of the Material without express written permission is prohibited.

Figure 7.1: Image Courtesy of the Advertising Archives.

Appendix B: Image Courtesy of the Advertising Archives.

Appendix C: Image Courtesy of the Advertising Archives.

Index